SUBURBAN TRUE CRIME

AUSTRALIAN CASES YOU'LL NEVER FORGET AND SOME YOU'VE NEVER HEARD OF

EMILY WEBB

Big Sky Publishing Pty Ltd
PO Box 303, Newport, NSW 2106, Australia
Phone: 1300 364 611
Fax: (61 2) 9918 2396
Email: info@bigskypublishing.com.au
Web: www.bigskypublishing.com.au

Cover design and typesetting: Think Productions

A catalogue record for this book is available from the National Library of Australia

SUBURBAN TRUE CRIME

AUSTRALIAN CASES YOU'LL NEVER FORGET AND SOME YOU'VE NEVER HEARD OF

BIG SKY PUBLISHING
www.bigskypublishing.com.au

EMILY WEBB

CONTENTS

ACKNOWLEDGMENTS

I respectfully acknowledge the Wurundjeri People of the Kulin Nation, who are the Traditional Owners of the land on which I live and wrote this book. I pay my respects to their Elders past, present and those emerging.

It's been several years since my books *Murder in Suburbia* and *Suburban Nightmare* were published in 2013 and 2016 respectively.

Suburban True Crime features some cases that were included in *Murder in Suburbia* and *Suburban Nightmare*, and it has been updated with new information and interviews. There's also two new chapters about the still unsolved 1967 murder of a woman named Margaret Pavarno in an armed robbery at her workplace, and the 1984 murder of six-year-old Kylie Maybury. Kylie's abduction and murder was unsolved for more than 30 years until a man was arrested and charged in 2016 and later convicted and jailed for life.

In 2017, I embarked on creating a podcast with Meshel Laurie called *Australian True Crime*. Neither of us could have imagined that our podcast, born from our interest in true crime, society and people would become as popular as it has. I first met Meshel when she asked me to be a guest on a podcast she was hosting at the time and talk about being a true crime writer.

I was excited to meet Meshel, and a little while after we'd chatted, she asked whether I'd want to do a podcast about true crime with her. I didn't have to be asked twice.

I can't put into words the privilege it has been to do this podcast and talk to so many incredible people – our guests, and our listeners.

Meshel, thank you for the opportunity.

Same goes for the people who have assisted me in the writing and content of this updated book (and who'd spoken to me for the original books). I am deeply grateful for their time: Lyle Allan, John and Helen Magill, Steve Dolman, Sandra Cory, Samantha Ellis, Craig Ellis, Janet O'Donnell, Kyle Simpson, Rebecca Redd, Shannon Connors, Jenny Convery, Cheryl Goldsworthy and John McManus, Janine Greening, Lisa Beverstock, Becky Melcher, Catherine Maree, Wendy Rawaday, Stephen Bennett, and the retired parish priest for his correspondence.

There are writers I look up to and consider friends and mentors who have encouraged me, advised me and supported my work: Megan Norris, Vikki Petraitis, Andrew Rule, Justin Smith, Dr Brian Williams, Sisters in Crime Australia (especially Lindy Cameron, Carmel Shute and Tara Mitchell) and Jason K. Foster.

Thank you to Diane Evans and the team at Big Sky Publishing.

And to everyone who has read my books. I really appreciate hearing from readers, and I hope some of you feel inclined to get in touch, especially if you have a connection to or memories of any of the cases in this book.

ACKNOWLEDGEMENTS

I don't take writing about true crime lightly. We all have a responsibility for doing what we can in our communities to reduce the systemic causes of violent offending and to help people who have been affected by crime and trauma.

If you have been affected by the content in this book, phone Lifeline on 13 11 14 or go to lifeline.org.au

If you have any information on unsolved crimes, phone Crime Stoppers on 1800 333 000.

SAME KILLER, DIFFERENT COUNTRIES

On the afternoon of 11 September 1985, in Melbourne, a young woman had a terrifying encounter with a man who would go on to murder two women, in almost identical crimes.

The woman, 30, was in the toilets at the Midtown Plaza (now known as Midtown) in Melbourne's central business district at the corner of Swanston and Bourke streets. It's an art deco building with a modest offering of retail shops, dining and six levels of office space and is located on one of the busiest corners of the city.

It was around 2 p.m., and the woman was washing her hands when she felt something hit her on the back. On turning, she saw a man standing there with a crossbow. Reaching around to her back, the woman could feel an arrow protruding out of her body.

It is not known whether the arrow fell out of her back, or the assailant pulled it out, but he then pushed her into a toilet cubicle and held a knife to her throat. 'Do as I tell you and you won't get hurt,' the man told the woman.

He demanded she take off her pants. Trying to stay calm in this life-threatening situation, the woman attempted to take control and asked the man to repeat what he'd said to her. It was a strategy to slow things down and buy her time. The woman told her attacker she was expecting a friend to arrive at any moment and that he'd be caught if he didn't let her go. The young man then hurriedly got his crossbow and left the toilets.

A few months later, the woman saw the image of her attacker on television and in newspapers. It was his eyes she recognised first … his frightening eyes. His name was Kurt Michael Dumas, and he was in the media because he'd been charged with murdering a young woman with a crossbow.

* * *

Kurt Dumas and Lyndell Martin were friends. The pair, aged 20 and 19 respectively, had known each other around three years. They had met when they were both patients at the Parkville Adolescent Unit in Melbourne in 1982 and had kept in sporadic contact. Ms Martin lived with schizophrenia, and Dumas had psychiatric conditions that had already seen him hospitalised several times.

On 18 November 1985, Dumas popped around to Lyndell's flat in Carlton and arrangements were made for her to come to his place in inner-city Fitzroy that night for dinner. It had been several months since they had seen each other.

What exactly went on in the flat that evening is not known, but Lyndell Martin never made it home. She would be found dead, by Dumas's mother Gail, in the bathroom/laundry of his Clauscen Street flat four days later. *The Sun* reported that a 14-centimetre steel-tipped arrow was embedded in Lyndell's abdomen.

The day after he'd killed Lyndell, Dumas fled to his parents' house in Chadstone (a south-eastern suburb) that's best known for being home to a mega-shopping centre. He took two .22 rifles, and the next day boarded a train to Ouyen, more than 400 kilometres from Melbourne, near the town of Mildura. Why Dumas chose this town is unknown.

He was arrested in Ouyen on 20 November and charged for being in possession of the firearms. Sergeant Paul Gunning, the arresting officer, followed his 'copper instinct' and spoke to Dumas just outside the town. Dumas told Sergeant Gunning he was in the area for hunting, hence the rifles. While Dumas pretended to look for his shooter's licence (he didn't have one), the policeman saw an array of other things in the bag, including a knife, which Dumas said he used for skinning rabbits. Dumas gave the sergeant a false name and address.

On 21 November, he returned to Melbourne, to his flat, where Lyndell was still on the bed. Dumas moved her body to the bathroom/laundry and covered it with towels, which is how she would be found the next day.

While his mother was discovering the horror of Lyndell's body in his flat, Dumas, using a false name, flew to Launceston, Tasmania. He was staying in a youth hostel when he was arrested. Police found a disturbing travel kit in his possession: 'a crossbow, ten arrows, some bullets, a pair of female panties, a lock of Lyndell's hair, a pair of handcuffs, some masking tape and a stainless-steel kitchen knife'.

Dumas was interviewed by both the Launceston Criminal Investigation Branch (CIB) and Melbourne detectives from the Homicide Squad who had travelled to Tasmania.

During the August 1986 Coroners Court inquest into Lyndell's death, the court heard that after his arrest, Dumas admitted that he had killed Lyndell. Dumas told detectives, 'I didn't mean to kill her; I just went off my head. It was Monday night at my flat and she just went crazy. She wouldn't shut up. I knew I had to fix her, so that's when I went and got it – the crossbow. It is the quickest and most accurate thing I have.'

Coroner Hal Hallenstein found that Lyndell died of blood loss resulting from the chest wound 'unlawfully and maliciously' inflicted by Dumas.

The details of Lyndell's last moments are among some of the most disturbing in Australian crime. *The Sydney Morning Herald* reported on 5 August 1986 that 'police alleged Dumas bound Lyndell with masking tape and crepe bandages before killing her'. Detective Senior Constable Rodney Wilson told the Coroners Court that Dumas had also admitted, 'I had sex with her after I shot her. She was still alive; she was resisting me.' Senior Constable Wilson said at the inquest that when he asked Dumas why he'd done that, Dumas told him, 'Well, it couldn't be any worse for me, could it?'.

The coroner's report concluded the stab wounds on Lyndell's body were inflicted after she died, possibly several days later. Police alleged Dumas told them he had returned from Ouyen to the flat a few days later and stabbed Lyndell in the stomach to test the sharpness of his knife. According to R v Dumas [1986], this detail was excluded from the trial.

Dumas's disturbed life was revealed at the coroner's inquest. His mother Gail gave evidence and detailed the hopeless facts of her son's condition and behaviours. From court records and newspaper archives, the picture emerged of Dumas as a dangerous young man.

Dumas was born in Michigan, United States, on 12 December 1965. Mrs Dumas told the Coroners Court that her son had suffered severe head injuries after falling from a table at the age of three months. She said that since that accident, Dumas had undergone several brain operations in the United States; one even required him to have a plastic plate inserted in his head to slow a leakage of fluid in his brain.

The operations changed her son. Mrs Dumas said he was violent, unpredictable and had been asked to leave three schools because of this behaviour. He also spent some years as an inpatient in psychiatric hospitals, including the one where he met Lyndell.

The Dumas family immigrated to Australia in 1972. Kurt Dumas returned to the United States for short time in 1978 but returned to Australia in 1979.

Dumas had younger brothers and had unpredictable violent outbursts towards them. He was also involved in petty crime and addictive behaviours, including compulsive eating. Court documents detail that in 1979, Dumas, then aged around 14, forced two young girls, aged 2½ and five years old, to undress, and then he also took his clothes off. He was sent to a child and family clinic for assessment.

The Dumas family was in crisis, and according to court documents 'Mrs Dumas made a premeditated attempt to kill Kurt to "save the world from him"'. Mrs Dumas was admitted to hospital for psychiatric care, and her son was sent to a state government centre for boys, called Baltara, then located in Parkville in inner-city Melbourne.

Shortly after this incident, the Dumas family decided to send Kurt back to the United States to live with his grandparents in Michigan. But his behaviour did not change, and somehow (it was not detailed how) it was discovered that the teenage Dumas had plans to kill his grandmother and aunt.

He was sent to Fairlawn Center in Michigan, a child psychiatric asylum (now closed), for assessment and treatment.

He returned to Australia in early 1981 and was again in trouble. *Serious trouble.* Suspended from school for physically hurting a classmate, Dumas ended up at the adolescent psychiatric centre in Parkville, and doctors believed he had psychosis. Soon after, Dumas was admitted to Larundel Hospital in Melbourne's north as an involuntary patient under the *Mental Health Act.* This admission was because Dumas had, according to court documents, attempted to 'extort money, sexually molest and kill a family of your acquaintance'.

Doctors who assessed him said his prognosis was 'extremely poor'.

* * *

After the coroner's inquest, Dumas was ordered to stand trial for the murder of Lyndell Martin in the Supreme Court. He entered a plea of not guilty. No application for bail was made, and he remained in custody where he had been since the murder.

The trial started in December 1986 and lasted nine days. The judge was Justice George Hampel, who sentenced notorious criminals, including Hoddle Street mass killer Julian Knight (sentenced in 1988), retiring in 2000 from the Supreme Court.

Dumas pleaded not guilty, and his story changed somewhat from what he'd told police after his arrest in Tasmania.

Mrs Dumas gave evidence in court she had seen her son on the morning of 19 November – the day after he killed Lyndell, and he told her he'd lost his job. The mother and son planned to catch up later that same day, but Dumas never showed up. Concerned when she hadn't seen him for a few more days, Mrs Dumas went to her son's Clauscen Street flat and found Lyndell's body on the floor of the bathroom/laundry, covered in towels.

When Dumas was being questioned in court the day after his mother, the jury heard Dumas had moved Lyndell's body so that he could sleep on his bed. This was not disputed by the accused.

In sworn evidence, Dumas said on the evening of 18 November, he and Lyndell 'started kissing and cuddling on the couch and eventually had sexual intercourse'. The pair then had dinner, and Dumas said Lyndell started 'yelling and screaming'. Dumas said he wound masking tape around Lyndell's mouth, which she ripped off and continued to scream. *The Age* reported Dumas said he told her to 'shut up or leave'. Dumas admitted to using the crossbow and that he 'blew my lid and fired it', but he said he'd put together the weapon to 'scare her into being quiet'.

Under cross-examination by Crown prosecutor Bruce Walmsley on 11 December, Dumas told the court he did not intend to harm Lyndell 'at all' and said the young woman was a 'good friend'. 'I was in a state of shock, not knowing what was going on, what was happening,' he said in court, as reported in *The Age*.

Dumas was 'quite stunned' at what happened. 'I was scared. I panicked. I packed some things and ran off, literally,' Dumas said.

Mr Walmsley asked Dumas whether it had been distressing for him, and Dumas responded, 'Well, I couldn't eat for days.'

Dumas denied raping Lyndell after he'd shot her with the crossbow. It was also alleged by police has Dumas had handcuffed her to the bed to stop her resisting him. 'When someone's dead or dying, that's sick, that's sick,' he responded.

Letters written by Dumas to a work colleague also revealed the depths of his disordered mind. The sentencing remarks stated, 'These letters provided graphic evidence that there was something very wrong with the applicant's mentality.'

John Bato, who had worked with Dumas at a smallgoods factory, gave evidence at the trial about a letter sent to him by the alleged crossbow killer. Mr Bato said that in the letter, Dumas wrote that his nickname in prison was 'William Tell. But tell all I believe it was an accident, which it was'.

Mr Bato also confirmed the contents, read out in court, which included, 'I'm sorry what's happened. I didn't plan it, the chance was there and I took it …. So John, I'm capable of killing someone and I'm not even feeling guilty. I'm not a mad killer'.

Dr Barnes, a forensic psychiatrist who studied Dumas's medical and social history, wrote in his report, referred to by Justice Hampel in his sentencing remarks:

I am quite convinced we are dealing with a person with significant psychiatric disorder and that a clear-cut diagnosis has not been possible, but there are certain neurological features relevant to his presentation which cannot be overlooked … his whole history is punctuated

with episodes of quite bizarre behaviour and in particular
of his having a chaotic and disturbed fantasy life manifest
by the writing of various notes, letters, plans et cetera ....
(R V Dumas 1986)

Another eminent specialist, Dr Bartholomew, described Dumas
in his report as 'markedly paranoid and close to psychotic'.

On 19 December 1986, Dumas was sentenced to life
imprisonment, but Justice Hampel fixed a minimum term of 18
years before the young killer could be considered for parole.

Justice Hampel said, 'The evidence and all the surrounding
circumstances, in my view, plainly demonstrate that there is a
real likelihood that a crime of the kind committed on Lyndell
Martin may be again committed by you.'

These words would end up tragically prophetic.

As for the assault of the woman in Melbourne's Midtown Plaza,
Dumas was questioned about it after his arrest in Launceston,
but the details of the crime were kept from the jury during his
murder trial. The case went to court in 1989. Dumas instructed
his counsel to say he had nothing to do with it.

The woman bravely gave evidence about her terrifying
encounter with Dumas, telling the County Court of Victoria on
6 February that she recognised Dumas as her attacker when he
appeared on television and newspapers after his arrest for killing
Lyndell Martin.

After the woman detailed her encounter with Dumas, the
prosecutor asked her if she had felt any pain from the arrow that
had embedded in her back.

'I think I did, but I was more aware of other dangers than the
immediate pain,' she answered.

The Crown prosecutor Tim Doherty said Dumas told police he intended to rob the woman and gave a detailed account of the attack to detectives. However, when he was charged over the Midtown Plaza attack (after he was sentenced for the murder of Lyndell Martin), he told his legal team to say he was not responsible.

On 7 February 1989, Dumas was convicted of unlawfully and maliciously inflicting grievous bodily harm and was sentenced to a minimum of three years to be served concurrently with his time for Lyndell's murder.

Chief Judge Glenn Waldron said, 'It must be said that this young woman firstly was fortunate in not suffering a more severe or lasting injury as a result of what he did, and secondly, I am sure, survived as she did only because of her presence of mind in what was a very perilous situation for her.'

In 2017, a retired Victoria Police officer Stephen Bennett contacted me after he'd heard me doing an interview on radio station 3AW. In an email dated 28 February 2017, Mr Bennett wrote he was the first police officer to respond to the assault in the Midtown Plaza by Dumas 'all those years ago and remembers it well'.

'I always hoped that the young lady managed to get over or at least manage what happened, to some degree,' he said.

'At that time, I was passing through the Melbourne District Traffic and Patrol Division, as a probationary constable … the girl was incredibly lucky to have lived, although we did not realise then how lucky she was. I left the force in 2002, after 19 years, and I certainly remember this one. I think about it often.'

Dumas served his time at various prisons in Victoria.

On the Australian crime website 'Aussie Criminals', one commenter 'jrcart' wrote on 17 January 2015: 'I remember Dumas from both pentridge [sic] and Barwon prisons. I'm surprised he was in mainstream, but most stayed well away from him anyway. Everyone called him Robin Hood ....'

Dumas's 1986 life sentence (with the 18-year minimum) was the first imposed in Victoria after legislation was introduced that meant a life sentence was not mandatory for murder. *The Crime Amendment Act* (1986) gave the power to fix a minimum term when imposing a life sentence. The thinking behind the changes to the act was that (among other things) at the time, all murders were treated identically under the act whether they were, for example, organised crime hits or family violence. The change gave the courts the power to set a minimum parole term.

Dumas's sentence was lengthy, but he was released after his minimum term, which would have been around 2003.

* * *

Dumas ended up back in the United States, living in the state of Michigan, his place of birth. From early January 2004, he rented the basement of a house that belonged to a woman named Denise Ann Howes, who was thirty-four. The house was in the township of Redford, in Wayne County. Denise still lived in the house with her ex-husband Mark Howes, but she was in a relationship with a man named Todd Neumann. There were problems with Dumas staying at the house and Denise had told some neighbours she planned to evict him.

Dumas would shockingly offend again, murdering Denise Howes on 7 December 2004.

In his statement to Redford Township Police Department on 8 December 2004, Mark Howes said he last spoke to his ex-wife at around 8 a.m. or 9 a.m. on 7 December, and she had told him Dumas's tickets to go to Hawaii had been cancelled, and he had then returned to the house. Mark was out of town in Ohio, a neighbouring state to Michigan.

It is mentioned in police statements that Dumas told Officers he was going to visit his daughter in Hawaii (there's no other mention of Dumas having a child, so whether the girl was born in the time when Dumas returned to the United States in the late 1970s, or when he returned after his sentence for Lyndell's murder is unknown) but his stepfather had cancelled the ticket. (This implied that Gail Dumas had also returned to live in the Unites States at some stage.) The flight was to leave at 5.30 a.m.

Mark said in his statement that he'd tried several times to contact Denise later that day on 7 December, primarily to ask if she could take his vehicle to get the brakes fixed, to no avail. He even called her workplace, only to be told she hadn't shown up.

Later that night, Todd Neumann phoned the Redford Township Police Department to report his concern about Denise's welfare because he had not heard from her all day. He also told police he started driving around the neighbourhood, checking for signs of Denise because when her drove past her house, her vehicle wasn't there. When he was driving around the neighbourhood he spotted her car – a 2000 Jeep Cherokee – but she was not the driver ... Kurt Dumas was. Todd followed the vehicle and ended up blocking it in a dead-end street. According to his statement, that's when he called police, and

Sergeant Eric Pahl and Officer Nicholas Lentine were first on the scene.

Investigating the 'suspicious situation', Sergeant Pahl saw the driver of the Jeep try to cut through a park that bordered the dead-end street, but the vehicle got caught in a ditch.

'I activated my lights and the Jeep tried to back out of the ditch,' Sergeant Pahl wrote in his 7 December 2004 incident report. 'I approached ... and saw a [white male] subject sitting in the drivers [sic] seat "revving" the engine in an effort to get out of the ditch .... I called for him to stop and he continued "revving" the engine. I went around and opened the drivers [sic] door and got the subject out of the vehicle.'

When Sergeant Pahl patted him down and asked his name, Dumas gave no response. Dumas did not have a driver's licence but he had his social security card and passport, and that's how the sergeant discovered his name.

Dumas was placed under arrest, and Sergeant Pahl put him in the back of the police car while he tried to find out more about the wellbeing of Denise. A search of the car uncovered a knife and a short-barrelled rifle found in a duffel bag. The rifle was loaded.

Two officers were sent to Denise's address to check on her – Timothy Paull and Lawrence Turner. They arrived at 11.10 p.m. to find the house in complete darkness. They had the keys to the house, which had been found in the Jeep, but they knocked first and rang the doorbell several times. Denise's dog was at the door barking at the officers, and they waited a few minutes until Todd arrived so he could calm the animal.

The policemen turned the lights on and called out, 'Denise! Denise!'

No answer.

Todd told the officers when they were approaching the main bedroom.

'As I opened the bedroom door, I saw a female lying face up on the bed,' Officer Paull wrote in his report.

He recalled in his statement, 'I saw that there was a piece of duct tape over her mouth. There was a green towel over her midsection ....'

There were no signs of life when Officer Paull checked Denise, and he immediately radioed to his colleague Sergeant Pahl to make sure Dumas was secure in the police car.

Officer Lawrence Turner interviewed neighbours. Some of them said they had been told by Denise that she was planning to evict Dumas from the house in December because she thought he was stealing from her. Some of the neighbours also told Officer Lawrence that Dumas did not drive, and that Denise would never have let him drive her vehicle. Dumas, who did not have a current driver's licence, told police he'd had permission to use the Jeep. Two neighbours described Dumas as 'very nosey' to Officer Lawrence.

Dumas was taken to the Redford Township Police Department to be charged and processed.

When the officer on the desk, Keith Cooper, checked Dumas and found a spent shell casing in the right front change pocket of his pants, Dumas reportedly said to Officer Cooper, 'Yeah, you will need that.'

Officer Cooper stated in his incident report (8 December 2004) that while fingerprinting Dumas, he said, unprovoked, 'They shouldn't have picked a fight with me, and I went back to check on her.' Dumas told Officer Cooper that he was in a bad mood because of his cancelled flight to Hawaii.

Dumas, handcuffed to the wall, then asked Officer Cooper, 'How's jail?'

Cooper responded, 'Why is that?'

Dumas answered, 'You know, you know I'm guilty.'

It was another strange exchange between Dumas and police. The Redford Police didn't know of Dumas's violent past and how he'd committed an almost identical crime nearly 20 years ago.

They would soon find out.

The officer in charge of the case was Adam Pasciak, then a sergeant. Sergeant Pasciak gave Dumas his Miranda Warning on 8 December at around 2 a.m., and he agreed to a police interview.

Dumas told Sergeant Pasciak that after he'd returned to the house on the morning of 7 December from the airport, Denise arrived around an hour later and started to question him about his job status and how he was going to pay his bills. Dumas said Denise was 'pushing his buttons'. It was at this point that he decided to go down to the basement and get his gun.

Sergeant Pasciak wrote in his report (8 December 2004):

Dumas stated that he stayed downstairs for a few minutes before deciding to come upstairs with the gun, which had a full magazine but no round in the chamber. At this time he brandished the gun (a sawed off .22 rifle) at Howes, telling her not to 'fuck with' him, and racked a round into the chamber. He stated that she looked afraid and made as if to reach for the phone. Dumas stated he panicked and pointed the gun at Howes [sic] head and pulled the trigger. Per Dumas, Howes fell to the floor but appeared to still be alive. He stated he carried her across to the master bedroom and attempted to put her on the bed, dropping her and causing her head to strike a dresser. He stated he put her on the bed, observing that she was still breathing but unconscious ….

Dumas told Sergeant Pasciak he sat on the couch for several hours. At one point, Dumas picked up the ringing phone. It was Todd Neumann, who wanted to speak with Denise. Dumas told him she was asleep, but like Lyndell Martin almost 20 years prior, Dumas had murdered and sexually assaulted Denise and was now plotting his escape from the house.

He gathered USD$178 in change from around the house, cashed it at a nearby bank and then bought supplies to help him survive in the woods. He had taken Denise's car, and he told police it was later that night, around 10 p.m., that he decided to go back to the house and check on her, and that's when he was spotted by Todd.

Like he told authorities after he'd killed Lyndell Martin, Dumas said that he hadn't planned to kill Denise. However, when searching the house and examining the home computer, detectives found something that demonstrated that Dumas *had* thought about harming Denise.

Sergeant Pasciak showed Dumas a printout from Denise's computer of a text message Dumas had written, dated 3 December 2004, stating she was 'condemned to death'. Dumas told the investigating officer he did write it, but he had no intention of actually hurting Denise, except in an extreme case where he needed money.

He also said he'd served jail time in Australia for killing a woman in 'similar circumstances' and that he had a problem with his temper.

Sergeant Pasciak sent a facsimile to Interpol to try to find out more about the murder Dumas said he'd committed in Australia. The fax, dated 13 December, read:

> I am investigating a homicide … in Redford involving Kurt Michael Dumas W/M 12-12-65 (our case number is 28356-04). The victim was a female he was living with, whom he shot and had sex with. He informed me that he had been arrested in Melbourne, Australia, November 18, 1985, for a similar offense and I am trying to get confirmation of this. He has been formally charged here in Redford and his next court appearance is 12-21-04 – Any help in obtaining information about the Australian incident before the hearing would be greatly appreciated. Thank you, Sgt Adam Pasciak..

Dumas was charged under Michigan state law with murder/non-negligent homicide.

According to an article from the *Redford Observer* newspaper dated 12 December (shared via findagrave.com), Dumas was arraigned on one count each of first-degree murder, felony murder, first-degree criminal sexual conduct and using a gun during a felony.

Dumas's legal team negotiated a plea bargain with the state that meant there was no trial. He pleaded guilty to second-degree homicide and felony firearms. He was sentenced on 8 April 2005 to a minimum of 43 years (maximum 80 years) for the homicide charge and two years for firearms offence. His earliest possible release date: 2049.

Denise's sister Rebecca Redd told me by message on Findagrave. com that Dumas had died of cancer on 14 September 2017. Dumas was serving his sentence at Oaks Correctional Facility in Michigan. Rebecca also told me that Todd Neumann died by suicide on 20 February 2016.

In a message to the author via Findagrave.com on 27 October 2019, Rebecca Redd said:

> Dumas died 9-14-2017 in a hospital of cancer. I sent for a copy of his death certificate to find out. Todd Neumann committed suicide Feb 20, 2016. A end to our families worries, that Dumas will never walk on this earth again, makes us feel a whole lot better. As far as Todd Neumann, well lets (sic) just say he (Neumann) was never convicted as taking part in Denise's death, after his arrest they didn't have enough evidence to hold him. So as far as our family is concerned, they both got what they deserved. It may seem harsh, but that's the reality of this horrific tragedy our family will forever suffer. We miss Denise, we will never be able to fill a void, Dumas and Neumann took that from us. May they both rot in hell for eternity.

When I asked about why the family felt that Todd was involved in Denise's murder, Rebecca replied via Findagrave.com on 28 October 2019:

Neumann was arrested, as was Dumas, the evening of Denise's death. I among with my mother, aunt went to the police station the next morning. Detectives talked to us, we ask (sic) why Neumann was arrested. The detectives said they would be letting him go, without further evidence they could not hold him. They told us "others were involved, just not enough proof to convict. After everything was said and done I knew and my family knew in our hearts Neumann had something to do with Denise's demise. He starting acting out, he became suicidal, and eventually did take his own life. Looking back, the day of Denise's funeral services, Todd had scratches all over his neck and face, deep gouges like he was in a fight. Denise would of fought and fought hard. Denise and Todd had a history of physical altercations between them on a regular basis. He was possessive, controlling. Mentally he was not very stable. There (sic) relationship was horrible to say the least.

THE ULTIMATE BETRAYAL

Imagine if in your final moments you knew the person you have loved most in the world was the one who was ending your life? The thought is devastating.

On 9 January 2000, during a routine check of Heathcote National Park in Sydney's south-west, a park ranger noticed a section of a mesh wire fence was missing. When he went to investigate why the fence on the fire service road was damaged, he saw a car – a Mitsubishi Magna sedan – down an embankment. There were two dead people inside – a man in the driver's seat and a woman in the passenger seat. The man was 'slumped in the footwell' and the woman was 'in the front passenger seat secured by her seatbelt'. (R v David William Weightman [2005] NSWSC 1354.)

The bodies were identified as being Sydney couple William 'Bill' and Pamela Weightman from Glen Alpine, a suburb considered to be affluent, family friendly, green and spacious. Bill, 51, and Pamela, 50, were childhood sweethearts and owned a childcare centre together. They worked hard to provide a comfortable life for themselves and their only child, David, who was just shy of 21 when they died. They had adopted David in 1979 in England when he was a baby. The young family immigrated from Birtley, Tyne and Wear to Sydney when David was three.

Pamela's sister, Margaret Urwin, and her husband, Alan, identified the couple. They had to attend the morgue in Glebe at 10 p.m. on the night Bill and Pamela's bodies were found. No one could locate David to tell him the shocking news that his parents were dead.

The Urwins found their nephew at 3 a.m. on Monday, 10 January. David was at a friend's house. When the distraught Margaret told her nephew about his parents' deaths, she was taken aback by his lack of emotion. His friend seemed more upset than David was at the news.

And in another strange response, Weightman put his parents' house on the market *on the same day* after he was told of their deaths. According to the Urwins, he did not even ask for any details about what happened to his parents.

The Urwins, on the other hand, were in shock, and nothing was yet clear about why Bill and Pamela had been in a car accident. However, even in their dismay, the couple could not understand the fact that their loved ones' bodies looked like they'd been assaulted.

Alan told ABC's *7.30 Report* aired on 6 October 2007, 'When we identified them at Glebe Morgue, I said it just looks like they've been in a fight because of the bruising on their faces ... and Pam's hair was all matted ... as though she'd been pulled through a hedge backwards, you know.'

The cause of the Weightmans' deaths was believed to be due to a car accident, and there was to be no inquest. The post-mortem examination found Pamela died from a blunt force head injury and the aspiration of gastric contents – in other words, she breathed the contents of her stomach into her lungs. Bill died from a probable combination of 'positional asphyxia' (when the position of a person's body restricts their ability to breath).

Police took a statement from Weightman on 11 January 2000. He said that when he went to his family home on 8 January, his parents were not there but he and his friend stayed at the Glen Alpine house that night. He didn't know where his parents were but he told police he was not overly concerned.

The matter seemed to rest after that, at least in the minds of authorities and David Weightman. He got on with life and took little time in spending, and enjoying, the sizeable amount of money – around A$800 000 – he got from the sale of his parents' estate.

The Urwins appeared to be only ones with doubts about what was believed to have happened. There were elements of the death site that did not seem right, even to the untrained eye. There were no skid marks on the road, and the car seemed to have rolled down the embankment. And why had Bill and Pamela been driving in the national park in the first place?

Alan and Margaret Urwin never felt like Bill and Pamela's deaths were accidental. 'I'm just a humble boilermaker, with no training of any detective work, but it looked wrong to me,' Alan later commented in a 16 October 2007 article by Kate McClymont for *The Sydney Morning Herald*.

Another thing Margaret noticed was that her sister's wedding ring was still at the house, and Pamela would never go out without it on. Also, the bed was unmade, and Pamela was one to always have the bed made before she went anywhere.

The Urwins expressed their deep concerns to coroner Dr Allan Cala, who allegedly assured them the injuries on the couple were consistent with the motor vehicle accident. Margaret told the *7.30 Report*, 'We took [Dr Cala's] word as gospel, so we did change our whole life to support David. And we brought him into our family situation and tried as best we could to get on with our lives.'

Immediately after the deaths, the Urwins took David into the home they shared with their three sons.

Life went on for David Weightman but not for the Urwins, who had deep suspicions that their nephew was involved in his parents' deaths. He had been a heavy user of cannabis and alcohol, and on the last Christmas his parents had been alive (1999), it had been clear to the Urwins that Bill and Pamela were frustrated with their son, who'd only shown up for Christmas day for a short time, having been out partying all night.

The Urwins weren't the only ones who suspected that Weightman may have had something to do with his parents' deaths. In an October 2007 article in *The Sydney Morning Herald* 'Couple's long road to vindication', Alan said he had a police clerical worker photocopy Dr Cala's report for him: 'She came back and said, "I think this couple was murdered, and I think you should go to the police .... I'm telling you he murdered them and he'll be coming after you and your family." '.

Weightman spent eight months travelling the United States by motorbike before returning to live with the Urwins at the end of 2001. However, by the end of 2002, he'd moved out – it was too painful for the Urwins to have him under their roof.

'At Christmas, 2002, we were obligated to invite him over for Christmas,' Margaret told the *Evening Chronicle* in an interview on 29 September 2004. (The couple did several interviews over the years with their local newspaper the *Evening Chronicle*, which kept a keen interest on the case.) 'It was the worst I've ever had in my life, wishing him Merry Christmas, knowing the feelings and the doubts that were going on in my mind,' she said. In early 2003, Margaret even suffered a mild stroke she believed was brought on from the stress and trauma.

In mid-2001, under advisement to have another look at the case, Dr Cala brought up the original post-mortem file on his computer. This second look revealed a mistake. When Dr Cala had determined Pamela died of head injuries from the car crash, he had actually been looking at the autopsy results from another patient's brain – and so, he'd typed the incorrect report number into the computer.

In 2007, Dr Cala was eventually censured and fined A$5500 by the New South Wales Medical Board for his mistake that led to the incorrect autopsy report. In 2003, Dr Cala had moved to South Australia to be the chief forensic pathologist. His New South Wales Medical Board reprimand did not affect his position in South Australia.

A police taskforce, named Tenos, was set up in mid-2001 to investigate the case, prompted by persistent calls from the Urwins. When the case was reinvestigated, an amended report was made on the deaths. The couple had been cremated, so there was no chance of re-examining their bodies, but the new report exposed the fact that the injuries to the couple simply could have not come from a car crash.

Bill Weightman had bruises on his face, but they didn't match up with the car steering wheel, suggesting the bruises were caused before the car 'accident'. He also had other bruises across his chest, arms and legs. The report drew particular attention to 'three spherical-shaped bruises to the left upper arm', which 'indicated he had been firmly gripped or pinioned by another person'. Pamela also had bruising on her face, both her arms and one of her legs. Like her husband, the bruising on her arms indicated she had been 'gripped or pinioned by another'. (R v David William Weightman [2005] NSWSC 1354.) There were also traces of a sedative found in their blood systems.

The report clearly vindicated the Urwins' belief that the couple was killed.

A reconstruction of the motor vehicle accident was performed in early 2003 at the alleged crash site.

During the years after his parents' deaths, Weightman had partied, spent his inheritance money, bought his own home and even got married and had a child.

On 1 February 2004, the Urwins confronted their nephew, again, at a family social gathering.

'All I want to hear from your mouth is what you did to my sister and her husband,' Margaret said.

Weightman confessed. 'Terry killed them,' he replied.

The 'Terry' that Weightman referred to was a man named Terry Donai. The pair had not been friends for long. They had a mutual love of motorbikes. Donai had some acquaintance with Bill and Pamela after he was hired to do trade work on the couple's driveway.

Margaret ushered her nephew to a quieter spot away from earshot of the guests. 'I killed them. I'm an arsehole,' Weightman allegedly told her.

The next day, police came to interview Weightman and videotape his confessions. He was taken to the Glen Alpine house and Pipeline Road where his parents were found in their car.

Here, the whole plot unfolded.

Weightman had planned the murder of his parents with Donai, and it was for no other reason than greed. Weightman had bragged to Donai about the money he stood to inherit in the event of his parents' deaths, claiming that in the two days prior to Bill and Pamela's murders, Donai proposed he kill them and offered to help. Weightman told Donai he did not want to be there, so he was not haunted by bad dreams, and he didn't want his parents to suffer.

The plan was that Donai would smother Bill and Pamela while they were unconscious or at least in a very deep sleep due to sedatives, and then the friends would stage a car accident. For his part, Donai would be paid A$17 000 – the cost of a particular type of motorcycle he wanted.

David told police he had no reason other than financial gain for killing his parents. There was no animosity. He'd had everything he could ever have wanted from his parents when it came to love, security and education.

The night of the planned murders, Weightman made cups of tea for his mum and dad and laced them with tranquilisers that he alleged Donai gave to him.

Expecting the couple to be out cold, Donai went to smother Bill and Pamela, but this proved harder than expected. There hadn't been enough sedative put in their tea, and they were not unconscious.

Weightman waited outside while his friend murdered Pamela, who was in her bed. Smoking a cigarette, Weightman heard his mum scream. Donai came outside a little later. He was sweaty and looked like he'd exerted a lot of energy to kill Pamela.

'[Terry] was stinking like death and he was like, "Gee, that took a lot out of me; I'll need a hand with your dad",' Weightman told the court at Donai's trial.

Weightman explained his rationale to the jury about what happened that night. 'Well, I thought my dad really, really loved my mum and he wouldn't want to keep going without my mum there and I thought ... it would be really weird if I pull the plug now. It doesn't work like that. It wasn't that I hated them, it was more I didn't want them to feel any pain,' he said.

After the murders, Weightman and Donai moved Bill and Pamela to the Magna sedan and drove to the national park where the car was pushed down the embankment at low speed into trees. Pamela had been dressed in a nightie when she was murdered. Weightman and Donai changed her into day clothes before her body was moved to the car. The matted hair her sister and brother-in-law had thought odd was from the struggle she'd put up for her life.

These details were reported only after David Weightman was sentenced in December 2005 for the murders of his parents. He pleaded guilty to the crimes and received 28 years' jail, with a non-parole period of 22 years. His sentence was reduced somewhat because he pleaded guilty. There was also the subject of his mental health and state of mind when the murders took place. He was diagnosed with a schizophrenia-like disorder, and his heavy cannabis use was thought to have made him more vulnerable to the influence of the older Donai.

Justice Peter Hidden said of David Weightman, 'If there was anyone from whom they should have feared no harm, it was he ....' (R v David William Weightman [2005] NSWSC 1354.)

The details of the murders (and the mistake made with the initial autopsy report) were subject to a suppression order. After David Weightman confessed, the police and the prosecution needed to build their case against his friend Donai, and he became a Crown witness against his former mate.

In fact, the secret operation to get Donai to admit his role in the murders was done with undercover detectives aiming to recruit him to a gang of successful criminals whose misdeeds included contract killings. This was a crucial part of the investigation because several years had passed after the murders, and the only word and recollections that could be used were Weightman's.

The details revealed in court of what happened the night of the murders came from Weightman giving evidence at Donai's 2007 murder trial. He had been arrested in 2006 and charged with the murders. Donai denied the allegations made against him.

More harrowing details of the crimes then emerged.

Weightman said he sat on his father's legs while his mate smothered him. Bill, who had been dozing on the couch, fought for his life. 'We went in and there was a shocked look on my dad's face … he put up a big struggle,' *The Daily Telegraph* reported Weightman said.

It's not hard to imagine the shock and distress Bill must have felt in his last moments and the deep sense of betrayal. His son told the court his father had managed to utter the words 'you bastards' as he desperately fought for his life.

Weightman also admitted in front of the jury that he'd faked his mental illness – one of the factors that got him a reduced sentence under 'diminished responsibility'. 'It's not really hard to make stuff up,' Weightman said. He confessed he lied to psychiatrists about hearing voices and seeing things, including 'little gremlins'.

In her 2008 sentencing of Donai, Justice Elizabeth Fullerton said:

> Given the toxicological report following [the] autopsy, she [Mrs Weightman] was unlikely to have been even mildly sedated when the offender fatally assaulted her. Whilst it is not clear whether William Weightman heard his wife's scream, it would appear that he did not react to it. This may have been because of the sedative effect of the [Temazapan] detected at post-mortem which was, in his case, within the therapeutic range. (R v Terry Mark Donai [2008] NSWSC 502.)

Donai was sentenced to life imprisonment for the murders. However, in 2011 on appeal, the sentence was quashed and a new trial ordered. A secretly recorded conversation with an undercover police officer was deemed to have caused a miscarriage of justice. Some of secretly recorded conversations, which were part of the undercover sting to get Donai to confess, were played to the jury. The conversation in question had Donai talking about whether he'd kill someone for money. Journalist Kate McClymont reported from the trial and detailed these tapes in 'Murder inquiry bungle: the secret's out', *The Sydney Morning Herald*, 24 May 2008.

'Is there anything that you wouldn't be prepared to do with us? Like, where would you draw the line?' an undercover officer said in the recorded conversation.

'I'd never kill a child,' Donai said. 'I wouldn't find it hard to kill someone. As long as it wasn't someone too close.'

In this particular conversation, Donai claimed he had 'knocked' a man who'd allegedly stolen 'cash and grass' from him. When the undercover officer asked Donai where he'd hidden the body, Donai said that the victim went in a vat of hot iron.

'His admission of having committed other crimes, and his willingness to commit crimes was not relevant to his prosecution for the present offences,' the appeal judges said. 'The evidence was … in any event wholly prejudicial to the appellant.' (Donai v R [2011] NSWCCA 173.)

Donai, by then 45, was found guilty again at his 2012 retrial. 'In the sanctity of their home, Mr and Mrs Weightman were killed in a brutal manner,' Justice Peter Hidden said.

Justice Hidden told the court he did not accept the Crown's proposition that it was Donai that came up with the plan to kill the Weightmans and convinced Weightman to do so.

'The fact remains that he [Weightman] was prepared to stand by while the offender killed them and, in the event, to assist in the killing of his father. It is, of course, also of significance that the victims were his adoptive parents, who had cared and provided for him,' Justice Hidden said. (R v Donai Terry Mark [2012] NSWSC 1102)

Justice Hidden also said he was at a loss to understand why Donai, who was of 'general good character' had committed such 'dreadful crimes'.

It was acknowledged by Justice Hidden that Weightman had essentially lied about the symptoms and his mental health, so he'd get a reduced sentence.

The court also heard that a teacher had sexually abused Donai, a father of two sons, when he was nine and then a Catholic priest when he was 11 years old. A psychiatric assessment for the court also found that a pattern of drinking and use of cannabis by Donai was problematic, and he had post-traumatic stress disorder from the sexual abuse and the enduring effects over the years.

Donai will be eligible for parole in 2039, and Weightman's earliest parole date is in 2026.

Outside the court after Donai was sentenced, Alan Urwin said to the press, 'For four years, we had to do the job for New South Wales Police. For four years, they were telling us that this was a motor vehicle accident, that we're being paranoid, and get on with our life.'

The Urwins' quest for justice came at a huge cost. Their marriage dissolved and the pair went their separate ways.

'It was easier to get our nephew to confess to murdering his parents than it is to get government departments to account for why they couldn't detect an obvious double murder,' Alan told the *Evening Chronicle* in January 2007 after Weightman was sentenced.

Margaret told the newspaper in 2008, when she was on a trip to her childhood home of Gateshead, in the north of England, that her nephew was 'pure evil'.

'They loved him so much. My sister couldn't have her own children, and she was the happiest she'd ever been when they got David.'

THE BROWNOUT STRANGLER

Melbourne was on heightened alert. The city was in brownout conditions. The lights were dimmed to reduce the threat of air raids from the Japanese, who had already bombed the city of Darwin on 19 February 1942. On that day, 242 Japanese aircraft attacked ships in the town's harbour and airfields.

Only one in four streetlights was lit, and train stations had their lighting subdued. Many workplaces would let women employees leave work early to avoid going home in the dark.

One of the consequences of these brownouts was an increase in deaths, especially on the roads. The advice to Melburnians from the Victorian State Government during the brownout was to remain indoors after dark and 'avoid unnecessary risks'.

Another big change for the city was the presence of American soldiers. American service personnel started arriving in Australia in December 1941, and it's estimated that for the next four years almost one million of them spent some time in Australia. There were thousands of young men stationed in Melbourne for recuperation. It was known as the 'friendly invasion'. US servicemen stayed in accommodation called Camp Pell, which today is known as Royal Park.

And some women of Melbourne were certainly enamoured of these young servicemen – they had sharper uniforms than their Aussie counterparts and knew how to dance and have a good time. The soldiers were greeted warmly at first, and then resentment grew among some local men because the intrigue about these visitors was competition for the home-grown blokes.

On 3 May 1942, a tradesman was on his way to work at 6.50 a.m. in the inner-city suburb Albert Park. He spied a man, who appeared to be in a uniform, rising from a crouching position in the doorway near the hotel on the main stretch of Beaconsfield Parade. The man, who seemed to be quite tall, walked away from the doorway where the body of a woman lay. The witness saw the body and immediately contacted police, though he did not get a decent look at whoever had just walked away from the scene.

The woman was Ivy Violet McLeod, 40. Her skull had been fractured.

In the days after the murder, the city was on high alert. The last person to see Ms McLeod (besides the killer) was a friend of hers who lived in Albert Park. Prior to her murder that night, the pair had enjoyed supper, talked and drank beer in his flat. Ms McLeod left the flat at 2 a.m. to catch the tram to her home in nearby East Melbourne. The friend offered to walk her to the tram, but he told police she'd said she wasn't afraid to go alone, despite the brownout conditions. Her tram was due around 2.45 a.m.

Less than a week later, another woman was found dead in the city. Pauline Thompson, 31, was found dead at 5 a.m. on 9 May on the steps of her residence in Spring Street in the city.

Mrs Thompson, whose policeman husband lived and worked in country Victoria with their children, had planned to meet an American soldier she'd made friends with, but when he was late, she didn't hang around and ended up in a hotel in Collins Place, in the CBD. Several people came forward to police to say they'd seen Mrs Thompson in the company of an American serviceman that night.

In the quest to find who killed her, Victoria Police did something they'd never done before. Using a recent photograph of Mrs Thompson, the photographic department superimposed the image on a picture of a dummy model that had been dressed to resemble what the dead woman had been wearing the night she was killed.

The investigation relied on eyewitnesses who had seen the victims with their killer or seen anyone acting strangely after the murders. There were no DNA tests or FBI criminal profilers who could shed light on the offender back then.

Mrs Thompson's husband Les was forced to defend his wife's reputation amid gossip about why she lived in Melbourne, away from her family. A distraught Mr Thompson gave an 'exclusive' interview to the *Truth* newspaper a few weeks after the murder.

The tearful and drained Mr Thompson said it was a mutual decision that his wife, who did some work on radio, move back to Melbourne from Bendigo after six years in the regional city so she could work and help the war effort through her talent as an entertainer.

'Pauline was always so bright, so entertaining and so full of life, that it was natural she was in great demand at parties and entertainments for various charities in the town,' he explained. 'She was a talented musician, and when war charities, concert parties, and camp concerts began to assume bigger proportions, she was itching to do more as some contribution to the war effort than was possible in Bendigo.'

The man who found Mrs Thompson's body, a nightwatchman named Henry McGowan, also spoke to the newspaper. 'The poor woman may have been lying there while I passed by before 5 a.m.,' he said. 'It's so dark there, it was just a lucky chance I happened to see her at all. She was lying there spreadeagled, and I immediately thought she had been outraged. She was a well-built woman and looked composed, but there were marks on her throat and her clothes were pulled down to the waist and up from the thighs, leaving her almost naked.'

Mr McGowan found the victim's handbag in a nearby lane while he was on his rounds an hour before he found her body.

For Mrs Thompson's husband, whom the *Truth* described as 'gaunt and hollow-eyed', the speculation about his wife's character was something that added to his pain.

Mr Thompson told the *Truth*, 'What makes it all the harder to bear was when young Bruce [their son] and I left her on the station a few hours before she was killed, she promised him she'd be home for his birthday on May 24, and she'd be home for good.'

The murders of the first two women in similar circumstances were being linked, and from tracing the movements of the victims' and eyewitness accounts, it was becoming clear that the murderer was likely an American soldier.

On 18 May 1942, the killer struck again.

At 6 p.m. that evening, 40-year-old Gladys Hosking left her office – the chemistry department of The University of Melbourne – and set off for home, walking several blocks with a friend. When the two parted ways, Ms Hosking continued walking towards to the boarding house where she lived in Parkville. She never made it home.

At around 9 p.m., at Gatehouse Street, Parkville, in the heart of Melbourne, an Australian soldier, who was on duty guarding some trucks, noticed a man crawling under a nearby fence. The soldier shone his torch on the man, who was covered in yellowy-brown mud.

'Where do I get a tram to Royal Park?' the muddied man asked. His uniform identified him as an American soldier. The American soldier was looking for his way to his accommodation at Royal Park, not far away.

The Australian asked, 'Where in the hell have you been?'

He replied, 'I fell over in a pool of mud going across the park.' He then set off in the direction of the trams.

In the early hours the next day, Ms Hosking was found dead facedown in a muddy trench. Not far from her body was a still-open umbrella and handbag. Her clothing was torn away, and she had been strangled. From the chaotic scene, it was clear to detectives that Ms Hosking had fought for her life.

The police were able to pinpoint Ms Hosking's killer from the mud trail that led from her body to the nearby Camp Pell. When police followed the mustard-coloured mud back to the camp, they were led to the tent of Edward Joseph Leonski, who was a young private with the 52nd Signal Battalion.

A fellow soldier at the camp was pivotal in identifying Leonski as the killer of the three women. This soldier was at the same camp and had known Leonski since their time in Texas. The soldier had seen Leonski at his tent on the night of 9 May at around 9 p.m. (Leonski had murdered Pauline Thompson in the early hours of that morning.) The solider said Leonski appeared drunk and was distressed, crying, 'I killed. I killed.' The pair caught the tram into the city, and Leonski continued to talk about the murder of a woman on a 'doorstep, doorstep'. Leonski kept muttering about murders and wiping fingerprints from the crime scene.

The next morning, the soldier saw Leonski, who asked him, 'Did you ever hear of a werewolf? Did you ever hear of Dr Jekyll and Mr Hyde? I'm like him – two personalities.'

The conversations disturbed Leonski's pal, and he said, 'This thing is driving me mad. I will have to turn you in.' Leonski reportedly shrugged and said he'd deny the crimes anyway, and the other soldier never reported anything.

It turned out that Leonski had attacked other women before the first murder.

In one case, he left a monogrammed singlet behind with the initials E L. The woman he'd attacked had met the smooth-talking Leonski when he struck up a conversation with her at one of Melbourne's busy train stations – Spencer Street – and asked if she could give him directions.

The married woman (the newspapers called her Mrs B) walked with the young man, who appeared charming and polite, and when they reached the doorstep of her inner-city flat, she wished the young man well and turned her back to open the door.

Leonski startled her when he pushed her inside and grabbed her neck when she screamed at him to get out. He disrobed, standing naked in her kitchen. The woman's screams alerted other people in the apartment block. Leonski fled the apartment, grabbing his clothes, but he left behind a singlet with his initials.

The woman didn't report that attack to police at the time, claiming she was too ashamed of what had happened. She had been set to fly to Brisbane, and she and her husband decided to go ahead with the trip and put the awful incident behind them. However, they kept the singlet.

By the time of the third murder, the woman, now living in Sydney, contacted police and told them what had happened to her. The fact she still had the singlet in her possession was a win to the investigators.

Another woman who escaped from Leonski with her life was a woman the newspapers dubbed Miss X. Leonski saw Miss X at the Melbourne Glaciarium – a large-scale ice-skating rink in the city – and asked her to skate with him. She politely declined the brash young soldier. When she left the ice rink, Miss X had no idea Leonski had been watching her and was following her home to South Melbourne. Leonski caught up to her as she alighted from the tram near her place. The woman told police that Leonski grabbed her around the neck and said, 'I was going to kill a girl tonight, you may as well be the one.' A passer-by heard Miss X's screams and ran to save her. ('Women who escaped killer', *Truth*, 15 November 1942.)

Leonski's brutal crimes raised questions about his sanity. The murders were committed when Leonski was under the influence of alcohol, but what was he like sober?

At Leonski's court martial, doctors detailed the young killer's disastrous family life. His parents – his father from Russia and his mother from Poland – were alcoholics. One of his brothers was in jail, another in a mental asylum. In one newspaper report, Leonski was described as 'perfectly built – about five feet nine inches (175 centimetres) tall with broad, powerful shoulders and hands'.

Dashing, handsome and somewhat cheery when sober, Leonski turned into a violent, angry killer, and he had, some press speculated, a mother fixation. His victims weren't young – they were more mature women in their thirties and early forties.

Leonski's unstable history raised questions about how he had even been allowed into the army. Before he landed on Australian soil, Leonski's unit had been in San Antonio, Texas. Shockingly, it was revealed Leonski had actually tried to strangle a woman while he was there. She didn't want to pursue an assault charge against him.

Sergeant Syd McGuffie interviewed Leonski in his cell and said the young man confessed, 'Fancy me a murderer! I guess that girl Thompson was the hardest. She was strong, and oh boy, could she drink gin squashes. She told me I had a baby face, but I was wicked underneath.' ('Queer mental quirk bared at soldier's murder trial', *St Petersburg Times*, 17 July 1942.)

Leonski also had a fascination with female voices. He said of Gladys Hosking at his trial, 'We came to a spot in the park. She had a lovely voice. I wanted it for myself. So I choked her! I choked her! She was a soft thing; she didn't even cry out.'

Leonski was actually never charged under Australian law with any crimes. The United States took charge of the matter with a court martial. Leonski pleaded not guilty to all charges, claiming he was insane.

Hayford Octavius Enwall was the trial judge advocate appointed to Leonski. Enwall was working as the chief legal officer of the US Army Services of Supply in Melbourne at the time. It was the first time a person was tried in Australia by a military tribunal for crimes that violated another country's civilian criminal law.

The court martial was held in a hall in Russell Street, Melbourne. It was heavily guarded, and press entry was very limited. The waiting press photographers could never get a clear shot of Leonski as he entered the hearing each day because he bowed his head and was flanked by military guard.

At the conclusion of the trial on 19 July 1942, where Leonski was sentenced to death, his trial judge advocate Hayford Octavius Enwall said, 'For five days this court has heard a story of human tragedy and depravity unparalleled in the administration of criminal justice in the United States Army.'

There were diplomatic tensions. Some believed the court martial and death sentence were a gesture by the United States to calm the Australian public who were seeming to tire of the American soldiers on their soil.

Leonski's mother back in the United States was shielded from the details, especially the fact that her son was going to die. Leonski's sister Helen was reported as commenting, 'It is unbelievable. My brother was a churchgoer, a high school honour student, and a model son. He never cared for girls, but seemed to be changed after being drafted into the army, when he began to drink.'

But Leonski seemed unperturbed by his death sentence. Newspapers reported that Leonski slept well, was jovial and 'plays checkers, reads and writes'.

A priest from the United States Army was organised to visit the condemned man at his request. Perth newspaper *The Mirror* reported, 'A padre was waiting for him, and they talked for a few moments in hushed tones. Then a US Army officer, in charge of the armed guard, touched Leonski on the arm and motioned to him that his time was up.'

Leonski continued with his jocular and odd comments. 'Well, they've measured me and weighed me. It won't be long now!' he said as he awaited his fate.

He was hanged at Pentridge Prison five days after his trial ended. The only Australian involved in any part of the execution was the hangman. Leonski was the first US soldier to be executed on foreign soil.

Leonski's remains have been moved several times since his death. He was first buried (and moved a few times on the same site) at Melbourne's Springvale Cemetery. The remains were then dug up and reinterred in an American war cemetery in Brisbane, Queensland. Later, the remains were shipped out of Australia and sat in a distribution centre for almost a year before the final resting place in Hawaii at the Schofield Barracks Post Cemetery in 1949.

A film was made about the case called *Death of a Solider*. Released in 1986, the Australian-made film received lukewarm reviews (the *New York Times* called it 'pallid'). James Coburn was the big-name star who played a US Army investigator.

Military police guarding the trial of Edward Leonski, known as "The Brownout Strangler" during World War II, Melbourne, 1942. Source: the Argus Newspaper Collection of War Photographs, *State Library of Victoria.*

THE VICIOUS MURDER OF ROSE BUDISELIC

In Perth in 1953, at the Home of Peace for the Chronic Sick in Subiaco, young nurse assistants Barbara Rose Budiselic (named Rose), 19, Ethel Rhodes (known as Ann), 17, and Lucy Kersley were asleep in the staff quarters. At around 4 a.m., Lucy awoke to the sound of screaming. What she thought was a bad dream was actually her roommate Rose being attacked by a man who'd entered their room. Lucy saw the man striking Rose repeatedly with what looked like a large knife.

Ann had awoken moments earlier and flicked on the light to see Rose being attacked. She had rushed towards the door, intent on getting help, but the man launched at her, stabbing her several times. She dropped onto the floor by Rose's bed and lost consciousness for a few moments. When she woke, Ann managed to flee the room and seek help.

Rose was found on the floor, bleeding and semiconscious. She had been stabbed five times. Ann had been stabbed eight times – three in her shoulder and five in the chest – but she was, incredibly, not critically injured. Rose was raced to hospital to undergo emergency surgery but died between the casualty ward and operating theatre. One of her wounds, under her collarbone, had severed an artery.

Detectives took possession of a bloodstained bayonet and a revolver found near the Rose's bed, as well as a bayonet scabbard found on the grounds. Newspapers reported the sad side story that the Home of Peace's resident dog Fifi 'refused to budge from the doorstep' of Rose's hut: 'Fifi was a particular friend of the victim.'

The man who had attacked Rose was not a stranger to the three women. He was 22-year-old RAAF aircraftman Duncan McColl Morton, and he had previously been 'friendly' with Rose.

After attacking Rose, Morton went to the home of one of his aunts, in Belmont, arriving at 6.30 a.m. She told police that he seemed 'a bit dazed'. They heard on the radio that Rose Budiselic had been stabbed, but when the aunt asked if the victim was Morton's girlfriend, he shook his head and left.

Detective Sergeant HD Burrows interviewed Morton at the RAAF Base Pearce, where he was stationed. At first, he denied any involvement in the attack and said he had last seen Rose a fortnight previously. He claimed he had been at another aunt's house in East Perth the night of the murder. Detective Sergeant Burrows asked, 'Who can prove you were at home all last night?'

'My aunt,' Morton replied.

'I have seen your aunt, and I am afraid she cannot help you. Were you at the Home of the Peace last night?'

'Yes.'

Morton was reluctant to answer further questions but eventually admitted to attacking Rose. He was arrested on a charge of wilful murder.

Details were reported in newspapers, including headlines like 'Broken romance motive hinted in Home of Peace tragedy' that showed the ideas of the time and the lack of understanding about violence against women.

Rose's fiancé, Herbert Harrison gave an interview to the *Sunday Times* in the days after the shocking attack that the night before she'd died, Rose, who was originally from Kalgoorlie, told him of a strange dream she'd had. The newspaper story, which ran on 22 March 1953, was titled 'Startling dream interrupted wedding'. Mr Harrison was a sapper – a combat engineer – who was due to go to Korea. He last saw Rose a few hours before she was killed. They had walked together in the streets of Subiaco, excitedly talking of their future. The couple had somewhat of a whirlwind romance, having only met five weeks before Rose's murder.

'She had dreamed of our wedding, and we were just about to move down the aisle of a church together when suddenly something black, and rushing – like a figure of evil – came upon us and came between us,' Mr Harrison said.

'Suddenly we were stopped, and then there was only darkness. She woke up screaming and couldn't remember any more.'

Giving evidence at Morton's trial a few months after the murder, Ann, dressed in black with a veil, recalled the night of terror.

'I turned on the light and made for the door. Morton was in the room with us. He was standing over Rose's bed. He seemed to be holding Rose down with his left hand and had something in his right. I never heard him say anything.

'As I made for the door, he grabbed me, and I felt something go into my right

shoulder. That's all I remember until I came to lying at the foot of Rose's bed.'

Ann told the court of the history between Morton and Rose. They had been 'keeping company' for several months, and there was even talk of an engagement. However, weeks before she was killed, Rose cooled the relationship with Morton.

Ann said she had seen Morton on 14 March, five days before the attacks, and told him Rose was seeing another man. She said that Morton said, 'Wish her luck for me.'

Lucy was also called as a witness at the trial and recounted the horror night. She said she woke to Rose's screams and saw 'Tex' Morton standing over Rose and striking at her.

'Rose was screaming, "Don't, don't",' Lucy said. 'I jumped out of bed and ran to the door. I heard him say, "If you don't wear my ring, you don't wear anybody else's".'

Morton was called on by the defence to tell his story of what happened that night. He said he was 'hurt and upset' by a letter from Rose to whom he'd been 'unofficially engaged'.

'I had a bad dream,' Morton told the court. 'I could see Ann [Ethel] Rhodes and Rose with the letter I had received on Monday, and they were laughing about it. This woke me up and I noticed the time was only three o'clock.

'I decided to see Ann Rhodes and tell her to stop interfering in my business. I also wanted to tell the truth to Rose about the letter.'

Morton said he hadn't meant to kill Rose but was angry with her. When she saw him in the room, she started screaming.

Morton said he told her to stop. 'She was pretty hysterical and grabbed [at] the bayonet,' he said. 'I tripped and fell, and the bayonet struck her. There had been a bit of a scuffle, and when this happened, I lost my block. Next I remember I was standing by her bed, and she was bleeding freely.'

Morton was sentenced on 11 May to hang for Rose's murder. The trial lasted one day, and the jury took 15 minutes to reach their verdict. However, they made a recommendation for mercy for Morton, owing to his young age. Addressing Morton, Chief Justice John Dwyer said, 'The stabbing of this girl was vicious, in my opinion, and at the time when she was helpless to defend herself.'

Newspaper reports said Morton 'showed no sign of emotion' as the sentence was handed down.

When it came to the death penalty, the ultimate decision was decided by the executive council of the West Australian state cabinet. On 28 May 1953, two weeks after the trial verdict, the state cabinet recommended that Morton's death sentence be commuted to life imprisonment.

Barbara Rose Budiselic, known as 'Rose', and her dog Fifi. Fifi reportedly refused to leave the hut where Rose was murdered. Source: 1953 'Murdered nurse HER PET DOG REFUSES TO LEAVE HER HUT', The Herald (Melbourne, Vic. : 1861 - 1954), *20 March, p. 1. (Via Trove)*

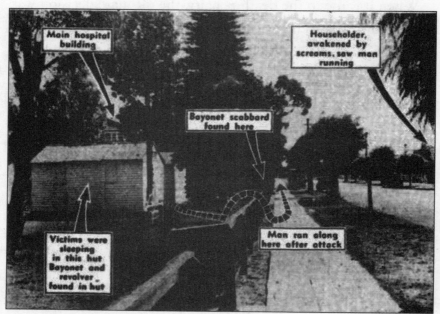

The scene where Rose Budiselic, a 19-year-old nursing assistant, was murdered. Source 1953, The West Australian (Perth, WA : 1879 - 1954), *20 March, p. 1. (Via Trove)*

THE FAMILY KILLER

In 1994, a suburban nightmare unfolded in Berkeley, Wollongong. The Velevski family lived in Castle Street, in a neat, three-bedroom brick home, with a double garage and lovely views. Husband and wife Ljube and Snezana had three daughters: Zaklina, six, and three-month-old babies Daniela and Dijana. The couple had met in 1988, when Snezana was eighteen. Ljube, three years older, had migrated to Australia from Macedonia in 1986. He was a shift worker at BHP, one of the main employers in Wollongong. Ljube's parents also lived with them, as is customary in Macedonian culture.

Sometime between 9 p.m. on Sunday, 19 June and 5 a.m. the next day, an event of unimaginable brutality happened in the master bedroom of the house. But this was not discovered until much later the afternoon of the Monday, 20 June.

It is believed the couple had a fight. The only person who could tell the story of the argument was Ljube Velevski. His story was that the pair argued at around 11 a.m. – he claimed Snezana had threatened to take the children and leave him because she was frustrated about living with his parents. He said she then retreated to their bedroom with the children, locking the door. However, unable to unlock the door (so he later claimed), Velevski went to bed in Zaklina's room at around 1 p.m., where he says he slept for 17 hours.

His story was that he awoke at 6 a.m. and could not find his wife. He stated the house was silent … no sounds of the babies gurgling or even crying. Velevski said he woke his parents quite early on the Monday morning and drove them to his sister's home, ten minutes away. His sister suggested he visit the Macedonian welfare centre in Port Kembla. The welfare centre was a community hub where Macedonians in the area gathered for social reasons and for support. He spoke to someone at the centre for advice about his marriage and reportedly said several times to the social worker that he could not gain access to the house and had concerns for his children. Staff there told him that he should check at Zaklina's school to see whether she was there. When he found out that Zaklina had not attended school, he decided to go to his neighbour for help.

Velevski asked his neighbour, Mr Jorge, if he'd seen his wife, and said, 'I don't know where my wife is. I don't know if she's in the room or if she piss off, because the door it's locked.' ('Bodies piled in bedroom', *The Daily Telegraph*, 23 May 1997.)

It was now 3 p.m. Mr Jorge called the police and mid-conversation asked Velevski when he'd last seen his wife. The neighbour got the gist of Velevski's weak English to tell police, 'He said since two o'clock this morning that door has been locked.' (Velevski v R [2002].)

Senior Constable Sonia Hayden attended the address with another police officer. Velevski showed them into the house and directed the pair to the main bedroom door where he told them his wife had been with the children since the previous day.

Kneeling to peer under the door, Hayden could see a pair of human legs. 'The skin appeared to be blue in colour,' she later recounted in the New South Wales Supreme Court.

Using a hammer to break in the door, Hayden was confronted with a devastating scene. Snezana was on top of a child – Zaklina – who was on top of a baby. None appeared to be breathing. Taking a closer look, the policewoman saw there was in fact another baby there too.

An officer from the police video unit was called to the scene soon after, at around 6 p.m. The gruesome scene had to be videotaped. It was a traumatic sight for the officers and other services at the scene.

The bodies appeared neatly stacked between the marital bed and a baby cot. Snezana's bloodstained body was lying face down. When she was removed from the stack, there was little Zaklina. Then after her body was lifted, the tiny twins were beneath, their heads almost severed from the cuts to their throats.

Crown prosecutor Paul Conlon told the jury that circumstantial evidence showed Velevski had killed his family after an argument with Snezana, and it was during this fight she said she would leave him and take their daughters too.

Two other alternatives were also considered. The first was that Snezana killed her children then took her own life. The second, that Velevski's father, Petre, was the killer. The theory on Petre Velevski was that he was angry about being told by Snezana the day before her death that she wanted him and his wife to move out.

The court document *R v Velevski* (1999) makes mention of Mr Velevski senior's devotion to his eldest granddaughter and that he would walk the little girl to and from school. How could anyone believe such a besotted and loving grandfather would kill his beloved grandchild?

Dr Peter Bradhurst, a forensic pathologist, gave his expert opinion in court that he thought Snezana could have cut her own throat. He told the Supreme Court there was no sign of a struggle or typical self-defence wounds on Snezana – the room was a 'quiet scene'. He did not observe any evidence that a struggle took place.

For the jury, this posed the question: were Snezana and the children killed while they were sleeping, or attacked from behind? Or did Snezana kill her own babies and then herself?

Conlon pushed Dr Bradhurst to expand on his view of the crime scene. The doctor conceded that in some homicide cases there could be a 'quiet scene' like the one at the Velevski home. He said it could be possible someone may not have typical self-defence injuries if they were caught unawares from behind or attacked while asleep. Referring to the parallel cuts, Bradhurst said they were generally typical of a self-inflicted wound but, from time to time, it could be a homicide wound.

If the timeline of the deaths were correct, then Velevski's parents were also in the house when the deaths occurred. And they reported that they heard *nothing*. Their bedroom was separated from the two other bedrooms by a corridor.

Why did Velevski want his parents out of the house? His explanation was that there had sometimes been antagonism between his wife and his parents, and on some occasions he had asked them to go the sister's house to relieve some of the tensions.

The Crown believed there was a window of time between Velevski taking his parents to his sister's and going to the welfare centre where he returned home. He said he did not check the room, which the Crown asserted could be an indication of guilt. The Crown also believed that it was at this time that Velevski cleaned up the home, because if the approximate time of death was to be followed, then Snezana and the children were already dead.

When Senior Constable Hayden first broke into the main bedroom, there was reportedly no light on and the curtains were drawn closed. So, if the defence's case of murder-suicide was to be believed then (between 9 p.m. on the Sunday evening and 5 a.m. on the Monday) Snezana slit the throats of her children, placing their bodies in a neat pile, and then slit her own throat, all in the dark. There was no blood found on the light switches, nor were any identifiable prints detected. The Crown asserted that Velevski murdered his family, with the lights on and curtain closed, and then switched the lights off when he left the room. Whether he wiped the light switch clean was not determined, only that no prints could be identified.

Velevski, by this stage 32 years old, was found guilty of murder and sentenced on each count to a minimum of 19 years' jail to be served concurrently.

Justice John Dunford thanked the jury in their efforts to find a verdict. The evidence, especially the photos and video of the crime scene, was extremely distressing.

'It has not been an easy case and there [have] been a lot of problems ... and it has been unpleasant,' Justice Dunford said on 15 July 1997, when the guilty verdict was announced.

Velevski maintained his innocence, stating to the media as he was led away, 'My whole life I have to suffer without my children ... and it's very sad on my innocent soul for me to be in jail for the rest of my life.' ('Killer: I'm innocent', *The Daily Telegraph*, 23 August 1997.)

In 1999, an appeal against his conviction was rejected at the New South Wales Criminal Court of Appeal. One of the three judges, Justice James Kirby, believed there was a 'significant possibility that an innocent person has been convicted'.

'Further, in respect of the medical evidence, I believe that there has been a miscarriage of justice, justifying a new trial,' Kirby said. ('Killer: I'm innocent', *The Daily Telegraph*, 23 August 1997.)

Questions were raised about the locked bedroom door, as Velevski claimed he could not open the door to check on or speak to his wife. With the defence's case proposing that the deaths were a murder-suicide at the hands of Snezana, the issue was bound to be raised whether Velevski could have killed his wife and children if he couldn't enter the room – as claimed – because it was locked.

Expert evidence from a locksmith determined the particular lock on the bedroom door was one that could be manipulated where you could very gingerly close the door so that it locked from the outside and give the appearance of it having been locked from the inside. And the lock could be opened from the outside, using an implement like a screwdriver and even an icy pole stick.

Velevski's lawyer in later appeals, Wollongong barrister and public defender Andrew Haesler (now a district court judge), told the High Court judges the defence could not rely on the locked door as proof of Velevski's innocence but that someone, if they knew what they were doing, could have entered the room and locked it as they left.

Velevski's team appealed to the High Court. During the criminal trial, pathologists and doctors had all given their opinions on whether Snezana killed herself or was murdered.

At the 2001 hearing, Haesler laid out the problems they had with the Crown's case and the conviction.

Haesler said, 'If you look for complexity in this case, you will find it, but we say there are some simple things and Mr Velevski is not the calm, calculated murderer he was made out to be. He did odd things and those odd things he did are relied upon to show his guilt when in fact all they are is ... "odd" ....' (Velevski v The Queen [2001] S197/2000.)

The appeal was rejected. Two of the three judges, Justices Ian Callinan and William Gummow said in a joint statement that there was a strong circumstantial case that Velevski killed his family, and his explanations were not credible in major aspects. The two judges also felt the conflicting medical evidence was not too hard for the jury to grasp and make a decision. However, the third judge, Justice Mary Gaudron, felt the appeal should be allowed.

In 2013, Snezana's family obtained court permission to sell the Castle Street house. The couple were joint owners, but in 1995, Velevski had the property registered in his name alone after he filed a notice of death about his wife.

Snezana's father Kiril Josifovski was appointed trustee for the sale of the property, which meant Velevski could not inherit her part of the estate. Snezana's stake in the house would stay in the hands of her parents and brother. The judge ordered Velevski to pay Mr Josifovski's costs and expenses of the sale of the property out of what would otherwise be his share of the proceeds of the sale.

In 2014, the house went to auction, selling for A\$382 500. New South Wales real estate agents are legally required to disclose if a violent death or suicide happens in a property. Estate agent Anthony Sorace told the *Ilawarra Mercury* in 2013 that the gruesome history of the house had not turned people off the property.

'Surprisingly, it didn't bother too many people, there were a very small percentage who were turned away and said no, I won't come to have a look at the property, no I'm not interested,' Mr Sorace said. 'Funnily enough … the husbands don't mind the situation, they're happy to live in the property, but it's the wives that are against it.'

In May 2021, Velevski chose not to apply for parole. It was the sixth time he had been eligible to apply since his non-parole period of 19 years ended in 2016, and he has declined to apply each time. Velevski's maximum sentence expires in July 2022.

A May 2020 media release from the New South Wales Parole Authority said since entering custody 'the offender has not engaged in any programs to address his violent offending, refuses to participate in any assessments requested by Community Corrections and declines to be interviewed by the Serious Offenders Review Council'.

THE MELBOURNE CUP DAY MURDER

Melbourne Cup Day is a public holiday dedicated to the horse racing event known as 'the race that stops the nation'.

But in 1984, the day was marked by a crime that shocked the public and terrified parents – the abduction, rape and murder of six-year-old Kylie Maybury in suburban Melbourne.

For Melburnians of a certain age the murder of Kylie is one they'll never forget. The school photo portrait of Kylie used in the media shows a sweet, freckle-faced little girl with mousey brown hair in a bowl cut.

Kylie had watched the Melbourne Cup race along with her mum – 24-year-old Julie Maybury – her sister and a neighbour at a pub local to their Preston home in Melbourne's inner north. They returned to their neighbour's flat. Kylie's mum and neighbour wanted a cup of tea and asked Kylie to go to the shop to grab some sugar. The Food Plus store in Plenty Road, Preston, was only about 150 metres from Kylie's home in Gregory Grove.

Kylie never made it back.

She'd not come home in 15 minutes from when she left – more than enough time to run the errand. Mrs Maybury looked for her at the Food Plus store, and when she was told that Kylie had left some time ago, alarm bells began to ring, and she immediately called the police.

In the early hours of the next day, at around 12.45 a.m., a motorist saw Kylie's crumpled little body, still clothed, in a gutter of Donald Street, just over a kilometre from where she lived in Gregory Grove. Police had searched the area thoroughly hours before. so it was believed Kylie was held somewhere for several hours and then her body dumped on the street.

It was the nightmare outcome police had hoped would not come true.

Victoria Police Homicide Squad Detective Inspector Peter Ryan told the media Kylie was the 'victim of a vicious rape and died as a result of that rape and probably shock'.

Victorians were reading about this horror crime in the newspapers in the days after Kylie was found, with headlines like 'Body of girl, six, found in gutter'. It was every parent's nightmare.

Detectives who were somewhat hardened to what they saw day in and out were devastated by Kylie's murder and the sight of her little body dumped in a gutter. The word 'monster' was used to describe whoever killed her.

The manager of the store, Kerry Margaritis, confirmed to police that Kylie went in to buy sugar. 'Between 5.30 p.m. and 5.35 p.m., I was serving behind the counter when a young girl approached me and placed a packet of sugar on the counter,' she said.

'She gave me a handful of small coins, and I put them in the till without counting them. I said, "That's all right, sweetheart," but she just stood there. I said, "That's all right, sweetheart" again and then she left. This young girl who purchased the sugar was the deceased girl Kylie. I saw her photograph on television, and although it is slightly different, I am sure that it was her. I have seen the deceased in the Food Plus on other occasions with her mother.'

Less than a week after the murder, newspapers reported there were two leads police were following up. One was that a man, posing as a photographer, spoke to Mrs Maybury outside her block of flats.

'He asked if she had any children he could photograph .... But this bloke didn't leave his name, he didn't have any camera gear with him and didn't leave a card or anything similar to allow her to contact him,' a detective said.

This lead came to nothing, as did a possible sighting in a Kentucky Fried Chicken of a young girl an hour after Kylie went missing.

The case went nowhere, but over the years, there were strange and tragic happenings and red herrings to do with the case.

There was some suspicion, soon dismissed, that either Kylie's maternal grandfather, John Moss, or her uncle, Mark Maybury, may have been suspects. Both have since died – Mark Maybury hung himself in his cell in Pentridge Prison in 1987. He had left a note naming a man he thought had killed his niece, as well as implicating himself in the murder of two sex offenders. Mr Maybury struggled with mental health and was on remand on violence and theft-related charges when he killed himself.

Kylie's grandfather, John, was the subject of rumours that gained enough traction that the Homicide Squad did interview him, but he was soon ruled out as the killer. The rumours and the shocking death of his granddaughter ruined his life, resulting in the deterioration of his marriage and health. Just before the first anniversary of Kylie's murder, Mr Moss took his life.

In 1985, nine months after the murder, a man put a massive urn atop Kylie's grave at Fawkner Cemetery, telling staff there he was a "gypsy" and he'd put a curse on the urn so if anyone moved it there would be severe consequences. Then a white statue appeared on the grave. After much publicity about the objects, a young man admitted to police that he'd put the items on the grave. However, he was not a suspect in the murder.

The autopsy found there was valium in Kylie's bloodstream. At the coroner's inquest in 1986, Coroner Hugh Adams presumed this was administered by the killer to subdue Kylie. 'The evidence tragically showed that she was sexually assaulted and murdered by a person, or persons unknown … despite intense publicity and police investigations, no one has yet been charged with the murder.'

From the evidence found at the crime scene, the police had a DNA profile for the offender but had no matches in the police database. For several years, they had convicted child murderer Robert Arthur Selby Lowe in their sights for Kylie's rape and murder.

Lowe, who was locked up and never to be released, raped and murdered six-year-old Sheree Beasley in Rosebud, Victoria, in 1991. The little girl was on an errand to the shops, just like Kylie, and was riding her pink bicycle when she was lured into Lowe's car.

Lowe died at age 84 in early November 2021 at the Hopkins Correctional Centre, a medium-security protection facility in Ararat, Victoria.

Lowe, a travelling salesman and churchgoer, had a holiday home in the town. Having seen Sheree riding around by herself before, he had targeted the little girl. He had been a serial public masturbator who, over 30 years, exposed himself to children but had managed to escape penalty for these offences. He was also able to hide a lot of his activity from his wife and two teen sons.

It was first revealed in 1995 that Lowe was a suspect in Kylie's murder due to the similarities in the natures of the murders of both the girls – they were both six; Lowe's salesman work placed him in the Preston area in 1984; and a month before Kylie was murdered, Lowe had exposed his penis at two schoolgirls near the crime scene.

The little Strawberry Shortcake purse Kylie had with her when she went to buy the sugar was found dumped in Wantirna, a suburb not far from Glen Waverley, where Lowe lived.

In 1997, police applied to take blood from Lowe. The Crimes Act allowed police to take blood from convicted prisoners for investigations into other crimes. However, it was a protracted fight to get the blood sample, and extremely distressing for Mrs Maybury, who'd become convinced that Lowe was Kylie's killer.

At a 1997 Supreme Court hearing into the police application to force a blood test from Lowe, Mrs Maybury was there to face the man she believed killed her child.

At the hearing, it was revealed Lowe had obtained Legal Aid to challenge the validity of the Crimes Act to fight the application, and the case was adjourned for several months.

Mrs Maybury told *Herald Sun* reporter Keith Moor she'd come face to face with Lowe as he stepped out of a lift at the court. She said, 'Our eyes met, and I said to him, "Are you looking at me? I hope you are because I am looking right at you, man".'

Mrs Maybury also voiced her disgust, as reported in Moor's 24 May 1997 article that Lowe was granted taxpayer funds via Victorian Legal Aid to fight having his blood taken for DNA. It was a move she said made her believe he was guilty.

'How come people who haven't been convicted of anything can't get legal aid, yet this killer can,' she asked. 'I wouldn't have thought he was entitled to any civil rights after what he did.'

The Office of Public Prosecutions, acting for Victoria Police, ended up withdrawing the application for fear any loopholes in the legislation could see Lowe's challenge succeed.

But in 1998, legislation was introduced in Victorian State Parliament that the Crimes Act would have no retrospective time limit (previously the legislation only extended back to crimes from 1992 onwards), and anyone who'd been convicted of a crime based on a forensic sample could be subjected to DNA comparisons to cold cases on file.

This meant police could obtain a sample of Lowe's blood. However, it was not a match to the DNA left by Kylie's killer.

It was a sickening blow for Mrs Maybury.

Speaking again to journalist Keith Moor for a 2 February 2001 *Herald Sun* article, who had covered the case since the discovery of Kylie's body, Mrs Maybury said she had really thought Lowe was the killer.

'Now we are back to square one, without a suspect,' Mrs Maybury said. 'I need to know who killed my daughter. It won't bring Kylie back, but at least I could begin to try to start a new life.'

Inspector Glenn Woolfe, a detective who doggedly pursued the case for years and prepared the inquest brief, told the *Herald Sun* he hadn't given up hope the murder could be solved by a deathbed confession or from a lead from someone with a guilty conscience who knows something.

For those who remembered Kylie, it was welcomed news that the Victoria Police was taking a fresh look at the case.

'We believe there is someone out there who knows who did it and for some reasons is not telling us,' Inspector Woolfe said. 'I was in the Homicide Squad for eight years, and this is the one murder that sticks in my mind as the one I would dearly love to solve. She was abducted and her body was later dropped in the gutter, just like a piece of rubbish.'

At the time of wrapping up the first edition of Suburban Nightmare in 2016, news broke that a man had been arrested and charged with the rape, false imprisonment and murder of Kylie. When I saw the breaking news that someone had been charged with Kylie's murder, I actually gasped, and I am sure I was not alone. I had written a chapter for the first edition of this book about the then unsolved murder, but the arrest in the case meant I couldn't include it.

The man in now in jail for the rest of his life.

Gregory Keith Davies, then 73, was arrested at the Waterford Park retirement village, in Knoxfield – an unassuming location in Melbourne's outer-east.

The expression 'hiding in plain sight' is often used to describe the lives of criminals who've gone undetected for years. In this case, the expression was absolutely appropriate. Davies had lived a seemingly normal life for decades.

Though he initially denied having anything to do with Kylie's abduction and murder when questioned by police in June 2016, at his committal hearing in 2017, Davies pleaded guilty.

While he was in custody, word got out among the prisoners about Davies' crimes, and he was attacked in his cell with boiling water, which caused serious burns to his neck and groin.

Davies was not unfamiliar with prison life. He spent most of the 1970s in jail for a horrific attack on a 14-year-old girl that almost killed her.

In September 1970, Davies targeted the young girl who was on a Hurstbridge line train travelling home. It was a sneak attack, and Davies bashed her skull, leaving her collapsed on the train floor and bleeding profusely. Davies fled and the girl was found when the train stopped at Eltham Station.

Davies appeared in the Supreme Court in 1971 and was found not guilty, by reason of insanity, of attempted murder and wounding with intent causing grievous bodily harm; however, he was detained in prison 'at her Majesty's pleasure' for many years, eventually being released in 1982. Davies was found to have an IQ of 84, which is slightly below average, and what was referred to back then as 'hysterical dissociation', which in modern diagnostics would be a personality or dissociative disorder.

In his sentencing remarks on 20 December 2017 for the murder of Kylie, Supreme Court Justice Lex Lasry noted that Davies received no medical or psychological treatment during this time.

Davies spent more time in prison in the 1990s for indecent assault and gross indecency against a number of young girls. He had been on the police radar for some time, with a tip to police in 1997 telling officers to take a look at him for Kylie's murder.

Justice Lex Lasry said of the police investigation and efforts into Kylie's murder, 'It is important for both the community and offenders to know that such serious matters are never left behind.'

After the sentencing, Julie Maybury told reporters outside the court that her family could finally move on. 'Kylie was a beautiful little girl; she was a little princess. She was so precious,' she said.

When asked by a reporter if she could tell Davies one thing, she said, 'I'd like to kill him myself.'

THE UNSOLVED UNIVERSITY MURDER

It was early in the morning on Saturday, 29 October 1977, and Annette Louise Morgan was on her way to visit a friend at St Paul's College at Sydney University.

Annette, 18, had been a science student at the university but had left three weeks earlier to train as a radiologist at the Royal Newcastle Hospital. She had moved back in with her parents in the suburb of Warners Bay, near Newcastle.

This jaunt back to Sydney saw her stay with a girlfriend overnight in Glebe, having caught the train from Newcastle on the Friday afternoon.

At around 7.15 a.m. on the Saturday, Annette left her friend's house at Wigram Road, Glebe, and started walking towards the college at Sydney University – a 2.5-kilometre walk. The route Annette took was a popular one that saw people cut through what is known as St Paul's oval to get to the college building. This was done by a gate in the fence.

The university, Australia's oldest, is centrally located in Camperdown, where the hub of the institution's administration and student accommodation is concentrated. The university is bordered by City and Parramatta roads.

At a leisurely pace, the walk would have taken around an hour. Annette was dressed in the fashions of the time, including blue platform-style shoes, which meant her pace may have been slightly slower than someone who had sneakers on. So realistically, Annette would have reached the oval sometime after 8 a.m. but well before 9 a.m.

At 9.50 a.m., a man walking across the oval found Annette. She had been bashed around the head and strangled. A post-mortem indicated that she had also been raped. No murder weapon was found. From the injuries Annette had sustained, it appeared that the man who attacked and murdered her had used his own fists. The post-mortem showed Annette had died of skull fractures. She had bruising on her neck where the killer had tried to strangle her too.

A couple of days later, on 1 November, police issued an identikit picture to the media of a man who had been seen leaving the grounds of Sydney University soon after Annette was killed. He was described as being aged between 35 and 40, and 173 centimetres in height, with a tanned complexion, a solid build, sandy hair and a crooked nose. Was this the killer?

Annette's funeral was held on 2 November at the Catholic church in her hometown. Detectives were part of the 500-strong congregation who came to mourn for a life taken so brutally and young.

Annette Morgan's brutal murder evoked shock and outrage from Australians, especially women students. It was said that her murder highlighted that the attitude towards women at the venerable university, and in society as a whole, was sexist and women were treated as objects.

Annette's murder brought into the mainstream media the discussion about the safety of women on university campuses. Welfare officer Michelle Martin commented that some areas of the university were poorly lit and not patrolled. 'I walked near the spot where the murdered woman was found. There are long grasses near the oval, which should be cut,' Ms Martin was quoted in a 1977 *The Sydney Morning Herald* article. She said the women coming to counselling services on campus was no indication of the true numbers that had been raped and assaulted.

A doctor who had worked at the university for eight years spoke anonymously to *The Sydney Morning Herald* and said the university's security had been inadequate for years.

Disturbingly, many women students came out and spoke of a culture of sexual humiliation of women on campus that was regarded by men as part of 'college fun'. This was detailed in a Letter to The Editor on 28 November in *The Sydney Morning Herald* from Carolyn Van Langenberg and Anne McCarthy titled 'The humiliation of women'.

Meetings and forums were organised in the wake of Annette's murder to bring to attention the patriarchal and sexist attitudes of men towards women.

Women on campus pushed for better security after Annette's shocking murder, with good results. Better lighting, gatekeepers at the main gates and phones placed around campus, with a direct line to a 24-hour security office, were implemented in the months after the crime. An evening mini-bus service operated at 20-minute intervals throughout the grounds of the university to transport women from the main library to bus stops, car parks and the colleges.

In May 1978, seven months after the murder, *The Sydney Morning Herald* reported a man had been questioned by homicide detectives. The article said the man was in custody on another matter. However, this never came to anything.

When this book was first published in 2016, Annette's case has not been mentioned much. A 2007 article in *The Sydney Morning Herald* made a brief mention of the case, which appeared to be long cold. The article said sources connected to the original investigation thought crucial evidence had been lost.

Award-winning investigative journalist, author and campaigner Nina Funnell, who is a rape survivor, has written extensively about sexual assault on Australian university campuses. In an investigative exclusive, she published on *news.com.au* in 2017, '"Rooting", "slaying" and "harpooning" women: sexism at elite St Paul's College exposed', and found that some deeply sexist attitudes still existed at the institution.

The 'root and boot' ethos that was revealed in a Facebook post on the St Paul's 2017 page gave tips for young men at the college to be 'rescued' after a one-night stand when they couldn't 'get rid' of the women they'd had sex with.

The post had almost 100 likes.

Nina created and manages the law-changing campaign #LetHerSpeak/#LetUsSpeak, established to overturn antiquated gag laws that prevented survivors of sexual abuse from talking publicly about their experiences, and to assist survivors to challenge these laws in court. The campaign overturned the laws in Tasmania, Victoria, and the Northern Territory.

WHO KILLED ELAINE JONES?

Melbourne couple Alan and Elaine Jones were like thousands of people who escaped from the suburbs each year to the idyll of camping in rural and coastal Australia.

However, what happened to the Joneses in the New South Wales border town of Tocumwal in the new year of 1980 was a violent nightmare that tore the happy fabric of their lives apart.

Mr and Mrs Jones were camping at the Town Beach Caravan Park in Tocumwal with their two daughters aged 15 and seven. Tocumwal, situated on the Murray River, is a popular tourist town and place to go boating and fishing. Back in 1980, it was a simple, relaxed location for a family getaway. The town's population could increase ten-fold in the summer with thousands of tourists from Victoria descending on the area for the summer holidays as well as itinerant fruit pickers. The Joneses had been holidaying in the town's caravan park for 18 years. The family was from Box Hill, an eastern suburb 14 kilometres from Melbourne's CBD and had travelled to Tocumwal to spend the New Year by the river.

On Thursday, 3 January, Elaine, 39, left their tent at 9.30 p.m. to walk to the town's shops for cigarettes and some chocolate. She set off along the quiet dirt road with a torch and was dressed in blue jeans, blue sneakers and a white knitted-style top. Alan Jones was reportedly not feeling well so he stayed behind in the tent.

Elaine never returned to the campsite from her walk. Her husband alerted the police early the next day. Alan was frantic trying to find his wife. Taking his youngest daughter with him, he took their aluminium run-about boat out on the Murray to search for any sign of Elaine.

Tragically, Alan found his wife's body snagged on a river log. When he was placing his wife in the boat, Alan saw that her throat has been severed and her head bashed. It was the most shocking and distressing sight for the 51-year-old, and in a tragic and rare twist, he collapsed on the boat and died instantly. The couple's seven-year-old daughter was left alone with the bodies of her parents until she could switch off the boat's motor, swim to shore and get help.

The shocking case made the front page of the *Sun-Herald* on 6 January with the headline 'GIRL'S RIVER TERROR – Mother slain, Dad dies of shock'.

A family friend in the town cared for the couple's two daughters until relatives could make the journey from Tasmania.

The police had the difficult task of trying to interview people. The investigation was hampered by the fact that hundreds of people had fled back to Victoria in fear following the news that Mrs Jones had been brutally murdered. And the fruit picking community also needed to be interviewed.

On top of this, the area's already large tourist population had swelled with an extra 2000 visitors for the annual convention of the National Nudist Federation, which was being held at the sprawling Bangalee Nudist Holiday Village. Newspaper reports in the days after the murder suggested police were worried that the nudist convention had attracted the killer to the town.

More candid with their language decades ago than they would be today, police were quoted in newspapers saying the murderer was 'obviously a maniac' and a 'cold-blooded killer who must be caught'. Elaine had also been sexually assaulted.

Several campers and residents of the town told police that they had heard a woman's screams on the night Elaine was killed. She had last been seen only 250 metres away from the shops.

The strongest lead for detectives came almost a week later when a local man said he had seen a stranger sitting in his car all day at the town's shops. This raised suspicions with the local because he wondered why anyone would sit in their car in such hot weather. The man's description was broadcast in the media, but detectives believed he would have fled the area, along with hundreds of other holidaymakers, soon after the killing.

A camper also reported seeing a car's headlights turn off moments after he heard a woman's screams. The camper, who was staying at the same caravan park as the Joneses, went to investigate. He and some other campers said they heard two 'blood-curdling' screams, a minute apart, between 10.15 p.m. and 10.30 p.m.

Head of the murder investigation, Detective Sergeant George Harvie, of the Albury Criminal Investigation Department, said the headlights had been seen 50 metres off the dirt road that

Elaine had walked down that night. Police believed Elaine was bashed unconscious and then driven to the riverbank where she was sexually assaulted, and then murdered.

When found by her husband, Mrs Jones was naked with only one shoe. Police divers failed to find her clothes or handbag when they searched parts of the Murray River.

From an identikit and information appeals to the public, detectives interviewed a Melbourne man and did forensic tests on his car. There had been reports that a man had been harassing women on beaches near Tocumwal. However, the man was eventually ruled out as a suspect.

The case went cold and there were sporadic public appeals over the years. In 1998, the strongest new development occurred when the *Herald Sun* reported that police had re-opened the case and were investigating the notorious convicted rapist and murderer Raymond 'Mr Stinky' Edmunds, also known as 'The Donvale Rapist', for the murder of Mrs Jones.

Edmunds, who got his nickname because some of the women he raped said he had repulsive body odour, was confirmed to have been camping on Ulupna Island, near Tocumwal, in the new year of 1980, and had left the campsite the night Mrs Jones had failed to return to her family.

Exclusive reports in the *Herald Sun* revealed that in 1985, detectives came tantalisingly close to getting a confession from Edmunds. Police reporter Mark Buttler spoke to Ken Mansell, a detective who interviewed Edmunds in 1985 over the murders of Shepparton teenagers Abina Madill and Garry Heywood in 1966. Mansell said he felt Edmunds was on the verge of confessing to the murder of Mrs Jones but a rule that meant police could only interview a suspect for six hours had ruined their best chance at cracking the case. The rule, which has now been scrapped, meant that the extent of Edmunds' offending could not be unearthed at that time. Mansell told Buttler that Edmunds had offered up information about the murder of Mrs Jones, as well as the 1973 abduction and killing of Bronwyn Richardson, a 16-year-old Albury girl. However, the day after admitting to the murders of Abina and Garry, Edmunds, on advice from his legal counsel, refused to say any more.

Shepparton, now a large rural centre, is in the north-east of Victoria, almost 200 kilometres from Melbourne. The Madill–Heywood killings haunted the Shepparton region for almost 20 years before Edmunds confessed to them. The teenagers went missing on 10 February 1966 when they left a dance in Garry's car. Their bodies were found three weeks later in a paddock in East Murchison, 32 kilometres from Shepparton. Abina Madill had been raped and then bludgeoned to death, and Garry Heywood had died from a gunshot wound to the head. Abina's former boyfriend Ian Urquhart was long suspected of the murders and had been brutally dealt with by police while being questioned. He lived under the cloud of being a double murder suspect and died in a car accident in Singapore six years after the murders.

It was the 1985 arrest of Edmunds in Albury for indecent exposure that cracked the case.

A re-examination of the Madill–Heywood murders had revealed fingerprints on Garry's FJ Holden car. These prints matched a fingerprint found at the scene of a rape in Melbourne's outer-east. When Edmunds' prints were taken on his arrest for flashing in 1985, they matched those on Garry's car and at the rape scene.

Edmunds is serving a life sentence, never to be released, though he did attempt a dramatic escape from Pentridge Prison in 1992, hiding in a steel cabinet on the back of a semi-trailer that was detected just before exiting the now closed bluestone prison. He was convicted of the double slaying of Abina and Garry in 1986 and also received a concurrent 30-year sentence for three rapes and two attempted rapes. Police suspect Edmunds committed at least 30 more sex attacks throughout Melbourne in the 1970s and early 1980s.

In 2019, Edmunds, by now 75 years old, was convicted of ten more charges of rape, indecent assault and false imprisonment that he'd committed in the 1970s and 1980s on women in Melbourne. Edmunds had confessed to police the year before about these violent assaults. Edmunds would enter the homes of the women he raped, armed with a knife and sometimes wearing a face mask with holes cut out for his eyes and mouth.

Victorian County Court Judge Susan Pullen, who sentenced Edmunds, said, 'It is difficult to find words to describe your horrific offending ....'

Renowned Australian true crime writer, journalist and podcaster Andrew Rule wrote his first book, *Cuckoo: A True Story of Murder and its Detection*, about the murders of Abina Madill and Garry Heywood and the life, crimes and eventual detection of Edmunds as a dangerous sex offender and killer.

In 2011, there was another public appeal for information about the murder of Elaine Jones, and the offer of a A$100 000 reward for information. The then New South Wales police minister Michael Daley said, 'Mrs Jones deserves justice, and police will never give up on finding those responsible.'

But without any new information, it appears that the secret of who brutally murdered the mother and wife in 1980 will die with the killer.

THE ADELAIDE ZOO KILLINGS

South Australia has been the location for some of the most shocking, strange and depraved crimes in the nation's history. There's the still unsolved mystery of the Beaumont children who went missing in 1966 from Adelaide's Glenelg Beach; the 1983 abduction and murder of 15-year-old Richard Kelvin; and the Snowtown 'bodies in the barrels' murders of 12 people between 1992 and 1999.

The crime described in this chapter is gut-wrenching and leaves the simple question, 'Why?'

On the morning of Monday, 25 May 1985, staff at the Adelaide Zoo turned up to work as expected to start tending to the menagerie and get the day started. What greeted them was absolute horror.

In the children's zoo area, cherished animals were dead in their enclosures. The body count was eight kangaroos, twelve rabbits, seventeen guinea pigs, eight sheep, two goats, an antelope, two turkeys, seven chickens, a duck, a pigeon and a deer. In another part of the zoo, three rhea chicks (a South American flightless bird related to the emu and ostrich) and an alligator had been slain. In total, 64 animals had been killed. But not just killed – these creatures had been butchered, bashed, stabbed and disembowelled. The alligator had one of its feet cut off.

Most of the animals in the children's zoo section were very tame and used to being around people. It would not have been hard to catch them. The poor animals had no chance of escape.

After the animal killers had finished their spree, they broke into the zoo kiosk and stole lollies. The brutal slayings, then the theft of sweets seemed at such odds with each other. What types of people steal lollies after they've bashed and hacked defenceless animals? It was almost certain the people who did this were young. It could have been a gang, judging by the number of animals killed. There were also rumours that quickly gained momentum that it was a former mental hospital patient who'd done the deed.

In the immediate aftermath of the slaughter, zoo director Robert Baker had strong words for whoever killed the animals – and those who knew something but had not yet come forward. These words were played on news broadcasts in Australia and overseas, including Great Britain's ITN:

Whoever has done it, and I suspect that there was more than one person – because these animals would require two or possibly three people to hold them – whoever has done it must have a lot of blood on them. There was blood everywhere, and if you start trying to cut a sheep's throat in the middle of the night you will get covered in blood. That person or persons must have gone home in something of a mess, and I would like to think that somebody will ask themselves what was going on ... and might come forward and say something ... because people just can't be allowed to get away with this sort of thing.

Adelaide CIB Detective Sergeant Jeff Lawrence told the media that police officers get somewhat desensitised to murder scenes, but what confronted them at the zoo was different. 'You can accept a murder scene, but to see innocent animals in a children's zoo slaughtered .... One's got to wonder what type of person this is.' (*The Day*, 25 March 1985).

A few days later, a 29 March editorial in *The Canberra Times* from the newspaper's South Australian correspondent wrote of the shock that rippled through the city after the zoo massacre, as it had been referred to: 'Not since the discovery of the bodies of the seven slain Truro victims – young women violated and killed between December 1976, and February 1977 – have Adelaide people felt so strongly that their picturesque little city is despoiled by recurrent acts of bizarre cruelty ....'

There was also speculation that the killers may have had a sexual motive to the animal killings. The zoo's veterinary surgeon, Dr David Schultz, told the media the day after the shocking discovery that at least four of the animals had injuries to the anus and vulva. Specialist pathologists had tested all the animal carcasses.

Dr Schultz said early tests indicated that a smooth blunt object had been inserted into the organs of some sheep and an Indian antelope. Whether these were pre- or post-mortem was unclear. 'If there were sexual connotations, it just might give the police a lead to a slightly different sort of a person they are looking for,'

Dr Schultz said. 'But there might not be any sexual connotations at all; it might have been done in the frenzy that was perpetrated with the knife.' ('Possible sex link in zoo slaughter', *The Canberra Times*, 27 March 1985.)

But Dr Schultz said he doubted a sexual reason was the main motive because of the large number of dead animals.

The hunt for the animal killers ended ten days later.

Two 18-year-old men, along with another friend, broke into a hardware store and stole almost A$6000 of goods, which were later recovered. The youths bent a roller door to make just enough room for one of them to squeeze through and gain entry to the shop in the inner Adelaide suburb Westbourne Park.

The boys had been on a crime spree. Four nights after killing the animals, the pair had broken into a horseriding store and stolen whips, bridles and other assorted items.

First Class Constable David Hunt interviewed the two main perpetrators on 2 April. They both confessed to killing the animals, although it soon became a case of each teen blaming the other for the worst of the killings. The pair told police they rode on their bicycles to the zoo, armed with knives and a torch, and scaled the fence. They wanted to kill 'a few' animals.

When police asked the obvious question, 'Why?' one of the youths replied, 'I don't know.'

Such was the revulsion and anger from the public about the crime, an interim suppression order on the names of the accused was granted. Their names were revealed publicly a few weeks later – they were both legally adults – but their addresses and that of their families were protected from being published by a court order. (The author has chosen not to use the surnames of the offenders, referring to them by the first letter of their surnames. The sentencing remarks are dated 6 September 1985.)

The men were granted bail and strict curfew conditions.

One of the youths, H, had already appeared in Children's Court and Magistrates' Court for break and enter and larceny. J had been fined in the Children's Court for not paying a taxi fare.

The preliminary hearing for the case took place on 10 July 1985, during which the police records of interviews with the men were read out in court.

When asked by police why he killed the animals, J said, 'The animals like the sheep and the roos – I didn't think were too bad as they get killed on the farm, but the animals like the guinea pigs and rabbits, um, I don't know ....'

J blamed H for the slaughter of the crocodile and described the crime in detail to Constable Hunt and how H had beaten the animal over the head with a signpost taken from the otter's cage.

'After a while he jumped in and hit the croc right in the eye,' J said, 'and it got stuck in there, and then he draped it out on to the grass and hit it a few more times – this took about half an hour to kill this croc – and he got it up by the tail and threw it out onto the outside and I didn't want to touch it and I don't remember if he cut it open or hit it a few more times or when he cut off the front paw using my knife.'

H told police J had been the one who'd suggested, one hour before the slaughter, 'Let's go to the zoo and kill some animals.'

The men were ordered to stand trial but both pleaded guilty to all the charges, which spared a costly and possibly lengthy trial and, no doubt, the pair's legal advice was also to spare themselves further media glare.

The young men's family backgrounds were considered by the judge.

'The material before me indicates that each of you come before the court with somewhat disturbed backgrounds,' Justice Burnett said. 'Whilst your backgrounds are not as underprivileged and distressing as those of others who appear in these courts, they are certainly not capable of being described as normal or comfortable.'

Justice Burnett continued and noted the men's poor education and employment records, and their immaturity were significant. H had also been involved in a serious car accident in Western Australia in 1983. He was a passenger in the car that collided at speed with another and had suffered major injuries to his head, knee, wrist and hands. The injuries meant he had a long time of rehabilitation.

'There may well have been an element of psychiatric cause or involvement brought on by your accident. That element may go some way towards explaining your actions, but it is quite inadequate to excuse them,' Justice Burnett said.

British child and adolescent psychiatrist Eileen Vizard has worked with children who have performed extremely violent acts, including interviewing Robert Thompson, one of the two ten-year-old children who abducted, tortured and killed toddler James Bulger in Liverpool, England in 1993. Dr Vizard's research and clinical specialty is with child forensic mental health, in particular, sexually abusive behaviour in children and teenagers.

Dr Vizard said in a 2000 article for the *BBC News* website titled 'The chain of cruelty' that there was a strong association with cruelty to animals in children and youth diagnosed with emerging severe personality disorder (ESPD).

Dr Vizard said those children who abuse animals tend to opt for ones unable to put up much resistance: 'They stamp on small hamsters or mice. Squeeze them or burst them, set fire to their fur. Gratuitous cruelty for which there can be no justification.'

In sentencing the pair, Justice Burnett said he had to repress his feelings of 'revulsion and indignation' and set to the side the massive public reaction against the duo. People were expecting a severe punishment for the zoo killings and the crime had garnered worldwide condemnation and shock.

'It is difficult to imagine a more cruel or callous series of acts against virtually defenceless creatures,' Justice Burnett said. 'There seems to be little doubt that you went to the zoo intending to kill some animals – the fact that you took knives with you makes that clear. You say that once you embarked upon your venture, things got out of hand. Well, that is an understatement if ever I heard one ....' ('Adelaide court told of zoo slaughter', *The Canberra Times*, 11 July 1985.)

J was treated as a first-time offender and given four years and four months, and H was sentenced to five years.

H had raised A$6000 in restitution, which was paid to the zoo. J was not able to raise any cash. The fact H paid money did not sway the judge to any leniency. He noted in his sentencing remarks, 'You have had your chances in the past and you have not, so it seems, benefitted from either those experiences of the leniency with which you were treated. You are not a newcomer to law breaking and cannot expect to be treated as such.'

However, the judge did acknowledge both the offenders confessed their guilt frankly and expressed remorse for what happened.

'It is all too obvious that these offences attracted to you notoriety and a degree of public exposure and condemnation which far exceeds that which is encountered by most offenders,' Judge Burnett said. The judge also said the public disapproval was in itself a form of punishment.

The young men attempted to have their sentences reduced, but the Supreme Court rejected the appeal in October 1985.

* * *

There were fears that copycat attacks could occur.

In Melbourne on 27 April 1985, seven horses were stabbed in a paddock in the south-east suburb North Dandenong. One of the horses had to be put down and several others suffered shock and blood loss.

A Victoria Police sergeant said they were investigating whether the bizarre and cruel attack was a copycat of the Adelaide Zoo killings. 'Obviously there are several possible motives,' he said. 'Spite is one. Or it was done by someone who was demented or sick or it was a gang of fellows having fun. There was nothing similar to the Adelaide attack, but it is just possible that someone listened to that and acted on it.' ('Seven horses stabbed in Victoria', *The Canberra Times*, 27 April 1985.)

In 2009, a blind, elderly male flamingo was bashed in the Adelaide Zoo. The majestic bird named 'Greater', aged 78, survived the attack – two 17-year-old males were arrested for the assault, but charges were dropped by police after 'numerous and repeated' calls for information from the public failed. It was believed two other young adults were involved in the attack, but there was insufficient evidence to charge them.

Like the 1985 animal attacks, the assault on Greater (who had lived at Adelaide Zoo since the 1930s and was one of the oldest flamingos in the world) sickened and angered the public, especially since the alleged perpetrators got away with it. In fact, Greater would have been there the night H and J massacred the animals in 1985. He survived that night but could have been killed in the attack almost 15 years later in 2009.

Zoos South Australia Chief Executive Chris West told the *Adelaide Advertiser*, 'What a victim – an ancient, innocent, half-blind flamingo.'

Greater died in 2014, aged 83.

* * *

You wonder what becomes of men who commit such acts at a young age.

According to death records found online at Australian Cemeteries Index, J died on 21 May 2000, aged thirty-three. His conviction meant J could never embark on a career in the Australian Army. Judge Burnett noted this fact during sentencing.

Did H make a better life for himself when he left prison? In 1987, the *Adelaide Advertiser* reported that H received A$114 000 in damages for the 1983 car accident he'd been involved in. At his trial, Justice Jacobs had said that the zoo killings had been 'wholly out of character'. Justice Jacobs said H had a 'demonstrated propensity to criminal conduct' but appeared to be honest, remorseful, and had a good rapport with prison officers and his family.

H declined to comment publicly on the damages award. He would have been eligible for release from jail in 1990.

THE WONGA PARK MURDERS

Bert Spinks nervously waited for the phone to ring. His daughter, Linda, a trainee teacher, was late back from a day out with her boyfriend, Neil Bray, 19. It was the first time Linda, 18, had been allowed to come home with a boy. The other times the young couple had been out together, Mr Spinks had picked his daughter up when it was time to go home. Neil and Linda had only been out together a handful of times and had met a month before at a dance in Balwyn, in Melbourne's east. Neil was a school athletics champion from the inner-north-west suburb Essendon, who was in his first year at Melbourne University studying applied science.

Earlier that day, 26 May 1965, the pair had gone off on Neil's scooter for a picnic at a Wonga Park nature reserve in Melbourne's outer-east. Linda knew the reserve well because her family sometimes went fishing there. Neil had picked up Linda from her Kilsyth home and from there it wasn't far to the reserve in the bushy suburb. The area is near a large campsite called Clifford Park, owned and operated still to this day by Scouts Victoria.

The couple had left for the picnic date at 11 a.m. However, when they had not returned to Linda's Hansen Road home by the early evening, Mr Spinks began to worry. 'When they hadn't returned by dark, I drove out to the reserve but could only find the scooter,' he later told reporters.

He contacted the nearby Ringwood Police Station to report his concern, and officers went out to Wonga Park to search for Linda and Neil.

When they arrived at the picnic spot at around 9 p.m., officers discovered a half-eaten picnic lunch in the shelter shed. Just metres away from the picnic shed, policemen found Linda's body in some shrubs. She was facedown, naked except for her cardigan, and there was a bullet wound in the back of her head. Neil's overcoat and her clothes had been placed over her body.

Neil lay metres away and had multiple gun wounds – in his head, hand and chest. He was still in his clothes, but his pants had bloodstains.

Surveying the scene, it appeared the couple's picnic had been interrupted by their killer, who forced Linda to take off her clothes and then shot her. Police thought that the killer then made Neil move her body, which would account for the coat and clothes covering her body. Then Neil, who fought for his life, was shot several times. *The Age* reported Neil 'appeared to have grabbed at a sapling above his head as he fell to the ground'.

It had been a busy 48 hours for the Victoria Police's Homicide Squad. On the morning of the same day Linda and Neil were murdered, the body of another young woman had been found at Woori Yallock, a town 56 kilometres east of Melbourne. The woman, known as Janice Freeman, was found in scrubland with bullet wounds to her head. Janice was from inner-city Collingwood, so detectives had to try and work out why she had ended up so far away.

Janice, a mother-of-two who was known by a couple of different surnames, was last seen in a Fitzroy hotel in the company of a man. A witness said he'd seen her with the man, and they'd travelled together in a 1938 green Buick to her house in Collingwood. Janice went in for a few minutes then came back out and went off with the man.

At first, police didn't think the Wonga Park and Woori Yallock deaths were related. But that all changed the next day when detectives found a suspect for Linda and Neil's murders. The man, 30-year-old John Desmond David, was seen in the Wonga Park death site. A policeman spotted David sitting in his green Buick parked near the entrance to the picnic ground.

When the policeman went to check out the car, he spied bloodstains on the passenger side door and a cartridge case that belonged to a .22 rifle. Bullets for a rifle were found in David's pockets. On this discovery, David told the policeman he always carried bullets around with him ... but he didn't own a gun.

Police escorted David to the scene of Neil and Linda's murders, and David told the officers he'd hidden a .22 rifle under a tree. They recovered the loaded rifle, and David was charged with the murders. Witness descriptions of his car matched up with that of the man Janice Freeman was last seen with in the city. David was subsequently charged with her murder as well.

David told detectives that when he and Janice had been drinking together, she'd mentioned that she wanted to go for a drive. David suggested they drive out to Warburton. Warburton is a town in the Yarra Ranges, attracting visitors who come for nature walks, world-class mountain bike riding and the stunning California Redwood Forest, among other activities.

The pair stayed in the town for a little while, and then David drove them to the Woori Yallock Creek.

David told the police that Janice, who was in the front of the car, made a comment about his family, which upset him. David was in the back of the car where his rifle was and said he remembered touching the weapon, but after that, he drew a blank. He had no memory of firing the rifle at Janice.

David said he thought Janice must have fallen out of the car when he drove off. He returned to his home in Bayswater, a suburb in Melbourne's outer-east.

Ballistic tests revealed that David shot his victims at close range. Detectives tracked down where the gun had been obtained. David had bought the rifle on 21 September, from a salesman named Norman Rae Staines who said David signed his name as 'Davis'.

David killed his victims over the course of two days. Had he not been caught, he could have continued killing.

The Age newspaper reported that at the coronial inquest into the young students' murders on 14 September 1965, Neil's father got out of his seat and lunged at David at one point during the police evidence. Mr Bray's family had to restrain him from attacking his son's accused killer, who was seated at the time, reading a book.

The judge committed David to stand trial for murder.

On 24 November 1965, David pleaded guilty to the murders. The judge presiding over the case, Justice John Barry, explained that the plea could only be accepted if the court was satisfied the accused *actually* understood the gravity of the plea. The penalty *would* be death. It was the mandatory sentence for murder. He had every right to plead not guilty and have the Crown prove beyond a reasonable doubt that he was responsible for the three killings.

The statement David made that was read to the court was eloquent for a man described by the court-appointed doctor as a man of 'dull normal' intelligence. Dr Alan Austin Bartholomew was tasked with determining whether David was fit to plead to the murder charges, and he concluded that he was.

David's lawyer, Phillip Opas, QC, read David's prepared statement to the court before sentencing, which read in part:

The statements obtained by the police from me in which I confess to the killings were fairly obtained. I was not ill-treated by the police in any way and I made such statements willingly without any threat or promise being made to me by the police. I also willingly accompanied the police to the scenes of the killings and voluntarily pointed out where the killings took place and described how they took place .... I have specifically instructed my council that I do not wish to raise any defence of insanity .... I consider that when the killings took place I knew what I was doing. I knew I was firing a rifle loaded with a live cartridge at a person and that there was a certainty if such a person were struck he or she would be at least seriously injured if not killed.

I knew also that such action on my part was wrong. It has also been pointed out to me by my council that the only penalty provided on conviction for murder is death and that if I plead guilty the Crown will not have to prove the case against me there will be no need to empanel a jury to try me but sentence will be passed immediately because by my plea of guilty. I will have admitted all the elements of the crime which otherwise the Crown would have to prove. I am extremely sorry for what I've done and I want to save the parents and relatives of the persons I killed from the terrible ordeal of a public trial which will go over all the details once again. I want to spare my wife and children any further sorrow on my account. My life up to now has not been any credit to me and at least I want it said that I did not try to back my way out of my actions by pleading not guilty …. ('Man admits three murders; death sentence', *The Age*, 25 November 1965.)

The Sun ran with the headline on 25 November: 'HANG DAVID, PARENTS OF COUPLE SAY' with Bert Spinks telling the newspaper, 'My family and I will not have any peace of mind until this man is hanged. We know he pleaded guilty so that the full facts of the crime would not be made public. As for him saying he wanted to spare us further grief – nothing he could do now would alleviate our pain.'

Neil's mum said she and her husband welcomed a death sentence for the man who took their only child.

'He pleaded guilty only so he would not be cross-examined. We would have welcomed a trial so that the evidence could come out,' Mrs Bray said.

David's young wife, Sadie, said that David had always been a wonderful husband and father to their children, Jennifer, four, and Johnny, two. 'He's never shown any violence in the house,' she said. 'I will do everything possible to save him from hanging.'

Mrs David visited her husband at Pentridge Prison with Johnny. 'I'd love to have taken Jennifer to see John, but it'd be no good,' she was quoted in *The Sun*. 'She'd fret more for him than she does now.'

David was the first man in Victoria to have his guilty plea accepted by the state's Supreme Court.

The guilty verdict did mean that details of the case were scarce. The families never discovered exactly why their precious children were so brutally – and randomly – murdered. There was no trial for the media to attend and cover. The public were safe from David but the reasons for his 'inexplicable' crimes went unanswered.

In early February 1966, news was reported that David's death sentence was to be reviewed. (Capital punishment was abolished in Victoria in 1975.) The State Executive Council (the group that advises ministers on decisions that need to be made under 'acts') met on 1 February to discuss David's case. The meeting included the Attorney General Arthur Rylah and Justice Barry, who initially sentenced David to hang.

David's sentenced was commuted to 40 years' jail with a minimum term of 30 years before he could be considered for parole. The triple killer's psychiatric background was the reason for the change of heart. Mr Rylah said, 'Although there was nothing specific, this suggested there was some condition which influenced him to commit his almost inexplicable crimes, having regard to his present background.'

Wendy Rawady was a student teacher with Linda Spinks at Burwood Teachers College (later absorbed into Deakin University). Now living in the United States, Wendy said she has never forgotten her friend.

At the time of the 2012 murder in Melbourne of young Irish woman Jill Meagher, Wendy left a comment on a 29 September 2012 *Irish Echo* article online. The tragedy stirred up memories from Linda's murder: 'I lost my friend and singing-partner Linda Spinks in 1965 in the Wonga Park murders. It has haunted me ever since. It's not something anyone ever gets over. The root causes of this violence have to be dealt with in society ....'

The author contacted Wendy, who said she was pleased Linda hadn't been forgotten. Wendy said she and Linda bonded over their love of musical comedy and she was sure Linda could have been a major star in the genre:

> We both liked the Beatles, and her boyfriend [Neil] had a motor scooter. I was very envious. Anyway, we were going out on a double date to a ball, and she didn't contact me to firm up the arrangements, and I was a bit hurt. Then on the way home from work, I saw her face all over the front page of the papers and I did go quite hysterical. The bus driver was very kind while the other passengers were freaked out. I never went near Wonga Park ever again after that as it was too creepy.
>
> Linda would have been around 68 now, I think. She was older than I am by a smidge. I think her folks went back to the UK after it all died down, but I am not sure .... I had never met them. We didn't even have a phone in those

days. Things were so very different. Burwood Teachers' College was taken over by Rusden, I think. Linda had a real way with children and would have been a wonderful teacher. We used to practise trampoline at the back of the college adjacent to Mt Scopus College, and she was so nice to the kids. Occasionally we would sneak them in to have a use of the tramps [trampolines] there.

Wendy said she had always wondered about what happened to Linda's family.

'I always looked for them also, but life was harder for contacting people in the 1960s, and she lived in a different suburb,' Wendy said. 'I think of Linda often. I hate the thought of our loved ones being swept away and forgotten. She was a really sweet girl.'

According to records from Melbourne's Greater Metropolitan Cemetery Trust, David died in 1994 at age fifty-nine.

NO JUSTICE: THE TYNONG NORTH-FRANKSTON MURDERS

It is hard to fathom how a spate of murders could go unsolved for so long. But that's exactly what happened with the killings of six women in Victoria, known as the Tynong North-Frankston Murders.

The murders of these women remain cold cases, and the likelihood of finding justice grows dimmer as each year passes by. For people who can remember, the cases hold an intrigue and a sense of bafflement that there has never been anyone arrested.

The youngest victim in the grouping of murders was just fourteen. Catherine Headland was a teen who loved horses and had a good circle of friends when she vanished on 28 August 1980. She was last seen walking from her boyfriend John McManus's house to a bus stop just 100 metres away in the outer-south-east Melbourne suburb of Berwick. Back then, Berwick was a rural haven for people who loved space, horses and to be away from the built-up suburbs. Now it's part of the massive south-east metropolitan sprawl that exploded in the 1990s when large chunks of rural land were subdivided for housing estates.

It was the school holidays, and Catherine had a part-time job at Coles supermarket at the Fountain Gate Shopping Centre in the nearby suburb of Narre Warren, where her mum worked. She wasn't too keen on the cashier job – it interfered with her social life and horseriding – and on that day in August, Catherine had remarked to her boyfriend, John, that she didn't really want to go to work. But she waved him 'goodbye' as she rushed to the bus stop.

Catherine never made it on the bus. Somehow, on that short walk, she disappeared. She must have got in a car – or been forced in – with someone. Did she know them? John and her best friend, Cheryl Goldsworthy, insisted that Catherine would never get into a car with someone she didn't know.

The weeks went by; Catherine didn't come home. Her friends still got together at Akoonah Park, Berwick, where they'd meet to listen to music. But now the gatherings took on a more sombre tone. Police dressed a mannequin in clothes similar to those Catherine had been wearing when she was last seen. The mannequin was placed at the bus shelter she was headed to when she seemed to vanish into thin air.

In December 1980, Catherine's decomposed body was found alongside the remains of two other women. The bodies were found near a deserted sand quarry in Tynong North, at that time a stretch of bushland in the West Gippsland region of Victoria.

Two men dumping lamb innards (to attract foxes) in a secluded bush area found the bodies. This was not a location someone would just stumble on. Being hunters, the men knew the area well – the killer must have too.

The first bones to be discovered belonged to Ann-Marie Sargent, 18, who'd gone missing on 6 October 1980 on her way to a job-seeker service in the working-class suburb of Dandenong.

A small drainage tube sticking out from the skull of the first body quickly identified her. Ann-Marie had undergone an operation to remove fluid on her brain and the tube was inserted in her skull. On her disappearance, pleas had been made to the public that she was vulnerable and any knock to the head could be fatal. Ann-Marie's devastated parents had known something was very wrong when she went missing. Her father Frederick later said he believed she had been picked up while hitchhiking and killed.

Close to the remains of Ann-Marie was the body of Bertha Miller, 75, still fully clothed. Bertha had been last seen on 10 August 1980, when she left her home in the inner-east suburb of Glen Iris to catch a tram to church. She never made it to the church service, which was completely out of character. Bertha was a woman of habit. Her disappearance gained increased publicity, as she was the aunt of the-then chief commissioner of Victoria Police, Mick Miller.

Catherine Headland's remains were the last of the trio to be found and identified. Her remains were found the day after Bertha and Ann-Marie, just metres from them. Three teeth were found nearby, and a specialist forensic dentist matched them to Catherine. A thin leather strap was also found on the ankle or the body. It had been a trend at the time among Catherine's friends to wear them as friendship bracelets around their ankles or wrists. It was one of the few things that could help identify the body, as well as a pair of earrings and the fact the victim had dark hair.

The length of time between the women's disappearances and the discoveries of the bodies – around four months – meant it was virtually impossible for the police to work out how they were murdered or obtain any substantial evidence to help catch the killer.

Meanwhile, there had been other disappearances of women in the south-east Melbourne suburb of Frankston.

Allison Rooke, 59, disappeared on 30 May 1980. She had told neighbours she was headed to the Frankston Shopping Centre. She waited for her bus on Frankston-Dandenong Road. Five weeks later, on 5 July, an off-duty policeman walking his dog found Allison Rooke's naked body in a shallow grave, partially hidden by scrubland, in McClelland Drive, Frankston.

Allison's son Ivan was, at the time of her disappearance and murder, a young policeman in South Australia. After his mum's body was discovered, Mr Rooke, then 24, was quoted as saying, 'When I heard the news that she was missing, I had the feeling I wouldn't be seeing her again.' ('The sorrow hits home', *The Age*, 10 July 1980.)

On 9 October 1981, Joy Summers, 55, was waiting for a bus on Frankston-Dandenong Road when she too vanished. It was the same stretch of road on which Allison Rooke had met her fate, presumably accepting a lift from her killer. Experiencing ill health, Joy had left a note for her partner to say where she'd gone.

It was the first time she'd been out alone since having a stroke, and when she hadn't returned by early evening, her partner contacted police. Her naked body was found six weeks later in scrubland not far away.

Around two years later, on 3 February 1983, more human remains were found in the Tynong North scrubland, around two kilometres from where the three women were discovered in 1980. A punctured trailer tyre caused two men to pull into an area opposite a truck stop on the Princes Highway. One of the men, former Victorian League Football player and coach Barry Davis, got out to stretch his legs. He spotted a bone sticking out of the scrubland, around 50 metres from the busy road, and instinctively took it to the Warragul Police Station. The bone was sent to the Melbourne Coroners' Court, where it was confirmed to be human.

A search of the area unearthed the bones from a badly decomposed body. The body belonged to 34-year-old mother-of-two Narumol Stephenson, who had vanished on 30 November 1980 from the inner-city Melbourne suburb of Brunswick. On the night she had disappeared, Narumol, who'd moved to Australia in the late 1970s from Thailand, had been waiting impatiently in the car while her husband socialised with friends in an apartment. She had not wanted to join in. Her husband had checked on her a few times during the evening, but when he went to leave at 6 a.m., she was gone.

Public transport would have been non-existent during those early hours, meaning she had either been offered a lift by her killer or forcibly taken. The distance between where she disappeared and where she was dumped was over 80 kilometres. Due to the decomposition of Narumol Stephenson's body, forensic testing couldn't determine how she was killed.

Then the disappearances of women seemed to stop.

Narumol Stephenson has always been linked with the other Tynong North-Frankston killings, but if you ask people who've been covering crime for decades, such as Victorian-based author and *Herald Sun* journalist Andrew Rule, they question whether Narumol was killed by the same person (or persons) who murdered Bertha, Catherine, Ann-Marie, Joy and Allison. 'It is true that Narumol Stephenson was abducted within weeks of the other three, and that her remains were found close to Brew Road. But nothing else suggests it was the same killer,' Rule wrote in March 2021. 'That she was picked up in Brunswick doesn't fit the pattern. Neither does the fact her body was left so close to the highway, and not hidden ....'

Police worked feverishly to find the killer – or killers (at certain points, investigators believed three separate killers could have been involved). Investigators interviewed 2000 people, including main persons of interest, offered rewards and did television appeals. A search was made of the dense scrubland and the water-filled disused quarry where the three women were found. No physical clues, such as tyre tracks or footprints, were left behind.

A 1985 police analysis of the murders, only publicly revealed in a 19 September 1999 article in *The Age* by John Silvester called 'Tynong: return to a killer's trail' said, 'There is nothing to suggest that the offender(s) selected their victims because of specific characteristics common to the women. It appears that each of them was selected at random. Who they were was not the criteria for their selection, but where they were was.'

Regardless, the case seemed to go cold.

A disturbing twist came in 1989, when a taunting letter was sent to police claiming intimate knowledge of a spate of unsolved killings of women: 'Is the Tynong file gathering dust? Did you know you are dealing with mass murder, in a scale never seen in this country?' The disturbing contents of the letter was published on 31 May 1989 in *The Sydney Morning Herald* and *The Age*.

The typed letter, postmarked 1 May, and addressed to the then chief commissioner of Victoria Police, Kel Glare. The writer immediately piqued the interest of police with tantalising information that was never released to the public: 'Did you find, the brooch that Miller was wearing on the day of her murder. Or the pair of sterling silver, blue birds, earrings. Belonging to Catherine.'

The accuracy of these words led police to believe the letter was not just a sick hoax, as such details had not been publicised. The writer taunted police with questions such as 'Have you ran into a dead end?' and 'Need help?'

The letter was traced to a typewriter from Melbourne's Pentridge Prison. However, the police didn't think the letter writer was the killer, but that the writer may have known who it was. Maybe he was paid or menaced to write the taunting notes?

The mystery of the letters has never been solved, or at least never revealed to the public.

Months before the letter was received, in December 1988, someone sent a Christmas card to Catherine Headland's mother, boasting that the killer's body tally would make Adelaide's Truro murders 'look like kid stuff'.

The Truro murders were a series of killings in 1976–77 by lovers Christopher Worrell and James Miller. The bodies of seven women were found buried in bushland of the South Australian town of Truro and its surrounds. Worrell died in a car accident in 1977 at age 23, and the murders stopped.

The message to Mrs Headland read in part:

> I hope in writing to you, I do not cause you or your family any stress. I can comprehend the pain the agony you have endured to lose a loved one Catherine, not knowing when or if the perpetrator will ever be caught? Well, the new year may be a good year for you! Things may unfold, the name of the perpetrator! Who's deeds make truro! Look like kid stuff! P.S. I'll keep in touch, sometime in the new year! Anon friend! ('Letter boasts of cold-blooded serial killer on grand scale', *The Sydney Morning Herald*, 31 May 1989.)

In 1999, a special taskforce, Operation Lyndhurst, was set up to reinvestigate the murders. Bertha Miller's nephew, Victoria Police Chief Commissioner Mick Miller, had quietly kept a very close eye on the case and, over the years, suspected a distant relative of committing the crime. Miller's theory and measured case for taking another look at the murders prompted the reinvestigation.

As part of Operation Lyndhurst, new technologies and methods were applied to the case. Witnesses were reinterviewed. The team used an FBI profiler for an expert profile on the likely killer. One of the main suspects was interviewed using a lie detector. And from this thorough relook there emerged a strong suspect. The man had been interviewed very early on, following the disappearance of one of the Frankston women in 1981. He had always been in the mix as a suspect, but the FBI profile determined he was the likely culprit. However, the team lacked enough evidence to charge the man.

The taskforce adopted a controversial strategy, and a press conference held in 2001 all but named the main suspect. The police revealed detailed information about the man, who by that stage was 68 years old. He was a Frankston North resident of many years, had a wife and three adult children and was a former film projectionist. It was the black panel van he drove at the time that drew the police's attention. Witnesses had reported seeing a man in a black panel van offering lifts to women in the area.

He had also worked in past years at the Frankston drive-in. This fact, combined with his penchant for offering lifts to people, led police to believe he was not a stranger to the area in which Joy Summers and Allison Rookes' bodies were dumped.

At the time, then Detective Senior Sergeant Clive Rust, now a commander, said the investigation into the murders had used modern analysis to narrow the field of suspects to one. 'We are confident we have identified the person responsible,' Sergeant Rust told the press conference. Rust confirmed that the man had been identified early in the investigation and was a suspect from the start. 'I'm sure that assistance from the public can only go to make this case stronger. This is probably one of the most serious cases that has ever been investigated by Victoria Police, and it involves probably one of our worst serial murderers.'

In an interview for the ABC radio news program *AM* aired 19 March 2001, Sergeant Rust said the suspect portrayed himself as 'Mr Average'. However, the outwardly devout church and family man had had previous dealings with police. And he had failed lie detector tests – not admissible in Australian courts, but a valuable tool for investigators.

'The lie detector test consists of a polygraph test, which is a very good scientific means which is indicative of a person's guilt or innocence. In this case, the suspect failed two lie detector tests in relation to the murders of two of these women,' Sergeant Rust explained to reporter Fiona Reynolds.

The police did not go so far as to name the man, but the information they released didn't make it too hard for media to track him down. The suspect refused to speak but had his lawyer make a statement of innocence on his behalf.

Any hope that his wife might recant her support for an alibi given to the police in 1981 – or reveal secrets about her husband – were dashed. A newspaper obituary revealed she died in 2006, aged seventy-three. On the day Joy Summers disappeared, this person of interest had told police that he and his wife had been shopping and gone to the bank. The man's wife backed up this alibi. There was no record of any bank withdrawals in their names that day.

In 2005, former policeman and journalist Wayne Jones interviewed the person of interest for a 22 October feature in the *Weekend Australian Magazine* called 'Under Suspicion'. When the reporter asked him if he had any police convictions, the man, who had been forthcoming and protesting his innocence, reportedly got agitated and his demeanour changed. 'I do not believe that I have been charged by police for anything,' he told Jones.

But it was reported that in 1997, this man was picked up for kerb crawling and trying to solicit an undercover policewoman for sex. Jones ended his feature article with the interesting vignette that when the man was taken to the police station to be charged for soliciting, he introduced himself as 'the prime suspect in the Tynong North killings'.

In August 2020, this man died at age eighty-eight. His name was Harold Janman. There has never been anything conclusive to link him with any of the murders, but he was a person of interest for a long time.

Journalist and author Andrew Rule, who also hosts his own podcast *Life and Crimes,* said of Mr Janman, 'The stridently religious husband and father and closet gutter crawler had never been the only suspect for the cluster of murders ... what everyone agreed was that Janman was a strange man who led a double life. The circumstantial case against him was damning ....'

* * *

There is another unsolved murder that has, over the years, been linked with the Tynong North-Frankston Murders.

On 15 April 1975, a young mum named Margaret Elliott kissed her husband and two sons, aged under two, goodbye and set off for Box Hill Hospital to visit a friend who'd had a baby. Mrs Elliott drove approximately 30 kilometres from her Berwick home to the hospital and arrived there at 7.10 p.m. She stayed at the hospital until 7.45 p.m. and should have been home at around 8.30 p.m.

When his wife didn't arrive home, Brian Elliott drove around the Box Hill Hospital area the next day, retracing her route, and happened to find her car parked some distance from the hospital. The sight of blood on the seat meant his worst fears were realised. The car also had a flat tyre. Police tests found the car had been driven many more kilometres than the distance from Berwick to Box Hill.

Margaret Elliott's partially clothed body was found the next day seven kilometres away in Gardiners Creek, Glen Iris. There had been football practice at the park, and a boy discovered her when he went to get his football from the creek. She had been beaten to death. The case is still unsolved.

In 2015, journalist Nino Bucci revisited the case in *The Age*. The article '40 years on, the killer of Berwick mother Margaret Elliott still on the loose', revealed that, tragically, Mr Elliott died at age 49, and the Elliott's eldest son, Chris, died by suicide when he was twenty-eight. The Elliott's youngest son, Ben Elliott, who said he was too young to have any memories of his mother, still held out some hope the case could be solved.

There were some facts that made police look at Margaret Elliott as a possible victim of the same killer. If she was, Margaret could have been his first victim. Margaret lived not far in Berwick from Catherine Headland's family home, and the area where her body was dumped was near where Bertha Miller went missing.

* * *

In 2006, Cheryl Goldsworthy and John McManus took part in an episode of a popular television series called *Sensing Murder*, where psychics help shed new light on unsolved murders. The episode, called 'The last goodbye', focused particularly on Catherine's murder. For reasons Cheryl and John weren't told, the episode never aired on Australian television, but it has been shown in other countries. The episode can be found on YouTube, uploaded by people who viewed it in other countries. The two psychics were taken to Brew Road in Tynong North where Bertha Miller, Catherine Headland and Anne-Marie Sargent were found. Psychic investigator Scott Russell Hill says to the camera, 'There are still bodies here that are yet to be found.'

To be chosen to be a psychic investigator for the episode on Catherine Headland, the *Sensing Murder* production team tested 100 psychics. The program gave these psychics 'two obscure murders' and only a photograph of the victims. According to the narrator of the program, the popular actress Rebecca Gibney, only five of the psychics could describe 'intimate details' of the cases.

The chosen psychics for the episode – Deb Webber and Scott Russell Hill – were not told the details of the case or the name of the victim, only that they were working on an unsolved murder. The psychics worked separately, were each filmed continuously over a day and were not interrupted or given any information by the film crew while they were doing the readings.

Deb Webber was given Catherine's earring wrapped in padding and in a sealed envelope. Webber did not know what the object was and felt its energy. She said it was found at the murder scene and asked, 'Is this an earring?' and motioned that she could sense the victim was tugging at her ear as an indication. And Webber also picked up that the victim loved horses. She said she believed Catherine was pulled into the car between two men, an older and a younger one.

Both psychics said the name 'Catherine' and/or 'Cathy' and said there was a strong connection with a school. Possibly one of the men was a parent from a school or an older brother of someone she knew.

Scott Russell Hill said he felt the energy of other women stepping forward along with Catherine. He kept emphasising the name Margaret and that she lived 'around the corner' or nearby to where 'this girl' (Catherine) lived. He said there was a girl with 'Cathy' he thought was named Anne or Anna. (Anne Marie Sargent's body was found close to Catherine's.)

The psychics were taken separately to the general area where the Tynong North victims were found. Eerily, Webber accurately pinpointed the location where Catherine's body was found.

Hill said he felt strongly that there were three killers operating separately but who were drawn to the same area in Brew Road. 'The number of people they killed and why they killed is all for different reasons,' he said.

In the *Sensing Murder* program, John McManus, who was sick on the day he last saw his teen love, said, 'My one big regret was that I didn't walk her to the bus stop.'

This has constantly haunted John, even though there was absolutely no way he or any of their friends could have anticipated what happened to Catherine.

'Berwick back then was very open. There was only one house between my place and the bus stop, but it would have been a straight 100-metre walk to that bus stop,' John said. 'If Catherine was to have been taken or kidnapped, she would have only hopped in the car with someone she knew, or I knew.'

John McManus was treated as a suspect in the early days of the investigation. He said there was a few initial theories police pursued – that Catherine had run away or run off to be with an older man. They even had a theory that John had got her pregnant and was hiding her.

Melbourne crime writer, former *Truth* newspaper editor and columnist Adrian Tame was interviewed for the program too. Tame had reported on the Tynong North-Frankston murders. Tame explained that there was a number of reasons the two victims found in Frankston were grouped with the Tynong North victims. 'One was that all of the victims were either waiting for public transport ... or hitchhiking ....' Tame told the program.

'They were all women. All of the disappearances were during the daylight hours; they were all in the same area within a 30–40-kilometre radius; they were all found in scrubland; and it is probably very significant that no tyre tracks, no footprints, no murder weapons, nothing whatsoever to identify the killer was found on or around any of the six bodies. So, there was a justifiable presumption that one individual was responsible for those first six disappearances.'

The *Sensing Murder* program detailed six suspects that police had identified over the years of investigations. One of these was convicted killer and rapist Raymond 'Mr Stinky' Edmunds.

Tame told the program Edmunds became a suspect after he allegedly told a cellmate in Pentridge Prison that he'd 'killed so many women he could barely remember'. It was alleged Edmunds hinted at one of the Tynong North victims in this jailhouse confession.

A taxi driver came up as a suspect; however, Tame said this man was tracked down and eliminated as a murder suspect but charged with unrelated 'unknown' offences.

Then there was 'the wobbly wheel bandit' who Tame described as a driver who drove alongside women drivers, pointed to the back wheel of their car and urged them to stop. If they stopped, he would tell the women their wheel was wobbly and ask if he could fix it. When he was underneath the car, the man would use it as an opportunity to look up the women's skirts and, according to Tame, there was said to be one time where the man raped one of the women. This man was convicted of rape but eliminated by police in the Tynong North inquiry.

That left three suspects.

One was a distant relative of victim Bertha Miller. This man also knew Catherine Headland, and Tame said there was a 'distinct possibility' he knew Ann-Marie Sargent. An alibi for the times of the murders meant early in the investigations this man was eliminated of suspicion. However, later there were allegations that the timecard the man produced as evidence of his alibi was not watertight.

Another suspect was a mystery man named 'Robert' who was said to be a close friend of Allison Rooke and played bingo with her. An article in *The Age* on 11 July 1980, featured a photo of the man they wished to speak to. The article said, 'The man, in his 50s, had been to at least one Seaford bingo night with Mrs Rooke before she disappeared on May 30.'

'Robert has never been identified and for that reason has never been eliminated,' Tame said.

Then Tame detailed the main suspect – the deeply religious, married father of three Harold Janman, a 'habitual offerer of lifts' who had failed two lied detector tests when questioned by police.

'Police obviously presumed they were dealing with a serial killer. At no stage has any police inquiry been able to find quite definitely that this was the work of one man, two men or even three men,' Tame said.

The families and friends of the murder victims hold on to hope that the case will be finally solved. Catherine Headland's best friend Cheryl Goldsworthy said she hoped someone would speak up and reveal what they knew. The constant thought, 'If only someone had been with her,' has plagued Cheryl ever since.

'But she should have been safe. It was broad daylight, and she only had to walk across the road to the bus stop,' Cheryl said. 'If anyone knows anything, it is time to say so,' she told the author for a 2015 interview for Leader Community Newspapers to mark the 35th anniversary of Catherine Headland's abduction.

Jenny Convery is the niece of Joy Summers. Jenny left a comment on the author's blog 'True Crime Reader' about her aunt's murder: 'Aunty Joy is never far from my mind and I have times where I get very angry and sad that her killer has gotten away with what he did.'

Like others affected by the case, Jenny has gathered whatever information she can via the internet and online message boards. 'I was actually living in London when it happened. I came home not long after,' Jenny said. 'Mum [Joy's older sister] had had a stroke and was extremely upset. Dad said they were visited by detectives who told him they reckoned they knew who it was but needed proof. For me personally, the effect has been a real awareness that awful things can happen to good people,' she said. 'Sometimes I picture how terrified she must have been when she realised he was going to kill her.'

Jenny believed her aunt was somehow convinced to get in a car by someone she thought she could trust. 'I doubt she was grabbed. She was not well and had had a small stroke herself,' she said. 'She would have been a pretty streetwise person after having lived a fairly hard life.'

Cheryl Goldsworthy urged people with any information about Catherine's murder to be brave and come forward. 'Everyone who knew Catherine has suffered with her loss for 35 years, and the person or persons who did this have not yet been held responsible,' she said. 'Solving this case may bring some peace to us all.

In February 2021, Dr Brian Williams, a Melbourne-based historian, researcher and barrister (now retired) released a book called *Somebody Knows Something: On the Trail of the Tynong North and Frankston Serial Killer*.

Dr Williams was a guest on the *Australian True Crime* podcast (co-hosted by the author) to talk about the research for his book and said these murders triggered in him the feeling that 'this could have been anybody. It could have been my mother; it could have been my sister as well. Like a lot of people, I thought by now we would have had some sort of solution.'

'There's so many angles to this. We're talking about six victims, maybe seven, which means there's quite a number of similarities between the people involved. There's lot of differences as well,' Dr Williams said. He also said there was still a 'feeling' that this case, though more than 40 years old, is still solvable. 'There's still enough around. There'd still be a witness around. There'd still be somebody around who knows something who could provide the vital bit of information here. (Dr Williams did, however, mention that the window of opportunity starts to close, especially as a case approaches 50 years unsolved.)

'I always say "he", knowing that it could be more than one person ... the way a person such as this would get somebody into his car would either be through force ... on a busy road that would be hard to do without raising some suspicion ... there would have been cars going past, and if you see a woman being pushed and shoved into a car, that's quite a memorable thing to see ... but the other way, of course, is to trick them into the car, and that seems to be more likely than not what occurred. We don't know what the little trick was ... somehow this person has managed to, fairly seamlessly, get people into his car, and he's off and away ....'

MISSING SOCIETY GIRL

The disappearance of Lucy Brown Craig from Sydney was the highest profile missing person case of its time in Australia.

Nowadays, Lucy's photo would be shared far and wide via social media and the New South Wales Police's social media channels. Online news would follow the situation and her case would be kept alive until she was found, or the public's interest waned from a lack of leads.

Back in 1940, newspapers and radio were the main form of communication, and the case of the missing young woman made headline news around Australia … until it faded into obscurity.

At around 4 p.m. on Friday, 12 April 1940, Lucy, the 19-year-old daughter of a prominent Sydney doctor, left her workplace at the BMA Building in the city's CBD.

The last known sighting of Lucy was when she stepped off a tram at King's Cross, in the company of a young man. The person who saw Lucy (described in the newspaper as 'the son of one of Sydney's best-known professional men and who knew Miss Brown

Craig well') said she was 'with an athletic-looking man of about 22 with a small toothbrush moustache and dressed in a grey suit'.

Lucy lived in Edgecliff Road, Woollahra, one of Sydney's premier locations not far from the CBD and Bondi Junction. Her life was one of privilege. Her father, Dr Francis Brown Craig, was a general practitioner who also worked overseas as an army doctor. Lucy was working as a secretary to a doctor in Macquarie Street at the time of her disappearance, and according to her father, she was very happy in her career.

That night, she seemed to vanish off the face of the earth.

Lucy was heading home for dinner then on to the theatre to see *The Pirates of Penzance* with friends and one of her sisters. When she didn't arrive home, her sister headed out without Lucy; however, it was out of character that she wouldn't contact her family to say she'd been delayed.

When she failed to arrive home late that night, her father notified the police. The family was not made to wait hours, or even days, before police started to look for her.

Police appeals for the man 'in a grey suit' to come forward were unsuccessful. Dr Brown Craig personally offered a reward of £200 (he offered this reward several times over the years) for any information on the whereabouts of his daughter.

The *Australian Women's Weekly* ran an article on 27 April and ran a photo taken by one of the publication's photographers of Lucy at a dance she'd attended at Royal Sydney Golf Club. The article described her as 'a pretty brunette, cultured, musical, with a winning and most amiable personality'.

The article also mentioned that the family had asked the *Australian Women's Weekly* to help in the search for their daughter, whom they believed was 'being held somewhere against her will', by publishing the photograph.

The police inquiries spread all over Australia, to New Zealand and New Guinea. A photo of Lucy was shown at cinemas before movie screenings in the hope it would jog someone's memory, and more than 1500 posters with her photo were distributed.

The sighting of Lucy on the tram to King's Cross was investigated with no success. Police concluded it was a case of mistaken identity. The 'man in the grey suit' never came forward to police.

The case attracted the cranks too. In a cruel attempt to menace money from the family, a Sydney woman, Ruby Gladys Evelyn, 27, appeared in court on 27 April 1940 (15 days after Lucy disappeared) after she rang Dr Brown Craig and demanded money for the return of his daughter. Evelyn knew nothing of Lucy.

The *Townsville Daily Bulletin* reported on 29 June that the family's former gardener said in his witness statement that he had seen Lucy at the corner of Edgecliff Road (which is a long stretch) at 4.45 p.m. on the evening she went missing. Dr Brown Craig believed this showed that his daughter had been on her way home. The newspaper recounted a theory Dr Brown Craig had in the absence of any shred of evidence about Lucy's whereabouts: 'This led him to the startling theory that possibly his daughter, crossing in heavy traffic, may have been struck by a car and injured, that the motorist may then have assisted her into the car with the intention of taking her to hospital, but alarmed at her sudden collapse had disposed of the body ....'

Three months after Lucy's disappearance, the *Truth* reported that 'police believe Lucy Brown Craig is dead' and that even her father had 'abandoned hope' for his daughter. Dr Brown Craig offered several rewards over the years, but on the 21 July 1940, in interview with the *Truth,* he said there was no way he could imagine his daughter had disappeared to start a new life interstate.

'She was happy, interested and contented in her work,' Dr Brown Craig told the newspaper. 'It was not that she had to go to work or that she was constrained to do work that she did not personally like. She wanted to work, and she liked the work as a trained and accomplished secretary.'

Lucy was not rebellious, and her father steadfastly denied his daughter would have eloped. Police even went to the lengths of checking wedding registries to see if Lucy had got married in secret.

'Her life and upbringing, and her nature and outlook were such that she would be unlikely to find any attraction in some capricious adventure,' Dr Brown Craig said.

The *Truth*, a tabloid-style newspaper that pulled no punches, was scathing of the police's handling of the girl's disappearance. 'The police are in the dark, too. And their groping, ineffectual, result-less efforts are an awful example of utter futility.' These words were highlighted in the newspaper – editorialising punctuated through the interview with Dr Brown Craig.

'It is positive that she never had an enemy in the world, nor had she ever been involved with anyone in a way which might lead to discredit, injury or foul play ... much less death,' the newspaper wrote on 21 July 1940. 'She was well educated; she was doing work that occupied her pleasantly; she was happy at home; she was immersed in the round of "doings" of her younger set circle ....'.

There would be the odd lead over the next few years.

Police investigated several reported sightings of Lucy. These included one from a man who said he was certain he saw her a week after she disappeared, in a car in northern New South Wales at a petrol station. The witness said the girl 'strikingly resembled Miss Brown Craig' and was with a man, around 35, with a thick toothbrush moustache. Another man rang police with a tip that he had seen her hiking with a man, aged around 40, at Orbost, Victoria. And yet another called police to say that the young woman was dead.

Lucy's father did not hold much weight in these alleged sightings, telling tabloid newspaper *Smith's Weekly* reporter Iris Dexter a month after his daughter's disappearance, 'I am inclined to doubt such a casual identification. I cannot see how anyone can tell the weight and height of a girl seated in a car. It is a new line of inquiry, of course – but I doubt that the girl was Lucy. I feel sure that the owners of that green car will come forward soon and make themselves known to the police.'

Dr Brown Craig told the reporter that he believed his daughter was being held against her will. 'After a month and the collapse of several theories and promising clues, I am more confident than ever that Lucy was enticed away on some pretext or by a misrepresentation – perhaps by someone professing himself to be a friend of mine – and that she was abducted and is now being held. I have implicit faith in the girl. If she were a free agent she would have communicated with me, or will,' he said.

In 1943, a handkerchief with Lucy's name embossed on it was found it a toilet block in Toronto, New South Wales. For a brief time, this renewed hope for the family that their daughter was still alive. However, the mystery was cleared up when it was discovered that Lucy's clothing had been given to a woman who had worked for the doctor. This employee had given the clothes to her daughter, who told investigators that she lost the handkerchief.

Her case was mentioned again in the newspapers when a young nurse went missing from Roma, Queensland. Scottish-born Sheila Proctor, 27, left Queensland on 8 May 1950 to head to Sydney. However, her luggage was never collected from Sydney, where it had been consigned. There were reports a woman of her description had flown to Brisbane and that a woman had stayed under the name Proctor at a nurses' hostel in the city from 9 to 11 May. Sheila had emigrated from Scotland in 1948 and only had one family member in Australia – a sister, Mrs Geoff Lee, who lived in rural Surat, Queensland. Newspapers reported that detectives feared Sheila Proctor has been murdered.

Unlike Lucy's case, Sheila's disappearance was solved. She was located 18 weeks later in Sydney, working at a private hospital, but police kept quiet on why the 'vivacious' young nurse had gone missing. Even her sister didn't know her whereabouts. And Sheila had been unaware her sister had reported her missing.

As for the unclaimed luggage, the matron of the hospital where Sheila was working said the nurse had not claimed the bags because she had no room to keep them.

In 1954, the *Truth* reported police were looking into a sighting of a woman resembling Lucy in Tamworth, New South Wales. However, in the same article, it was also reported that police were 'absolutely convinced' Lucy had been murdered.

According to the *Truth*, one of New South Wales' 'most notorious' criminals named a well-known Sydney man as the killer. The criminal offered to name the killer in court for a reduction of his lengthy prison sentence. He also claimed Lucy's body had been dumped at sea from a private vessel.

Police did some digging about this criminal's credibility and decided that he could not be trusted, and no jury would believe him.

Lucy's mother Mary died in 1957 and her father in 1964, never knowing what happened to their daughter. All of Lucy's siblings – two brothers and two sisters – have also died. Her sister Anne, who was closest in age to Lucy (less than two years apart), died at the family home in Woollahra in 1995, where she and Lucy had been raised.

Have You Seen Her?

Miss Lucy Dulcie Brown Craig, whose disappearance from her home in Sydney has led to an Australian-wide search. Her father, a prominent Sydney doctor, has offered £200 for information about her.

Lucy Brown Craig, 19, was last seen stepping onto a tram in Sydney's CBD in the early evening on 12 April, 1940. Her disappearance remains unsolved. Source: 1940, The Courier-Mail (Brisbane, Qld. : 1933 - 1954), 25 April, p. 11 (Via Trove)

THE BUTCHER OF WOLLONGONG

It was the housekeeper who found her boss's body.

When Maria Subotic arrived at the home of Frank Arkell to deliver his newspaper on 27 June 1998, she discovered the 68-year-old dead in the bedroom of his granny flat in Wollongong, New South Wales. It was a shock for the woman who had worked for Arkell for more than 40 years (and before that, his mother) and lived a few doors down from the address.

It wasn't natural causes that killed the former Lord Mayor of Wollongong. Arkell had been bludgeoned to death in an attack so vicious there was blood spattered all over the small unit.

Wollongong was known for decades as 'Steel City'. Steelworks owned by Broken Hill Petroleum (BHP) and manufacturing drove the city's economy. Wollongong was a blue-collar community (until recent years where it has had a cultural, professional and entrepreneurial makeover) and probably the best-known champion for the city was Frank Arkell.

Arkell lived a life of civic service. He was born and bred in Wollongong and worked in finance and then his family's farming businesses before entering local politics. Arkell was Lord Mayor of his beloved city from 1974 to 1991 and was also elected an independent member for the New South Wales upper house until 1991. He was everywhere and was passionate about his city, so much so that he was nicknamed 'Mr Wonderful Wollongong'.

Rumours had swirled around Arkell for years. It was in the seven years after his political career ended that Arkell's life was put under the spotlight. The man who many considered 'wonderful' was linked with a paedophile ring that included politicians and businessmen.

In fact, Arkell had been charged with multiple sex offences against boys as young as 13 during the 1970s, when he was mayor, and was due to face court in September 1998.

He had already appeared before the Wood Royal Commission into the New South Wales Police Service, which was where his involvement was first revealed by a member of Parliament named Franca Arena. Mrs Arena named Arkell, as well as former judge David Yeldham, QC, during a 1996 debate in the House regarding the Wood Royal Commission. There had been suppression orders on Arkell's name and several other high-profile people, and Mrs Arena had questioned whether they had received preferential treatment by the commission. Arkell was codenamed 'W1' by the commission, and witnesses had given evidence of sexual encounters they'd had as boys during the 1970s with Arkell. *The Sydney Morning Herald* reported Mrs Arena asking: 'What about former member of Parliament Frank Arkell, known to the commission as W1, who was summoned and did not attend as his lawyers said he was too ill?'.

Another former Wollongong mayor, Tony Bevan, had been an alleged key player in the paedophile ring Arkell was accused of being part of. On Bevan's death in 1991, tape recordings and other communications and notes of customers and the boys they allegedly abused were found among his possessions.

Arkell maintained he was 'set up' by Bevan because of a property deal gone badly during the 1970s. (Arkell, who was mayor at the time, had stymied Bevan's attempts to buy a historic Wollongong mansion, convincing the council to buy it instead.) Arkell claimed the allegations were born from a malicious grudge Bevan had against him.

'I hated his [Bevan's] guts,' Arkell told *The Daily Telegraph* newspaper in 1996, in response to Ms Arena's parliamentary outing of his identity as an accused paedophile.

Mrs Arena also named Justice David Yeldham as another prominent person who may have been protected by the commission in the course of its investigations into paedophilia. The retired Supreme Court judge Yeldham, 67, was one of Australia's highest profile and respected legal identities. Days after Mrs Arena named him, he died by suicide.

In the hours before his death, Yeldham had told the Royal Commission he had spent years paying men for sex in public toilets in Sydney. At least twice police had questioned him about his conduct at railway station bathrooms, but the respected judge had been let off the hook. He told the commission that yes, he had paid men for sex and was bisexual but would never, ever have engaged in sex with a minor. It was a tragic and sad end to a successful life on the bench and devastating for his family.

Arkell's address was no secret to anyone in Wollongong and his property had been subject to vandalism since he was outed as a suspected paedophile.

The savagery of the attack on Arkell led some to speculate that someone who'd experienced childhood sexual abuse – possibly one of his alleged victims – had been his murderer. Arkell had been bashed over the head with a wooden lamp around 34 times. The wooden lamp had splintered and broken, such was the ferocity of the killer's rage. The killer had also tried to strangle Arkell with a belt and the lamp's electrical cord, which were both still partially around his neck when the body was found. Three tiepins were inserted deep into each eye and one of Arkell's cheeks.

On 12 June, two weeks prior to Arkell's murder, another Wollongong man – well-known neighbourhood shopkeeper David O'Hearn – had been savagely murdered and mutilated in his Albion Park home. Police were reluctant to publicly link the two murders, but there were real fears there was a vengeful killer out there, stalking the streets and targeting men he thought were perverts. Mr O'Hearn was gay, but according to his family, quietly so. Unfortunately, the media made assertions about Mr O'Hearn being linked with Frank Arkell and the paedophile network that were simply not true and caused great hurt to his family, who were already reeling from his horrific murder.

The crime scene was grisly – Mr O'Hearn had been mutilated in the extreme. He had been decapitated and his head was found in his kitchen sink. The killer had disembowelled Mr O'Hearn, mutilated his penis and cut off his left hand, which was found on a lounge chair. In a further act of defilement, a hammer had been inserted in his rectum. Some of Mr O'Hearn's bowel was left on a silver tray, and sections of his intestines were scattered on the kitchen bench top. The word 'Satan' was written in the victim's blood on a mirror and a wall, and a pentagram and inverted cross were also painted on some walls – the killer used Mr O'Hearn's severed hand to trace the bloody messages.

The implements of the murder were laid out next to the defiled body. Used in the slaughter were knives, string, a hacksaw and a hammer – all found at the victim's house. The killer had crafted his own murder kit in what was a suburban horror story.

In regards to Arkell's murder especially, there was shock but little sympathy from the community. The then editor-in-chief of the city's newspaper *Illawarra Mercury*, Peter Cullen, said in a 1998 editorial in *The Australian* 'Killer wins kudos in a city as hard as steel' that paedophiles would be 'shaking in their boots' after Arkell's murder. The newspaper had been relentless in reporting the paedophile underbelly of Wollongong and the sexual abuse of children by clergy and other men in power.

The men who'd accused Arkell of molesting them had been questioned by police about their movements on the night of the murder, and all had alibis.

Criminal psychologist Dr Richard Basham, who had worked with the taskforce that captured serial killer Ivan Milat ('the Backpacker Murders'), wrote an opinion piece for *The Daily Telegraph* on the profile of the killer. At the time, there was also speculation that the December 1997 murder of a convicted paedophile, Trevor John Parkin, in Sydney, could have been the work of the same killer as that of Arkell and O'Hearn. Parkin had been stabbed multiple times in the stomach and groin and partially disembowelled. (Another man later confessed to the murder.)

Dr Basham wrote, 'Who might have committed these murders? Since they bear the hallmark of revenge killings for paedophilia, the murderer must see himself as a victim of his victims …. The young man barely out of his teens had not targeted his victim for any specific reason … given the apparent absence of forced entry; however, his victims must not have realised how deeply he hated them … one can imagine the murderer as a lowly, powerless young man exposed to the despised and ravishing eyes of an older, powerful man ….'

Dr Basham concluded the likelihood of more murders was 'very high indeed'.

After Mr O'Hearn's murder, police started looking into people in the area who had an interest in satanism and the occult. This led them to a man named Keith Schreiber, who lived a few doors down from Mr O'Hearn's Albion Park (a suburb of Wollongong) townhouse. When they knocked on the door of Schreiber's house, his flatmate answered. The flatmate, Mark Valera (previously known as Van Krevel), 19, spoke with police and let them have a look around the place, including Schreiber's bedroom where they found satanic-inspired music posters and some disturbing hand sketches of people disembowelled and beheaded. However, Schreiber had a solid alibi.

The police knew they had to act fast. At the Arkell murder scene, the killer had left items of bloody clothing that was not characteristic of anything the victim would have worn. There was a pair of boots that were not the same size as any of Arkell's shoes and a pair of Nike track pants. After a public appeal for information, several tips came through to police, including one from a woman who said her ex-boyfriend had worn similar clothing. This boyfriend was Mark Valera, the man who'd lived with Schreiber. The woman told police he'd become fascinated with the murder and had reacted aggressively when she'd questioned him about the clothes she'd seen on the television appeal.

A few months after the killings, on 29 September, Mark Valera surrendered himself as the killer of Arkell and O'Hearn. His Taekwondo instructor, Rodney Day, accompanied him. Mr Day was someone Valera trusted and looked up to.

Just prior, Valera had mentioned to his ex-girlfriend (the one who'd called the police) that he'd done 'some really bad things' and confessed to Mr Day that he'd killed the men. The martial arts instructor convinced his student to go to the police station.

With no prior criminal record, the young man spent 20 hours being questioned by detectives, during which he confessed to the murders. He was detailed and cooperative with detectives, walking them through the crime scene in a calm manner, pointing out to the police where he'd found the murder weapons and how he'd drawn the satanic symbols on the walls and mirror. Handcuffed and barefoot, Valera is seen in the video with detectives (shown on the television program *Forensic Investigators*) at Mr O'Hearn's home dressed in a T-shirt that reads, 'I live with fear every day'.

The nightmarish details he revealed so matter-of-factly included that he'd cradled Mr O'Hearn's severed head for several minutes, contemplating whether he'd keep it as a trophy. One of the interviewing officers, New South Wales Police Detective

Inspector Russell Oxford, said, 'He [Valera] wasn't confused. He was very sure of what he was saying, and the Frank Arkell interview was no different.'

Valera was on a mission to be a serial killer. He'd made notes in a book – *The A to Z of Serial Killers* – that indicated he'd derived pleasure in recalling the crimes. According to court documents, written in the cover of the book were Valera's disturbing handwritten notes:

My List

Who will be my No. 3.

The possibilities are endless including [there then follows a large number of names, in excess of 40, and then some categories]

Some Satanic faggot

Some horny faggot

Some sexy prostitute male or female

The list ends: 'Not anyone in particular'. (R v Valera [2000] NSWSC 1220.)

Valera told the police on the day of killing Mr O'Hearn, he just wanted to kill someone and went to the victim's house 'just random'. In the initial 'Electronically Recorded Interview of a Suspected Person' (the technical name for recorded interviews at a police station), the young killer said he had only seen O'Hearn from sight when he was walking around the neighbourhood.

'I had it in my mind that I just wanted to kill someone that day,' he told the police. 'I asked him if there was any accommodation around, like boarding houses, and he invited me inside to talk about it. We sat down and he offered me a drink, and when he got up and turned his back, I picked up this heavy, like, bottle and hit him on the back of the head.' The heavy bottle was a wine decanter, and Valera told the detectives he'd counted the number of times he'd smashed the heavy decanter ('fancy glass bottle' is how he'd described it initially to police) into Mr O'Hearn's skull – ten times.

Watching footage of Valera talking to police at the crime scene and in a police interview room, it is chilling that the young killer speaks so matter-of-factly of the crime. Tragically, David O'Hearn was targeted for no other reason than he was there and was friendly enough to talk to Valera.

Interviewed for a 2005 Australian television program, *Forensic Investigators*, Mr O'Hearn's sister said of her brother, 'He liked to help people he thought needed a hand.'

Valera didn't know Arkell either, though owing to the former mayor's high profile, the killer said he knew about the man and had a hatred for him. The pair were, until the murder, strangers. Valera told police, 'All the nasty things he has done to kids. Read about him. Heard about him in the papers and the media ....' Valera and his mates had sometimes prank-called the well-known man, calling him a 'poofter' and 'child molester'. (R v Valera [2000] NSWSC 1220.)

This time, Valera said he'd ended up at Arkell's home after phoning him claiming to be gay and inviting himself over. Arkell had not tried to dissuade the young stranger.

However, when it came to preparing for the trial in 2000, Valera claimed provocation as his defence for both murders – that the men had both propositioned him for sex and this made him explode and lose control. Valera pleaded not guilty to murder but guilty to manslaughter.

The stories had now changed, and Valera claimed to have met Mr O'Hearn before when he'd bought some drinks at the deceased's corner shop. Valera said he felt Mr O'Hearn had been suggestive to him, and then on the morning of the murder, he'd turned up at the shop again and Mr O'Hearn had masturbated him in a closet. Then the pair had gone to Mr O'Hearn's home to have a drink and watch a pornographic video. The accused said he'd launched into the frenzied attack when he was 'put on the spot' and asked for sex by the victim, who had removed his pants.

Forensic evidence proved this a lie (along with Valera's whole story about that day) because blood spots on Mr O'Hearn's jeans indicated they were being worn at the time he was attacked. Valera also said he'd taken the pornographic tape from the video machine but not replaced it. The video found in the machine at the crime scene had a segment recorded about Her Majesty the Queen.

Defence outlined Valera's alleged deeply unhappy childhood, which he claimed included sexual abuse and brutality inflicted by his father, Jack Van Krevel, who raised his son and a daughter alone after their mother left them as infants. (Valera's birth name was Van Krevel, but he said he had changed it to distance himself from his father.) In the initial police interviews, Valera had said he'd had a rough upbringing and his father had been physically abusive. However, weeks before his trial was set to begin, the story emerged of alleged repeated abuse by his father. This was a shock to the people who knew Mr Van.

Supreme Court Justice Timothy Studdert said, 'Whilst he freely admitted to physical abuse of the prisoner, Mr Van Krevel continued to deny throughout a testing cross-examination that he had ever sexually abused his son ....' (R v Valera [2000] NSWSC 1220.)

In sentencing on 21 December 2000, Justice Studdert said, 'The level of heinousness involved in these two killings does not allow for the imposition of anything less than imprisonment for life.'

At the time, Valera was the youngest person in New South Wales to be sentenced to life in prison – never to be released.

There was an appeal in 2002 against the severity of the sentence, but this was dismissed. One of the Supreme Court justices, Anthony Meagher, said, 'Using language as restrained as possible, I find the circumstances of each murder disgusting.'

* * *

In a shocking postscript, just ten days after Valera was sentenced to life imprisonment, his father, Jack Van Krevel, was murdered. The man Valera tried to blame for making his life miserable and causing him to kill was hacked to death as he slept.

The killer was Keith Schreiber, the good friend and former housemate of Valera and the boyfriend of his sister Belinda. While it was Schreiber who carried out the brutal murder – Mr Van Krevel's head was almost severed – it was Belinda, the dead man's 20-year-old daughter, who had orchestrated the whole thing.

The young woman claimed her father had sexually and physically abused her for years, and had even been abusing her young daughter and she'd had enough. She had left a window open for her boyfriend so he could enter the house, and also left the killing instruments out for the deed – a fire poker, knife and tomahawk. Belinda Van Krevel was in the house with her little girl as her father was killed. Schreiber told police he killed Mr Van Krevel for Mark Valera. 'I told [Mr Van Krevel], "This is from Mark, you fucking paedophile bastard. You'll never molest another kid again."'

Schreiber was sentenced to a minimum of 12 years in jail, and Van Krevel six years for soliciting the murder. She has become one of Australia's most notorious women and is thought to have been the inspiration for the 2006 black comedy movie *Suburban Mayhem* about a teenage mother who gets her dim-witted lover to murder her father as she sits in the next room.

Van Krevel and her brother won A$300 000 from their father's estate. Van Krevel gained the greater part of estate, and many who knew the family believe that money was the motivation for her to incite Schreiber to kill her father.

She was released in 2007, but that wasn't the last the woman dubbed 'Evil Van Krevel' and 'killer vamp' would see of a jail cell. In 2010, Van Krevel was again back in prison for a few months for stealing a woman's handbag and punching her in the face.

Then in 2013, she attacked her boyfriend – a man named Marshall Gould – stabbing him five times during an argument at their home. Mr Gould tried to protect Van Krevel, saying he'd been mugged and attacked by three men. However, a search at the couple's home revealed large bloodstains, indicating the story was false. Mr Gould said to reporters after Van Krevel was sentenced to three years' jail, 'I love her, and I support her, and she has had a troubled childhood.'

The Daily Telegraph reported Van Krevel whispered to Mr Gould, 'If anyone asks why you're sticking by me, tell them it's because I'm sexy.' Van Krevel was released in mid-2015.

On her release, she gave an exclusive interview to the Sunday night television program *60 Minutes*. When asked by reporter Allison Langdon if people could feel safe with her out in the community again, Van Krevel smiled and said, 'Why not?'

In one of the most dramatic moments of the interview, Langdon handed Van Krevel the *The A to Z of Serial Killers* book that had her brother's handwritten list of intended victims. Van Krevel had never seen this book up close before. Written on the 'hit list' was her name. She looked shocked but then said, 'This is just him being angry.'

Langdon shared her thoughts on Van Krevel after spending weeks with the complicated woman. 'Everything she has done is because of her love for her brother; she thinks he's innocent, not in the sense that he didn't kill the men, but that he was driven to do it,' Langdon told news.com.au in 2015.

'I found her such a compelling character .... I surprised myself that I actually enjoyed her company, but then there was a switch, and there were times when her eyes would go really black and I would think "this is a scary person, someone capable of real evil".'

The horrific murders were a true suburban nightmare. As for the legacy of Frank Arkell, who was part of making the city what it is today, it depends on who you speak to.

'To many in high places, he was the city's saviour, but to others who knew his dirty secrets, including his predilection for young boys, he was a "rock spider" who deserved what was coming to him …'wrote ABC Illawarra journalist Nick McLaren on abc.net.au in 2018.

MURDER OF A COMMUNITY ICON

As the licensee of one of the most famous pubs in Wollongong, Lucy Barrows, aged 53, was a strong, forthright woman who was respected in the community. Mrs Barrows, who was also heavily involved in the local racing industry, ran the Oxford Hotel in the heart of the industrial city.

The widow had moved to Wollongong in the early 1940s from Tumut, a town in New South Wales's Riverina region where she had also run a hotel. When Mrs Barrows took over the license for the Royal Hotel in Tumut in 1932, it made the local newspaper: the *Tumut and Adelong Times*. One of Mrs Barrows' sisters and her husband had run the hotel years before.

The Oxford Hotel was lively and an iconic spot in the area. It only closed down in 2010 and was well known for its live music scene in later years. In March 1951, police raided the hotel for unlawful trading (they found three men there on a Sunday afternoon), though one of the policemen who attended said the premises was 'well conducted and was a first-class hotel'. . .. (*South Coast Times and Wollongong Argus*, 8 March 1951.)

As the licensee, Mrs Barrows appeared in court along with the three men found in the saloon bar. She was fined £2 (around A$82 today) and also had to pay ten pence (A$20 today) for 'being the licensee of premises on which persons were unlawfully found'. No conviction was recorded for Mrs Barrows, and she could continue to operate the hotel. It wasn't even Mrs Barrows who had let the men into the hotel under the auspices of having lunch – it was her sister, Mary Burke, who helped her run the place. But as it was her name over the entrance door of the hotel, Mrs Barrows was responsible for everything that went on there.

Mrs Barrows lived at the top storey of the building, so she lived and breathed the hotel life.

There was plenty to keep on top of with the running of such a busy place ... including the inevitable clean-ups from alcohol-fuelled bar-room bust-ups. In April 1951, two men appeared at Wollongong Court over a brawl that smashed a plate glass door at the hotel. The criminal damage was reported in court to be £10 (around A$412 today), and the men were each fined and ordered to pay damages to Mrs Barrows.

Just a few months later, something much worse happened.

On Sunday, 10 June at around 10.30 p.m., Mrs Barrows retired for the night to her bedroom at the top of the building. There was nothing unusual about the night. The next morning at 6.30 a.m., housemaid Mary Deady was going about her duties and went to check on Mrs Barrows. She found her boss lying in a pool of blood on the floor. A pillowslip was tied tightly around her neck, and she'd been viciously assaulted. Ms Deady ran to tell one of the barmen, and he called the police.

The room was ransacked with suitcases rifled and furniture strewn all around. There were items of jewellery missing too, including rings that police believe the offender ripped from Mrs Barrows' fingers. Mrs Barrows wore her wedding band, four diamond rings and a delicate watch. These were all missing, as well as the keys to the hotel and safe, which she placed under her pillow at night. A locksmith was enlisted to try and open the pub's safe to see what was in there. There was money and jewellery still in the safe, and it looked as though the killer had fled the hotel without trying to open it.

The post-mortem of Mrs Barrows revealed her killer had been merciless. The medical officer determined Mrs Barrows had died from shock and strangulation but had also been severely bashed. She had a broken nose, five bruises on her head and face, which had most likely been caused by a clenched fist, two black eyes, and one of her bottom teeth had been knocked out.

At first, police believed robbery was the motive, but whoever killed Mrs Barrows also missed a wallet in a cupboard containing £100, and almost £50 in notes and coins that were clearly visible in a vase on the mantelpiece. There were some suggestions the killing could be relate to someone – or something – from the woman's past.

Guests at the hotel told police they heard nothing. No screams or a scuffle. There was a guest – a visiting bank inspector – sleeping on the verandah near Mrs Barrows' room (back then, a verandah was used as an extra room for buildings, especially hotels). He reported he heard only footsteps and voices – two men talking to each other – but no banging about or screams from the victim.

The police investigation focused on what the newspapers described as 'new Australians', mainly because many of the hotel guests were migrants. A witness had placed a man with an 'unusual gait' leaving the hotel around 1.40 a.m. This man was reportedly six feet (183 centimetres) tall and had his hat pushed down over his face.

The crime made headlines around Australia, and the city of Wollongong was in shock that one of its prominent community members had died in such a brutal manner.

Mrs Barrows was buried around 48 hours after her body was discovered. The *South Coast Times and Wollongong Argus* reported the funeral was the biggest the area had seen in living memory. The whole community was represented – council, sports and recreation clubs, police and businesspeople. There were people who came from all over New South Wales to pay their respects to the popular Mrs Barrows.

At the same time as the funeral, some council workers trimming grass found a bloodstained cotton scarf pillowslip and sheet in blackberry thickets at a vacant allotment near the hotel. The sheet and pillowcase were from Mrs Barrows' room. There were also some missing pages of a newspaper from her room that were found strewn nearby. Police checked with Mrs Barrows' sister and others close to her to see if the scarf was hers; however, after the investigation, it appeared the scarf belonged to the killer.

Another big break in the case came quickly when on Tuesday evening – a day after the body was discovered – a diamond ring pawned at a Sydney pawnbrokers turned out to be one of the ones taken from Mrs Barrows' fingers.

Police strongly suspected an employee, or ex-employee, of the hotel was involved. This would prove correct.

Just days after the murder, three men were arrested. The men, all Hungarian, were George Gach, 22, Instran Gal, 22, and Laszlo Kerekes, thirty-six. All were from Sydney. Kerekes had worked at the hotel for a few weeks earlier in 1951, and under police questioning, Gal and Gach admitted being at the hotel in the early hours when the murder happened.

'Did the boys tell you they do the strangle and I wait outside?' Kerekes, known as 'Peter', asked Detective Brian Doyle during his police interview.

But the other men told police that Kerekes had strangled Mrs Barrows, and when Detective Doyle told him this, he replied, 'Please believe me, they tell lies.' ('Thought Mrs Barrows was still alive', *Illawarra Daily Mercury*, 7 July 1951.)

Detective Doyle relayed Kerekes' statement to the inquest into Mrs Barrows' death.

It was Kerekes who showed the two other men how to get into Mrs Barrows' room and instructed them on how to subdue the woman while they robbed her. He told the pair he couldn't be part of the robbery. 'I say I don't go in room because Mrs Barrows know me,' he told police. He headed down to the nearby golf club where he could see the view of the hotel from the street.

Kerekes said, 'I saw George [Gach] go slowly in Mrs Barrows' window. I saw George jump, then I hear screams. I go down in Corrimal Street and after a while Steve [Gal] come down and I ask him what happened to Mrs Barrows. He tell me he didn't know what George did, but he go back to see. After a while I see George and Steve and Steve get a parcel under his arm. George tell me Mrs Barrows is very strong woman. George tell me pillowslips, sheet, and scarf in his parcel. Steve tell me he had tried to hit her two times in chin.'

The Canberra Times reported on 7 July 1951 that Kerekes said, 'I miss her chin and hit her eyes left and right.'

According to Detective Doyle, Kerekes told them to tie her legs and wrists and put something in her mouth to stop her screaming. Mrs Barrows bit Gach's hand when he placed it over her mouth and gave him a bloody nose when she punched him in the face.

When the two men left the room after bashing Mrs Barrows, they told Kerekes she was still alive.

When Kerekes saw a newspaper headline that Mrs Barrows had died, he said to the men, 'Why did you lie to me?'

Gach reportedly told Kerekes, 'She was still and alive because she was making noise.'

Gal then said, 'Yes. That's right. She was making noise and taking in and putting out air.'

A Czech migrant named Vaslav Flieger appeared at the inquest and admitted he had pawned the diamond ring that belonged to Mrs Barrows, but he claimed he was unaware of its origin at the time. Mr Flieger said Kerekes showed him the ring outside a club in Sydney and said he'd brought it with him from Europe.

Other pawnbrokers also appeared at the inquest and identified either Gach or Gal as men who attempted to pawn the jewellery, including an opal brooch and watch taken from Mrs Barrows.

On each day of the inquest, the court and public gallery were packed with onlookers. At the time it was one of the longest inquests the state of New South Wales had ever had.

The inquest was high on drama too with one of the accused, 22-year-old Gach, collapsing from a suspected heart attack on the first day of the hearing. Gach reportedly fell against the back of the dock, tears streaming down his face when Detective Doyle confronted him about the strangulation of Mrs Barrows.

Gach recovered, and it was thought by doctors the suspected 'heart attack' was actually an anxiety reaction to the proceedings.

The men were sent for trial, which began on 18 September 1951. The men were tried together and were all found guilty of the murder.

Judge Herron said to the men, 'You have all three disgraced the name of the New Australians. This was a defenceless woman, a decent citizen of these parts. I believe that you, Gal, and you, Gach, attacked her with a ferocity quite foreign to our way of life, and you, Kerekes, aided and abetted them.' ('Three sentenced to death; murder at Wollongong', *Daily Advertiser*, 25 September 1951.)

The automatic penalty for murder was the death sentence, but these sentences were commuted to life imprisonment, as was the policy of the New South Wales Government at the time.

It was quickly reported that the men would be deported after they'd served a portion of their sentences.

An editorial in *The Sydney Morning Herald* on 26 September 1951 stated:

This case, the latest brought to issue in an upsurge of crime in which migrants have been conspicuous, has drawn attention to the provision for deporting criminal aliens. If the Wollongong murderers are not to be hanged, Australia is surely under a moral obligation not to loose them upon some other community when they have served merely a portion of the substituted term of imprisonment.

A cynic could suggest that deportation might also give these criminals an opportunity to return to Australia at some future time, through the loopholes of our selection system in Europe. Mr Holt's praise of that system, and his insistence that there is no cause for concern over criminality among foreign migrants, are not likely to reassure an increasingly worried public.

The Mr Holt referred to in the editorial was Harold Holt, a future Prime Minister (January 1966–December 1967, when he disappeared while swimming at Cheviot Beach on Melbourne's Mornington Peninsula) who was then Minister for Immigration and Labour and National Service.

The men all appealed their sentences. The basis of Kerekes' appeal was that he was prejudiced by having to stand trial with the other men and that he had not ordered the attack and robbery on Mrs Barrows. The Court of Criminal Appeal rejected all their appeals.

The Wollongong community remembered Mrs Barrows by dedicating several sporting events to her name, including a memorial surf carnival and trophy competition between two local surf clubs.

Some say Mrs Barrows' spirit stayed in the hotel for years after the murder. In a 2010 *Illawarra Mercury* article marking the final closure of the Oxford Hotel, a former bar manager, Alby Fares, said that Mrs Barrows 'lurked in the many dark corners of the historic building'.

Fares said, 'One staff member always claimed it would be about ten degrees colder than the rest of the building in the upstairs room where the murder happened.'

Pub licensee Lucy Barrows, 53, was murdered in 1951 in her room at the top of The Oxford Hotel, Wollongong, New South Wales. Source: 1951, Brisbane Telegraph (Qld. : 1948 - 1954), *14 June, p. 7. (Via Trove)*

The Oxford Hotel, Wollongong, where Lucy Barrows was murdered. Source: 1951 'Scene Of Murder', Brisbane Telegraph (Qld. : 1948 - 1954), *13 June, p. 3. (Via Trove.)*

THE SALON
MURDERS

Eric George Nydam had known Katherine Joan Stradling, 55, for five years. The pair had met through a pen friends club, and after a long while corresponding to each other, Ms Stradling, who was an occupational therapist from England, decided to move to Melbourne with her sister in 1974.

Nydam, who was married, left his wife and son to live with Ms Stradling and her sister for a while. However, the relationship faltered, and Ms Stradling and her sister moved back to England. The pair kept in contact, and he convinced her to come back to Australia in 1976. The sisters rented a flat in Balaclava, not far from St Kilda.

The relationship was unhealthy, and the pair essentially 'broke up' again. However, Ms Stradling signed an odd document in the presence of Nydam's adult son that stated:

I agree to see Eric Nydam on either Saturday or Sunday every week on condition that he does not bother me at any other time and behaves in a reasonable and civilized way when we are together. My sister and I will also go to his flat for Christmas Day lunch. I undertake to be perfectly truthful in reporting on this association and I ask Paul Nydam to believe what I say. If anything I consider untoward occurs I wish to terminate the association and disclaim any further responsibility.

[Signed] Joan Stradling

Nydam was obsessed with Ms Stradling and her comings and goings. In January 1976, Nydam got the idea in his head that Ms Stradling and her sister were going to move back to England. Ms Stradling had allegedly told him, 'I may not be able to see you again, something big is going to happen.' (Nydam v R [1977].)

On the night of 14 January, Nydam waited outside the sisters' flat to find out more, and they arrived in their car with a man, whom they introduced to him. The man had a British accent, and Nydam started to obsess over whether that meant the three of them would definitely go back to England.

He lay awake all night obsessing over these thoughts. The situation, as he perceived it, was making him feel depressed.

Early the next day, at 7 a.m., Nydam got a taxi to near Ms Stradling's flat. He asked the driver to stop in a location where he could see her exit the building. He told the cabbie that he was a suspicious husband spying on his wife who he thought was having an affair. The sisters came out of the flat, and Nydam had the taxi follow them. Satisfied he knew where Ms Stradling was headed, he got the taxi to drop him off near his Blessington Street house. Nydam only had to walk a short distance to find Ms Stradling.

Just after 8 a.m., Ms Stradling walked into the Coiffure Roundabout Ladies' Hairdressing Salon on Acland Street for a shampoo and set. Nydam followed her in and the manager of the salon, Margaret MacConachie, heard Ms Stradling tell him to go home and she'd see him there. He then left. A young apprentice hairdresser, Karen Brush, shampooed Ms Stradling's hair, and when Ms Stradling was about to get it set, Nydam entered the shop again, this time holding a yellow bucket full of liquid.

He threw the liquid, which was petrol, over Ms Stradling and set her alight with a cigarette lighter. Ms MacConachie later told police, as reported in *The Age* on 15 July 1976, that she heard Nydam say, 'You will pay for this.'

The salon was filled with screams and engulfed in flames. Ms Stradling was burning to death, and the young hairdresser, Karen, who had been near Ms Stradling was also badly burned. Karen died of her horrific injuries five days later.

In the process of setting Ms Stradling on fire, Nydam was caught alight, and police found him outside the shop, lying on a tram track and moaning, 'I'm going to die. Don't worry about me, I want to die. I should have died but I got her.'

When interviewed by police, Nydam claimed he had only intended to 'stage a dramatic act' and denied he'd deliberately thrown the petrol at Ms Stradling. 'It was only a gesture. I wanted to gain her sympathy,' Nydam said. 'I intended to go and tell Joan that I intended to take my life, for her to see it happen, and to do this I was going to pour the petrol over myself and set fire to myself,' Nydam told police.

At the coroner's inquest in May 1976, the coroner Mr Pascoe found that the women died from burns 'maliciously inflicted' by Nydam.

The horrifying details of the crime emerged during the hearing with detective Senior Constable Graeme McDonald of the Homicide Squad, detailing how he found a burnt body in the shop ruins. The body was so badly burned, he couldn't tell whether it was a man or woman.

Nydam was eventually convicted of the murders of the women in 1977, but it took a few false starts. The first jury was discharged without a verdict because one juror told a court official they'd already made their mind up about Nydam. The second jury deliberated on a verdict for more than 24 hours but could not agree. The third trial resulted in a guilty verdict, but the conviction was quashed on appeal because the trial judge did not direct the jury adequately.

On 7 March 1977, the fourth jury to hear the case found Nydam guilty. He was sentenced to life imprisonment.

Karen Brush's distraught mother Ethel had been denied Victims of Crime Compensation and appealed this decision.

In March 1979, Mrs Brush appeared at the Country Court with her lawyer arguing for her that she had suffered mental distress (these days it would be called post-traumatic stress disorder) from her daughter's death and seeing Karen in hospital with the horrific burns caused by Nydam's violent actions.

Earlier in 1977, a few months before Nydam was found guilty, a skeleton found in Trentham, a small town in Victoria's Hepburn Shire, was identified as Peter Alexander Nydam. Peter, a 19-year-old laboratory assistant who had been missing since

1968. The cause of death was believed to be suicide because there was a bullet hole in the skull and a rusted rifle beside the skeleton. A wallet found with the skeleton helped identify Peter's remains.

Peter was Eric George Nydam's son.

Nydam's wife Claire died in 1985 at age seventy-one. On her gravestone, there is no mention of Nydam.

Going back through newspaper records, the name Eric George Nydam came up decades before the horrifying 1976 murders.

In 1944, a man named Eric George Nydam, then aged 29, was convicted in Queensland of unlawful assault against a man named Joseph Patrick King, who was the foreman of a woollen mill in Ipswich where a teenage girl, Jean D'Arth, also worked. Nydam had become obsessed with Jean, and he showed up to the mill to see the 16-year-old, whom he'd wanted a relationship with, but she'd written a letter to him to 'break off the friendship'.

Mr King tried to get Nydam to leave the workplace and leave the girl alone, but he headbutted him.

Police believed Nydam intended to abduct Jean.

A woman who befriended Nydam appeared at one of his earlier court appearances in January 1944 to give evidence about threats he'd made about Jean, including that he'd shoot the teen if she ever 'turned him down'.

Newspapers, such as *The Queensland Times*, reported that the witness Florinda Ethel Walker said Nydam had handed her a letter he'd written and asked her to keep it for a few days before reading it.

'I opened it that night. I later gave it back to defendant who destroyed it. In the letter, Nydam stated that there was no happiness for Jean and himself on this earth, so they would find it elsewhere,' Ms Walker told the court on 4 January 1944.

Ms Walker said she'd given him back the letter, telling him not to be 'so silly'.

A few weeks later, she saw Nydam, who told her that he had 'got Jean back' and then made the ominous threat: 'If Jean ever lets me down, or goes with anybody else, or loses any of her ideals or morals, I will kill her no matter how long I will have to wait ....'

She said she believed Nydam was serious about carrying out his threats to kill Jean and himself.

Nydam was sentenced to a year's jail with hard labour for the assault of Joseph King at the woollen mill, but the judge said he could be released on condition he stayed out of Queensland for 12 months.

In a strange addition to the story of Nydam, his father, Niels Oswald Nydam, killed himself – blew himself up – on 4 January 1944 with an explosive in an air raid shelter at the South Brisbane Auxiliary (Diamantina) Hospital where he'd been a patient since March 1943.

UNSOLVED 1960S MURDERS: THE WORK OF A SERIAL KILLER?

There are several unsolved murders in Australia from the 1960s, but four in New South Wales that took place in 1965–66 have been highlighted as possibly being related and committed by a serial killer.

These cases are the infamous killings of teenagers Marianne Schmidt and Christine Sharrock at Wanda Beach, Sydney, in 1965, and the murders of Wilhelmina Kruger and Anna Dowlingkoa in 1966. In 1990, the Canberra-based Institute of Criminology commented on these cases, 'Police suspect that there are links between the Wanda Beach murders and the other two murders. Indeed, there appears to be striking similarities between all three murders.'

* * *

There has been much written about the 'Wanda Beach Murders', which remains one of Australia's most notorious unsolved cases.

On 11 January 1965, Marianne Schmidt and Christine Sharrock, both 15, friends and next-door neighbours, took Marianne's four younger siblings to Cronulla Beach. The Schmidt family had immigrated to Australia from Germany several years previously. The family had had a tough time, with Mr Schmidt dying of cancer six months before and Mrs Schmidt ill in hospital. While Marianne took the younger children out, her two older brothers remained at home to clean the house.

Years later, Trixie, Marianne's younger sister, said in an interview that the children were all excited to have a day out and to catch the train from their home in West Ryde. However, when they arrived, they found that Cronulla Beach was closed due to strong winds. So, the party-of-six stashed their beach bags and walked towards the sand hills behind Wanda Beach Surf Club. It was a hot and windy day though, and the children quickly became tired.

In the early afternoon, Marianne and Christine told the youngsters to wait for them while they walked back to where they'd hidden their beach bags. They said that when they returned, they would all go home.

The girls never returned.

The children waited until 5 p.m., and then retrieved the beach bags themselves and went home.

The girls were reported missing at 8.30 p.m. that night.

The next day, the girls were found partially buried in some sand dunes. Their injuries were horrific – both had been stabbed multiple times, bashed, and there were signs of sexual assault. The man who found the girls initially thought they were mannequins dumped in the dunes.

So began one of the most exhaustive criminal investigations in New South Wales.

Derek Ernest Percy, who died from cancer in hospital in 2013, remains a prime suspect for the murders. Percy abducted, tortured and murdered 12-year-old Yvonne Tuohy in 1969. He took her from Warneet Beach in Victoria. Initially found to be criminally insane, Percy was jailed indefinitely. However, psychiatrists later found that he was not mentally ill at all.

During the investigation into Yvonne's murder, Percy was linked to a number of other child murders, including Marianne and Christine. It was thought that Percy's job in the navy gave him the opportunity to access victims in a variety of locations. Seven-year-old Linda Stilwell was snatched from Melbourne's St Kilda Foreshore, near Luna Park, in 1968. In 2009, a coroner's inquest found Percy was responsible for Linda's death, but her body has never been found. Whenever Percy was questioned about Linda's murder and any other crimes he was suspected of, he feigned memory loss.

A 2014 ABC article said the injuries found on Marianne and Christine 'were similar to those inflicted on Yvonne Tuohy'. A number of other clues point to Percy being responsible for the girls' deaths. However, there was not enough evidence to be certain, and detectives were unable to obtain a confession from Percy on his deathbed.

* * *

The murders of Wilhelmina Kruger and Anna Dowlingkoa are lesser known and have slipped from memory over the more than 50 years since they happened.

Wilhelmina 'Emmy' Kruger was a 56-year-old cleaner who worked at the Piccadilly Shopping Centre in Wollongong. Mrs Kruger's body was found by a butcher on his way to work at 6 a.m. on Saturday, 29 January 1966, at the base of a stairwell in a parking area of the shopping centre. Mrs Kruger had been strangled – with a cord or piece of material and by the killer's hand – as well as terribly mutilated. Mrs Kruger was naked apart from shreds of her dress around her neck.

In an initial newspaper report about the killing, police said the killer attacked Mrs Kruger while she was cleaning part of an arcade near the main shopping centre and threw her down a flight of stairs, strangled her, and then 'tore her to pieces'. In fact, there was speculation whether a wharf labourer's hook was the implement used to mutilate Mrs Kruger, or a knife six inches (15 centimetres) or more in length; her body sustained severe internal damage. There were also signs that the killer had sexually assaulted Mrs Kruger. There was no attempt to hide her body.

A month later, the decomposed body of Anna Dowlingkoa was found in a carriageway of the New Illawarra Road, Lucas Heights, Sydney. Anna, 24, who went by several names, including Tomlinson and Dowling, was a sex worker who was last seen alive on 16 January 1966 at a club in Kings Cross. Examination of her body revealed Anna had been stabbed, strangled and mutilated.

Police drew comparisons to Mrs Kruger's killing, so much so that they believed the same man killed the women. The murders would have happened within days of each other. Police believed the killer returned to Ms Dowlingkoa's body a few weeks after he killed her and dragged her further away to where she was found.

At the 1967 inquest into Ms Dowlingkoa's death, the coroner stated her murder bore a 'close resemblance to what are commonly known as the Jack the Ripper Murders'. The coroner found the stab wounds were made after death and that the place of death could not be established.

Police followed several lines of inquiry into the brutal killings.

In March 1966, it was reported police had interviewed a man from London, who'd only been in Australia since late 1965. The man had tried to strangle a woman in a Kings Cross house. Police told the newspapers the man was not being sought for the murders of Mrs Kruger and Anna.

The team handling these cases was nicknamed 'the Mutilator Squad' in news reports. The team spoke to the man about a series of killings of women in London dubbed the Jack the 'Stripper' Murders, also known as the Hammersmith Nudes Murders. At that stage, six women had been killed and their bodies dumped along the River Thames in West London.

There have been several books published over the years and many articles pointing to the identity of the man known as Jack the Stripper. Former British boxing heavyweight champion Freddie Mills has long been in the mix as a suspect. Mills died in July 1965 in an apparent shotgun suicide. He was associated with the underworld, including the Kray Twins, and one gangster suggested Mills killed himself because he had a dark secret – he was the killer of the six women.

A writer called Neil Milkins wrote the book *Who is Jack the Stripper?* and named a man called Harold Jones as the killer.

Jones had been jailed for 20 years in the 1920s in Wales for the murders of two children aged eight and eleven when he was only fifteen. On his release, Jones moved to Fulham in West London and was living there at the time of the Jack the Stripper Murders.

The Sun newspaper reported in 2011 that the suspect favoured by the police boss in charge of the investigation was Scottish security guard Mungo Ireland. Ireland killed himself soon after the last murder and left a note saying, 'I cannot stick it any longer. To save you and the police looking for me, I'll be in the garage.'

The identity of the murderer remains a mystery. The police investigation looking at possible links between these murders and those of Mrs Kruger and Anna came to nothing.

At the time, police linked the murders of the two women with the Wanda Beach Murders, as the cases were close in time and location. However, there were other similarities, as the Institute of Criminology noted, 'In each case, a body was dragged along the ground with no real attempts made to conceal the bodies. Sexual molestation after the slaying was involved in all cases, and the victims were murdered near or in Sydney.'

* * *

Another suspect in the Wanda Beach Murders, who could therefore reasonably be a suspect for the killings of Wilhelmina Kruger and Anna Dowlingkoa, is the man known as 'the Beauty Queen Killer'.

Australian-born Christopher Wilder moved to the United States in the 1970s and abducted, raped and murdered at least eight women in a cross-country killing spree across America. The spree lasted six weeks and came to an end in 1984 when Wilder,

39, died during attempts by law enforcement to capture him in a New Hampshire village. There's debate about whether Wilder shot himself deliberately with his .357 Mangum or whether the gun was accidentally fired when a state trooper tried to restrain him in a 'bear hug'. There had been a nationwide manhunt for Wilder.

Nonetheless, Wilder, who was described in the media as a 'millionaire Australian race car driver', was suspected of killing many more women. The FBI connected him to at least 11 abductions, including four murders where bodies were found.

Untasteful headlines appeared in newspapers, including *The Tuscaloosa News*: 'Christopher Wilder a real "killer" with the ladies'.

He was bailed to appear at court in Sydney for the assaults of two 15-year-old girls but never appeared. At the time of the offences in Sydney, he'd been visiting his parents – his father was a retired US Navy officer so Wilder had dual citizenship.

Wilder has also been named as a possible suspect in the abduction and murder of Sydney teen Trudie Adams in 1978. Trudie had been at a dance with her boyfriend at the Newport Surf Lifesaving Club. She left the dance alone in the early hours of 25 June and was seen getting into a light-coloured 1977 Holden panel van. Trudie has never been seen again. Wilder was visiting his parents in Sydney at the time of Trudie's disappearance.

Wilder lured girls with promises to help them launch modelling careers and claimed that he wanted to photograph them. He'd already been charged several times in the United States in the 1970s for sexual misconduct, and in 1980, he was arrested for raping a woman after he'd told her he could make her a model.

His parents put up their home as surety for his $400 000 bail.

Wilder disappeared from his Florida home on 17 March 1984, leaving an estate of houses and land worth at least US$1 million. He was placed on the FBI's Most Wanted list on 5 April and was dead a week later. It was one of his victims who helped police find Wilder. He abducted 16-year-old Dawnette Sue Wilt from a shopping centre in Indiana, stabbed her and left the teen to die. Dawnette described Wilder's vehicle, which helped police in their search.

Wilder was a convicted rapist, having taken part in a pack rape in Sydney in 1963, two years before the Wanda Beach Murders. He was a suspect in the murders of Christine Sharrock and Marianne Schmidt and was living in the Sydney area at the time; he immigrated to the United States in 1969.

* * *

A blog called *Forgotten Illawarra* detailed that in 1975, Detective Cec Johnson, who had worked on the Wanda Beach case, was given 'an abstract landscape painting' by Alan Bassett. Alan Bassett, at the time aged 21, had been arrested in June 1966 for the rape and murder of 20-year-old Carolyn Orphin, in Wollongong. He had met his victim at a dance. He was sentenced to life imprisonment for Carolyn's murder.

During his time in jail, he presented the abstract landscape painting to Johnson, and certain details on the painting immediately caught the detective's attention. Johnson claimed that the painting 'contained images of the positions of the bodies in the Wanda Beach Murder, as well as details of the murder never revealed to the public', and also 'contained clues to the Piccadilly murder'.

Johnson wrote a book discussing his theory but was killed in an accident before the book was finished, and it was never published.

Could these murders still be solved more than 50 years on?

'TIL DEATH DO US PART

The message was scrawled in lipstick on a notepad, but the page was so bloodstained police could barely make out the words. The writer seemed to be accusing a woman of 'not playing straight'.

It was the afternoon of 23 October 1950, and police found a shocking scene at the room of the boarding house at Surry Hills, in Sydney's south-east. Young wife and mother Betty Fay Kennedy was lying motionless on the bed. The 24-year-old was wrapped in a blanket, and a man, bleeding profusely from slash wounds to his arms and wrists, draped over her with his head resting on her left shoulder.

Detective Sergeant Dimmock, of Darlinghurst Police, said to the man, 'What's going on here?' The man was weak from blood loss and didn't answer. Detective Sergeant Dimmock and his colleague lifted him and tried to wake Betty.

It was Betty's cousin, a woman named Patricia Buxton, who had contacted police to say that Betty's husband was at her back door, covered in blood. He spoke to her, saying he'd killed his wife, before staggering back to his accommodation a few doors' away.

So it was no surprise to police when the man found sprawled over Betty's body was her husband: Athol William Kennedy.

The Kennedys were taken to St Vincent's Hospital in nearby Darlinghurst, but Betty was dead on arrival – strangled and with a serious head injury.

Kennedy, 28, had killed his wife, that much was clear to police, and he'd tried to end his own life too. His wounds needed 45 stitches. Kennedy was subsequently charged with his wife's murder.

The Kennedys' five-year-old daughter was at school when the murder and attempted suicide took place. *The Sydney Morning Herald* reported she was placed temporarily in Mrs Ruxton's care. Mrs Ruxton said, 'We did not tell her that her mother was dead. We told her she was in hospital …. the girl said, "It is silly to cry, as mummy will soon get better."'

It wasn't until 21 December 1950, almost two months after the murder, that Kennedy's bail application was heard. He'd been remanded in custody for all that time and was considered at high risk of suicide if he was given bail.

The coroner's inquest was held a few weeks prior. Detective Sergeant Dimmock recounted his statement from the day of the killing. He said Kennedy had confessed, 'I found out that Betty was running around with another man and I killed her. I strangled her, but God knows how I loved her.'

The *Truth* newspaper reported others gave evidence at the hearing, including Mrs Ruxton, who said she'd seen violent episodes before from Mr Kennedy. 'On one occasion when Kennedy was on leave from the army during the war, Betty came downstairs crying and showed us a mark across her back,' Mrs Ruxton told the inquest.

Mrs Ruxton disputed Kennedy's story that it was his wife's 'cavorting' with other men that drove him to kill her: 'I have never seen Betty with any man other than her husband. She had never been friendly with any other man and was a good-living woman.'

On 17 April 1951, the case came before court. Kennedy pleaded guilty to manslaughter.

Having been chastised by the judge for 'sitting there for the whole morning looking down at your boots', Kennedy then launched into an hour-long explanation for his actions.

The newspapers lapped up the drama of Kennedy's account, which was reported as a melodrama rather than a fatal act of violence against a woman.

'She was making love to me,' Kennedy told the court. 'I noticed a sly look on her face and I accused her of going out with other fellows. Her sly look said, "If I do, they give me a better time than you do."'

'All I know is that I had no intention of killing my wife or of strangling her because I was very much in love with her,' reported the *Brisbane Telegraph* with the headline 'Ten years' jail for jealous strangler'.

Kennedy based his paranoid and controlling suspicions, which snowballed into murderous rage, from alleged conversations with his landlady Rita Darby. 'About last September, I was talking to my landlady, and she was telling me about my wife and other women,' Kennedy said. 'I said I was glad I had nothing to worry about and she said, "You don't want to be so sure." Nothing more was said, but I had a very nasty taste in my mouth ...' the *Truth* newspaper reported.

This conversation seemed to flip a switch in Kennedy's mind, and he became obsessed with catching his wife out with other men. He resorted to methods like placing his wife's shoes in a position where he'd know if they'd been moved – in his paranoid mind, indicating she'd snuck out.

He also admitted he accused his wife of being unfaithful and looked feverishly for clues to back up his suspicions. He took to following Betty when she went out with other women, including the landlady Mrs Darby.

In court, he recounted another conversation he alleged he'd had with Mrs Darby. 'I said, "I followed the three of you last night and saw you go into the pictures." And she [Mrs Darby] said, "How long?" I said, "Not long." She said, "You didn't stay long enough to see Betty come out of the pictures and return just before the end!"'

He then continued, 'My mate told me if I didn't stop worrying, I would go off my head.'

He also commented, 'On the Sunday, my wife was getting ready to take our little daughter down to see all the dolls in the shop windows, and when she was ready to go I said, "When you go to the pictures, you are all dolled up, and when you go out with me, you are like an old hag!"'

He also said, 'I was worried and upset and drinking a lot. I just couldn't get it out of my mind.'

Sentencing Kennedy to ten years' jail for the murder, Mr Justice Clancy said, 'Kennedy, I think your judgment was affected by this belief, which you held as to your wife's infidelity. If your version is correct, then your sole source of information was this Mrs Darby. I am loathe to criticise this Mrs Darby because she is not here to give her version of it. But whether that version is correct or not, I am satisfied that your mind was affected by that belief.'

Mrs Darby told the *Truth* she was shocked at Kennedy's allegations that she had told him his wife was not 'true'. 'I am deeply distressed at Kennedy's charges. I think he must have said those things out of spite,' she said.

According to records found on ancestry.com.au, Kennedy died in 2010 at age eighty-eight.

WHAT LIES BENEATH

In 2011, the Sharma family was taking a scenic drive in the Dandenong Ranges, in Melbourne's outer-east. The drive is world famous for winding through the forests and lush greenery of the Dandenongs, with little towns such as Olinda and Sassafras punctuating the drive. Hundreds of thousands of tourists each year visit these little spots to have Devonshire teas, a kitsch smorgasbord experience and traditional German entertainment at the world-famous Cuckoo Restaurant (it closed in 2021) and take in the natural beauty of the area's national park and stunning gardens.

Nilesh Sharma, 36, his wife Preetika, 35, and their young children – son Divesh, five, and daughter Divya, three – lived in the eastern suburb Glen Waverley where they'd settled after moving to Australia from Fiji in 2003. Sharma was driving his family in their Honda east along Mountain Highway, near Sassafras, when the car drifted into oncoming traffic then veered to the left side of the road and ran down the embankment. The vehicle stopped when it collided with a tree.

The family were dragged to safety by passers-by moments before the car burst into flames. The children were unhurt, but Preetika sustained injuries that required a hospital stay, inpatient rehabilitation and time off work.

Sharma, who also suffered some injuries that needed outpatient rehabilitation, told police he had blacked out at the wheel.

The family moved on and recovered from the frightening crash. However, six months later, the accident took on a potentially sinister significance.

Sharma, a finance manager, was suffering headaches from the head and neck injuries he received in the car crash. An assessment from a neuropsychologist showed he had some impaired brain function and memory processing issues resulting from the car crash. The neuropsychologist was working with Sharma on relaxation techniques to help manage the headaches and stress.

On 1 May 2012, Sharma's nephew, Shane Chanel (the son of Sharma's sister), rang triple-0 with some concerns for the family. Mr Chanel had been contacted by Divya's childcare centre because the little girl had been absent for two days with no forward notice. Her older brother, Divesh, had also been absent from school. When Mr Chanel couldn't get in contact with the Sharma family by phone, he drove to their Marcia Court house. He found the curtains closed and the family car in the driveway of the brick house but couldn't get any answer when he knocked on the door.

The police investigated. Peering through a window, officers saw a child's body motionless in bed. When they forced entry inside, their worst suspicions were realised. The whole family was dead. Divesh was found lying in his bed with a pillow over his face. Preetika and Divya were dead together in another bedroom. Both were facedown, each with a pillow over the back of their heads. Both children were dressed in pyjamas, and Preetika in a tracksuit. According to the Coroners Court of Victoria report, there were no outward injuries to any of the bodies.

In the hallway, police found Nilesh Sharma, who'd hung himself.

According to the police evidence brief, the house was orderly and tidy. There had been no forced entry in the house. It appeared Sharma murdered his wife and children then killed himself.

Forensic examinations of Sharma's laptop found that a website called 'Buy Chloroform' had been accessed 27 times. The person using the computer was logged in as 'Neil', Sharma's nickname.

The State Coroner, Judge Ian Gray, who was at the helm of the inquests into the Sharma family deaths, said in the inquest finding dated 8 May 2015, 'I am satisfied, on the balance of probabilities that Mr Sharma exposed Ms Sharma, Divesh and Divya to chloroform, disabling them so that he could then cause their deaths by smothering or suffocating.'

At the direction of Judge Gray, the deaths were also investigated by the Coroners Prevention Unit, a service that helps the Coroners Office play a wider role in prevention issues surrounding public health and safety.

The investigation uncovered a history of family violence within the Sharma marriage. Some of Preetika's relatives and friends said Sharma was controlling and isolated his wife. Outwardly,

Sharma seemed to present a different face at work. As noted in the coroner's findings, Sharma's manager said he was a 'diligent and responsible worker'.

Sharma was born in Ba, Fiji, in 1975, and migrated to Australia in 2000. He had lived with his sister and her family in Wheelers Hill, and then bought the Glen Waverley house with his mother and lived there with his parents. In 2002, he returned to Fiji with his parents and was introduced to Preetika through family connections for an arranged marriage.

Preetika's sister, Ashika Prasad, told investigators that after Divya's birth in 2009, the landline was disconnected from the family home, and Preetika told her it was because Sharma wanted to be in control of whom his wife spoke to. Ms Prasad also said her sister told her that early on in the couple's marriage, Sharma would slap her 'whenever she questioned him'.

A work colleague of Preetika made a witness statement that she offered to help her after Preetika confided in the work friend that she was physically abused by her husband.

There had also been a period of separation in the marriage. It was instigated by Sharma soon after Divya's 2009 birth. According to the inquest report, Sharma had found an email to his wife from a man she had once been in a relationship with. The relationship happened before Preetika and Sharma had even met each other, but Sharma accused his wife of infidelity. It was he who initiated the separation where they took to separate bedrooms under the same roof. Sharma also discovered his wife had been pregnant to this man and had had a termination. Although this was personal information that Preetika did not want anyone to know, Sharma told people about it, including Preetika's father and family.

Expert evidence was given for the inquest by Dr Ruchita Ruchita, then a case worker at inTouch Multicultural Centre Against Family Violence and she said 'cultural and religious beliefs could have been a major contributing factor' in the murder of Preetika, Divesh and Divya.

Some of Dr Ruchita's recommendations to the coroner were for there to be an increase in Culturally and linguistically diverse (CALD) specific services at magistrates' courts, programs targeted at international students and for CALD media to run violence prevention messages and content. She also called for communities to work in changing behaviours and attitudes to educate about gender equality.

Judge Gray said, 'The unexpected and violent death of a person is a devastating event'.

'Violence perpetrated by an intimate partner or a family member is particularly shocking.'

In the decade since Nilesh Sharma murdered his family, awareness of family violence and the services available to keep women and children safe has increased, though there is much more work to be done.

THE MURDER OF BEVERLEY KEYS

The fatal bashing of a Canberra hotel receptionist in 1961 shook the quiet capital, which was not used to such violent crime.

Beverley Irving Keys was found unconscious in her bed by her mother on the morning of Friday, 22 September 1961. Beverley had a large gash on her head, and it appeared she had been attacked sometime overnight in her bungalow, while her parents and 20-year-old brother slept just metres away in the family home in Geerilong Gardens, Reid.

Reid is one of the most established suburbs in Canberra and located directly next to the city. It is named after Sir George Reid who was Australia's fourth prime minister (he was in power just shy of a year between August 1904 and July 1905).

Beverley never regained consciousness and died in the Canberra Community Hospital 40 hours later.

At the time, the murder was the biggest investigation ever undertaken by ACT Police. Immediately after Beverley died, 20 detectives and uniformed police canvassed the suburb and searched all over, including in sewer drains and manholes, for the murder weapon.

As with all other investigations, the acquaintances of Beverley were questioned, and her family were fingerprinted and eliminated as suspects. She was described as a popular, friendly and well-presented young woman. She had spent four years living in England and had returned home to Australia to live with her parents in May 1961.

Detectives also spoke to known thieves and criminals in the city. Whoever killed Beverley had also stolen her pay packets and handbag.

One clue that bolstered the detectives' hopes was the discovery of a cigarette butt – Carlyle brand – on the corner of the lawn opposite Beverley's bungalow.

Beverley had finished work at the Hotel Rex in the city at 11.45 p.m. on Thursday, 21 September and arrived at her home in a taxi at midnight. She had been paid that day so she had her pay packet from the Hotel Rex, which was her regular employment. Beverley also worked casually as a receptionist at another Canberra hotel, the Ainslie-Rex, and had also been paid for work she had done earlier that day.

These pay envelopes had been stolen. The same night of the murder, another home had been broken into nearby and a transistor radio had been stolen.

Meanwhile, women in the suburbs were terrified by the prospect that a brutal killer was in their midst and prowling the streets as they slept. Five days after Beverley's death, *The Canberra Times* reported that streetlights in the northern suburbs would be kept on all night. Member for ACT, Mr JR Fraser said it was at the request of 'many housewives'. The newspaper reported that the lights usually went out at 12.30 a.m.

Police worked around the clock to capture Beverley's killer, and on 30 September, they charged 45-year-old cook Daniel Norris Nicholls with murder. It was an unusual arrest in that Nicholls was charged at a special bedside court at the Canberra Community Hospital where he was recovering from a shotgun injury.

Nicholls became only the third person in ACT history to have been charged with murder. The first was a man named Bertram Porter, who in 1932 force-fed his 11-month-old son rat poison; he was charged with the boy's murder but was eventually acquitted on the grounds of insanity and sent to a psychiatric hospital. In 1957, Elaine Kerridge was acquitted of murdering her abusive husband with an axe.

Nicholls came to the attention of the police on 28 September, a week after the attack.

On that day, Nicholls was at a sprawling property in Top Naas where the owner had given him permission to shoot on the land. The landowner, Max Oldfield, had taken up Nicholls' invitation to look at fox skins in the cook's utility truck, but the mood changed quickly.

Nicholls pointed a shotgun at Mr Oldfield and demanded to be taken to the house for a meal and so that he could write a statement.

He spent two hours painstakingly writing a statement that outlined his innocence on the murder of Beverley. However, he did write: 'Due to my past I must eventually become a suspect and undergo an ordeal I am not prepared to face.'

Nicholls wrote the statement in point form, which was basically the circumstantial evidence that he believed would render him guilty in the eyes of the law. He admitted, among other things, he smoked Carlyle brand cigarettes – the brand found outside Beverley's sleepout – and that he had stolen from bedrooms in the past. 'I am caught in a web of unfortunate circumstances, which at this stage I feel I haven't the strength or youth to fight. I could not face the thought of possible conviction and spend the remainder of my days in prison.' He also mentioned, 'I wish this to be published so that a few – very few friends can sum up things for themselves.'

Nicholls fully intended to kill himself by shotgun after he had written his last testament, and he had it witnessed by Mr Oldfield and his wife Dulcie. The Oldfields, including their two young daughters, must have been terrified, especially when Nicholls ordered Mrs Oldfield to tie up her husband's hands. While Nicholls was tying up Mrs Oldfield's hands, her husband freed himself and lunged for a revolver, which he fired into the wall. In a mad grab by both of the men for the shotgun, it accidentally discharged, and Nicholls was injured.

Mrs Oldfield, the postmistress at Top Naas, phoned the police at around 9.15 p.m. 'Come at once,' Mrs Oldfield said. 'The man who killed the Keys girl is at Max Oldfield's.'

Mr Oldfield told investigators that Nicholls had begged the couple to 'finish him off'. Nicholls was begging the man to shoot him or give him the shotgun so he could kill himself, but Mr Oldfield refused. When police and ambulance arrived, they found Nicholls writhing on the lawn.

Mr Oldfield's extraordinary life as a stockman in ACT's high country was documented in a book *Max Oldfield: The Story of his Ride.* Author Richard Begbie wrote of the family's encounter with Nicholls, 'Although post-traumatic stress had not been identified then, the effects of that night would haunt them for years.' The family moved from their Top Naas home a few years after the frightening night with Beverley Keys' killer.

At the inquest into Beverley's death, her father gave evidence that at 9.10 a.m. on 22 September, he had noticed a Carlyle brand cigarette stub, some ash and 'human excreta' in his garden but did not realise the significance of them until his wife discovered their daughter in her bloodstained bed at around 10.30 a.m.

Associates of Nicholls told police that they noticed that the man had money on the day of 22 September, when the day before, he had complained he was broke.

There was also the matter of the transistor radio that was stolen on the same night and found in the accused's possession. The homeowner, Richard Prowse, gave evidence at a court hearing for Nicholls in November 1961 that he last saw the transistor on the windowsill of his 12-year-old daughter's bedroom.

The lead investigator on the case, Detective Sergeant Ray Kelly, had no doubt as to the accused's motives: theft and sex. Kelly told the court on 26 October 1961 that he believed the young woman had been killed for 'some reason of sexual gratification' but would not give his opinion on which came first.

The judge presiding over Nicholls' Supreme Court trial adjourned proceedings so that the defence could make more investigations to prepare its case.

Nicholls pleaded not guilty to the charge of murder and appeared before the Supreme Court in March 1962. He did not deny that he entered Beverley's room and stole money and her purse, but he claimed not to remember the events afterwards.

On 8 March, he was found guilty and sentenced to death. Newspapers reported that Nicholls was impassive when he heard the verdict and quietly left the courtroom, smoking a cigarette, to be escorted back to prison.

Nicholls successfully appealed his sentence and a retrial started in March 1963; however, he was again found guilty. This time his death sentence was commuted to life imprisonment.

AN AFTERNOON OF RANDOM VIOLENCE

Getting attacked in your bed by a member of staff is certainly not what you expect during a hospital stay, but that's what happened to Melbourne man Ralph Lowther. On Saturday, 7 September 1974, the elderly man was in his bed in Ward One South, St Francis Xavier Cabrini Hospital, Malvern (the hospital is now known as Cabrini Malvern), when a male nursing assistant smashed a half-pint bottle of milk over his head. The nursing assistant, a fourth-year medical student, ran out of the room after the bizarre, unprovoked attack, which left Mr Lowther dazed and bleeding, with cuts that needed stitches.

The events that unfolded after the attack were nothing short of suburban mayhem that would leave a child dead and 13 people seriously physically attacked (not to mention their trauma and that of the people around them that day).

Martin Phillip Parkinson, 21, had been at work at the hospital since 7 a.m. For some unfathomable reason, he snapped at 11.50 a.m. with the attack on Mr Lowther. Following this, he told the nurse on duty, Sister Gray, that he was going home. Sister Gray asked him if his shift was finished, and he replied, 'No, I'm leaving.' Then he hit her on the side of her head. Sr Gray fell, and Parkinson fled the room.

Parkinson, dressed in a white uniform, bolted to his car – a white Ford Cortina – and drove off. Where he was headed was unknown, but it was fair to assume he might have been going home to the house he shared with four other medical students in Inverness Avenue, Armadale. He had only lived in the share house for two months, having moved from his family home in the eastern suburb of Vermont.

Sister Renee Kittelson, a nun and the matron of the hospital, was paged just after 12 p.m. and told she was needed at Ward One South immediately, but she was given no explanation as to why. She was off duty at the time but headed straight over, sensing this must have been something serious.

When she arrived at the ward, she found a shaken Sister Gray who told her what happened, and that Parkinson had run out of the ward. After checking on Mr Lowther, the patient who'd been attacked, Sister Kittelson rang reception to find out if anyone had seen a medical student exiting the hospital and was told that yes, a student had been seen running out the doors, but no one knew who he was.

Sister Kittelson rang Parkinson's share house, to warn his housemates that Parkinson was in a 'disturbed mood' and to keep him contained if he showed up. When a woman answered the phone, telling Sister Kittelson no one was home, Sister Kittelson told the woman what had happened and to get out of the house, in case Parkinson returned.

In what would be a decision later criticised, the hospital did not tell the police of the assaults by Parkinson until 1 p.m., an hour after the young man had fled the building. Between Parkinson fleeing and the police being contacted at 1.p.m, Sister Kittelson rang Parkinson's family home and spoke to his stepfather who, after hearing what had happened and that she intended to phone police, asked her not to and that the family would 'look after everything'.

Unimpressed by this reaction, Sister Kittelson rang the hospital administrator, Sister Irene, who advised to wait until a doctor came in (which was around 1 p.m.), and he then told her to phone the police, who arrived soon after.

Two constables from nearby the Malvern Police Station were first on the scene at the hospital and were told by Sister Irene, 'A medical student who works here part-time went berserk and struck a patient across the face with a bottle. He then attacked Sister Gray.' When they asked Sister Irene why police weren't called sooner, she told them, 'I was more concerned with contacting the doctor and tending to the patient's injuries than calling the police.'

Parkinson's brother, a barrister, and his stepfather later arrived at the hospital.

No one at the hospital that day could have known what would then unfold.

Parkinson's first stop was Elsternwick, a suburb less than five kilometres from his Armadale share house. It was around 2.40

p.m., almost three hours since he had assaulted the patient and nurse at the hospital.

Parkinson stopped outside a house in St Georges Road, where Joan O'Shea and her son Jon, 17, were gardening in the front yard. Parkinson had no links to the property and didn't know the family. Still dressed in his hospital whites, Parkinson got out of his car and approached the property, walking through the gate towards Jon and said, 'How are you?'

Trying to work out if he knew the man, Jon had no time to reply before Parkinson grabbed the garden spade from his hand and launched into an attack, hitting him across the head and upper torso. Joan O'Shea, weeding the garden at the time, heard her son yell, 'Mum' and turned around to see 'a man in white coveralls standing in the centre of the lawn' with a shovel in both hands and holding it above his head. Jon was lying on the lawn and she saw the man 'hitting him about the head'. She was quoted in *The Age* saying that the attack was so bizarre, she thought Parkinson was joking at first. However, she instinctively ran to her son. 'I ran to protect Jon, and he [Parkinson] hit me across the head and shoulder,' she said.

Hearing their screams, Joan's husband Hugh ran from the house to find his wife and son covered in blood on the lawn.

It was ten minutes of hell for the family, and while Hugh tried to help his wife and son, Parkinson fled in his car, taking the O'Shea's shovel with him.

Joan and Jon O'Shea were taken to The Alfred Hospital with serious injuries. Joan's head wound needed 22 stitches.

A weary, shocked O'Shea family were pictured in *The Age* newspaper in their home the day after their ordeal. In a description that conjures up images from a horror movie, Hugh O'Shea described to reporters how he saw Parkinson: 'I saw a very pale figure standing about four metres away. His face was expressionless, and his eyes were staring vacantly and glazed.'

Meanwhile, Parkinson drove three kilometres to Alma Road, Caulfield North. There he stopped and attacked a middle-aged woman, Jean Ferguson, who was standing on the footpath. She was seriously injured. In fact, her injuries were so severe, she was left with brain injury that caused partial loss of movement and meant she needed to use a wheelchair. Ms Ferguson, a former secretary, was also left unable to speak and with severe emotional trauma. She was awarded the maximum A$3000 by the Crimes Compensation Tribunal in 1975. The Tribunal admitted the amount was clearly not enough to compensate her for her life-altering injuries.

A witness, Linda Walsh, who lived in Alma Road and was in her front garden when Parkinson pulled up in his Cortina outside her house and walk across the road, towards Jean Ferguson's home, heard loud screams and ran out of her gate to confront Parkinson as he returned to his car. 'You bastard, what have you been up to?' she said.

He made no reply, and Linda recalled his eyes were 'very wide and glassy'.

Linda rushed over the road to find a woman lying on the nature strip, with bleeding head wounds. She shouted out to another neighbour to phone the police, and then she told them the registration number of Parkinson's car.

After attacking Jean Ferguson, Parkinson drove half a kilometre to Orrong Crescent, Caulfield, where he targeted two teenage girls. When I first wrote about this case, I'd read an article from *The Age* that had a timeline of the events of this horrid day, and it reported that the girls were attacked as they were walking along the street. The truth is that Parkinson randomly chose one of the girl's homes and walked up to the front door.

I spoke to Sandra Cory by phone in January 2021. It was her family home that Parkinson arrived at on that Saturday afternoon.

I was pleased when she agreed to talk to me, but I was a bit nervous about bringing up the past for her.

'It was a long time ago and I'm over it,' Sandra told me when I asked what it was like to be contacted out of the blue over Facebook Messenger.

Sandra is in her mid 60s now, still living in Victoria, and works as a horticulturalist.

Here's Sandra's recollection of that day:

'I was 17 and three quarters. Both my parents were overseas in San Francisco, visiting my second oldest brother who lived there at the time. And an old friend of my mother's was staying on his way to somewhere, so he was there. And then my oldest brother, he was resident doctor at St Vincent's Hospital. So, he was living there while Mum and Dad were away. And anyway, one Saturday afternoon, my friend who lived up a side street near me came down to the house. And she comes in the back door, just as a member of the family, sort of thing. I had a Doberman dog and the dog started barking.

Our front door knocker was not that easy to hear sometimes, if you're at the back of the house. So, I went down to the front door and there was a guy in whites, as in a medical, nurse person, and he was carrying a shovel. And my mind just said, 'Oh, that's somebody that my brother David knows. He's obviously in his white gear and he's borrowed Mum's shovel and he's bringing it back', because he'd come up to the front door and then walked down the steps and was walking up the driveway. So, I just said, 'Oh, what do you want, mate?' And he just walked up and drove the shovel straight into my face, between my eyes, and then clipped me again under the right nostril. I can remember my friend tried to hide in my parents' bedroom, and all I can remember seeing was this guy push the door open and was just bashing the spade towards her. I ran up to the room where my mum's friend was having a nap and he woke up with all this din going on. And I don't know why, whether the dog scared him off or whatever, but he took off. And then, of course, we immediately rang the police. And then the ambulance came and took us into St. Vincent's, where my brother was, and we got stitched up. And my sister was living in Gippsland, so we went up there for a few days, just to get away from everything, because the reporters were going nuts'.

Sandra says her injuries were minor compared to what happened to the other people attacked by Parkinson. She had a cut between her eyes that got stitched up and told me her friend had stitches in her scalp. However, the mental effects were longer lasting.

185

'It was a little bit scary for a while because prior to this happening in North Caulfield, there'd been a lot of burglaries. A lot of Jewish people lived there, and a lot of wealthy Jewish people had been burgled by someone they named the "cat burglar". And he would go into people's houses and steal jewellery off their fingers. And we'd had a few creepy people around, so I was pretty tentative. But it didn't take me too long because I moved off into the country to work the following year, or two years later. So, I got away from it all,' Sandra told me.

While Sandra said the attack happened so fast, she does remember one thing about Parkinson.

'He had piercingly blue eyes. And probably to this day, whenever I see anyone with those, I'm a little bit like, "you can keep away from me. I don't want to know you",' Sandra recalled. 'He didn't say anything to me. He didn't say, "Oh, good day", or anything like that. He obviously had this vision, I don't know, of killing somebody or whatever. But he was certainly pretty hyper.'

I asked Sandra what kind of support she and her family received after the attack, with the thought that in 1974, the services in place and awareness of trauma after crime would not have been as evolved as it is nowadays.

'Well, it was very traumatic for my parents because they weren't there, and my mother wanted to jump on a plane straight away. And my brother said, "Look, no. Enjoy the rest of the holiday and everything and stay there. She'll go down to Jill's (Sandra's sister) place and get away from everything," which I did. And then the only thing I can remember from being down there is I had to go into the hospital to have the stitches out. And then I took a bit of time off school, but I went back to school and the school was very supportive. I don't think I went to any counselling. My mother was a social worker, so she was pretty good at listening if I ever felt a bit worried.'

Sandra said she did receive victims of crime compensation, which she thinks was around A$1000 at the time.

We finished our chat and Sandra told me she wondered why the family's pet Doberman never lunged at Parkinson.

'The dog didn't seem to bite him or do anything like that. He wasn't trained to do that, but he was a fairly big, stocky dog. And I thought: "why didn't you do anything, dog?" I think maybe he was a little bit stressed because there was blood and screaming,' she said.

Parkinson continued his aimless journey of suburban terror.

The only clue for police about his whereabouts as he journeyed through the suburban streets was when he attacked someone. There were a number of police cars out, searching for him and following the next lead they received.

His next stop was Park Crescent, Caulfield North. Friends Janet, 15, and Angie, 12, were walking across the street and Parkinson drove at the girls, hitting Janet, before speeding off. Janet had bruising to her leg and a lump on her head. She was taken to The Alfred Hospital by ambulance.

Parkinson then headed to Glen Waverley, an eastern suburb. Why he chose this destination was a mystery, but in Westlands Road, a 20-minute drive from the scene of his last assault,

Parkinson mounted the footpath with his car and struck a seven-year-old named Paul who was out riding his bike. The car dragged Paul for 25 metres while his horrified ten-year-old sister, Susan, watched on. Susan was photographed by *The Sun* with her brother's mangled bicycle and spoke about what she saw.

'I turned around when I heard the car and all I could see what his [Parkinson's] head over the wheel. He didn't seem to care what he was doing,' she said. 'I was near a lamp post and saw Paul go under the front wheel and be dragged along.'

Parkinson hit another child, a ten-year-old named Luke, with his car on Gallaghers Road. Luke was outside his house, talking to a friend, when he was knocked down, and he was lucky to escape with minor injuries.

However, even worse was to come.

Just a few kilometres away in Vermont Street, Glen Waverley, three-year-old Rachel Grahame was playing with a friend, a little boy, also aged three. They'd been playing at Rachel's house then moved on to the boy's house.

At around 3.30 p.m., Rachel's father was in the garage of their Vermont Street home and heard his wife yell for him.

The little boy's mother had Rachel in her arms, who had visible injuries to her head that were bleeding.

Rachel was carried inside, and Mrs Grahame phoned the ambulance.

Rachel was then taken to nearby Box Hill Hospital, but her injuries were so severe she was transported to The Royal Children's Hospital. Despite trauma surgeons working throughout the night to save her, Rachel died the next day.

Rachel's parents spoke to the media. Mr Grahame said he was working in the garage when his wife came screaming, saying Rachel, his 'beautiful little child', had been badly injured. 'We thought at first she had just fallen off the fence. It was five hours before we realised what had happened,' her father said.

In his statement to the coroner, Mr Grahame said he asked the little boy what had happened, and he said, 'A man in a car with a shovel hit Rachel.'

Mr Grahame said he could not believe what the boy told him and thought that Rachel must've fallen from a fence.

Another little girl aged three, named Daina, was attacked around 4 p.m. in Winston Street, approximately four kilometres from where Rachel was attacked. (In some newspaper articles in the days after the shocking attacks by Parkinson, Daina's name was reported as Dianne.)

It appeared that Daina must have been riding her tricycle outside near her house when it's thought Parkinson targeted her. Her older sister, aged five, had alerted their mother that Daina was injured. Daina's mum saw her little girl lying on the footpath, covered in blood, and nearby, the tricycle was overturned. This led to her mum thinking that Daina fell from the tricycle, but the doctor who attended her asked whether she may have been hit by a car.

She was rushed to The Royal Children's Hospital, and she survived.

In her statement to the coroner on 27 November 1974, Daina's mother said her older daughter was not able to say what happened to her little sister, and they didn't know how she got her injuries.

A woman who lived on Winston Street, a nursing aide at St Francis Xavier Cabrini Hospital, spotted Parkinson sitting behind the wheel of his Cortina. She didn't know it was Parkinson at the time, but later she said in her statement to the coroner that she knew of him from the hospital. Her attention had been drawn to the sound of 'metal hitting metal', and her teenage daughter pointed towards 'two cars, bumper to bumper'. That's when she saw 'a youth dressed in white, sitting behind the driver's wheel'. The driver then reversed the car and drove off.

As she and her daughter walked down the street, they heard a woman scream, 'What's happened?' The woman saw Daina's mother bending over her daughter, and the fallen tricycle nearby.

Parkinson took his final ride to Grantley Drive, Glen Waverley. It only took a few minutes.

Barry Simpson, 37, was sitting in the front room of his home in Grantley Drive. Around 4.10 p.m., he noticed Parkinson with a spade over his shoulder walking onto his property. Mr Simpson got up to see what this stranger wanted. But Parkinson had already entered the house and was in the kitchen.

'He just walked in like he belonged there, and when I said, "What do you think you're doing?" he just hit me over the head with the edge of the spade,' Mr Simpson said.

Dazed, Mr Simpson later told the coroner he pulled out a handkerchief and held it to his head, asking Parkinson, 'What did you do that for? I don't know you and you don't know me?' He said he kept asking what the man in white wanted, but Parkinson remained silent.

Mr Simpson told his wife Claire and one of his three children to go to the neighbours to call the police. His wife came back, and fearing for her safety, Mr Simpson told her to 'go, get out!' Not wanting to aggravate the frightening situation that was unfolding, Mr Simpson made no mention of the police to Parkinson, who was 'menacing with the spade again' and moving towards him. Mr Simpson then ran out his front door, heading next door.

Reading the newspaper and coroner reports about what happened next, it almost seems like Parkinson had a robotic quality about him. Parkinson followed Mr Simpson to the neighbour's house. Mr Simpson had just hung up his neighbour's phone to police when Parkinson smashed through the front window.

While the others fled through the back door, Mr Simpson stayed to fight off Parkinson with a chair that almost broke in half when again, Parkinson tried to assault him with the shovel. Mrs Simpson came into the room where her husband had Parkinson pinned to the wall. She had a knife in hand, and said to Parkinson, 'You've had it.'

And then Parkinson uttered his first words, this whole time. 'I know,' he simply stated.

Officers from the Dandenong Crime Car Squad arrived just as Mr Simpson tried to escape Parkinson by throwing the chair across the room. The two officers had been patrolling the area around Monash University in Clayton when they head reports on the radio about various attacks in the suburbs on adults and children and to look out for a young male, dressed in white, driving a Cortina.

The two officers were driving the streets of Glen Waverley, stopping to talk to people milling about where attacks had taken place. They entered Grantley Drive and spotted the Cortina parked the wrong way on the street. Then, they heard screams coming from one of the houses near where the Cortina was parked.

One of the policemen, Senior Constable Steven Dolman, ran towards the house, then entered through a side gate where he saw a number of women and children huddled. Sen. Constable Dolman told them he was police and asked, 'What's happening?'

Claire Simpson screamed, 'He's trying to kill my husband!'

Sen. Constable Dolman ran inside and saw Barry Simpson with blood all down his face and shirt.

Mr Simpson said, 'It's not me, he's in there. Get him!'

Sen. Constable Dolman was then confronted by the sight of Parkinson carrying a spade. He shouted for Parkinson to drop his weapon.

However, it was to no avail.

Parkinson ignored the warning, lunging at the senior constable with the shovel. Sen. Constable Dolman was backed into a corner of the family room, unable to move backwards or sideways. 'He kept on rushing towards me, and as he came into the room, he raised the spade higher,' he said in his statement. 'He had a maniacal look on his face.'

Sen. Constable Dolman, with his pistol drawn at waist height, was forced to shoot Parkinson to stop him and said he didn't have time to take aim.

Parkinson dropped to the floor, facedown, still gripping the shovel.

It wasn't over though.

'He seemed to just shoot forward from the floor with the spade in his hands,' Sen. Constable Dolman said.

Parkinson kept on at the police officer as he moved backwards out of the house.

'His eyeballs seemed to be protruding from his head, and he looked absolutely insane,' Sen. Constable Dolman said.

Parkinson ran at Sen. Constable Dolman as the constable moved backwards out of the patio door. He was waving the shovel above his head and about to attack. Sen. Constable Dolman then raised his pistol at shoulder level and fired a shot.

Parkinson fell forward at the constable's feet. However, he still had to be restrained, first by Sen. Constable Dolman, who'd grabbed the spade and 'skidded it along the concrete' out of Parkinson's reach.

Sen. Constable Dolman's partner, Constable William John Hall (known as John), ran over – he'd just been at the police car radioing for an ambulance. More police arrived at the scene, and Sen. Constable Dolman wrote in his statement that it took five officers to restrain Parkinson, who was still forcibly struggling.

Constable Neville McMaster was stationed at Ferntree Gully Police Station, at the foothills of The Dandenongs, and was on duty that day, driving a divisional van. While in the van, he was instructed to attend the intersection of Stud Road and High Street Road and stop the Cortina if he saw the vehicle. Another call came through for any police vehicles near the 10 Grantley Drive address to give urgent assistance to the police unit.

Constable McMaster was one of the officers who had to restrain the wounded Parkinson while they were waiting for the ambulance.

'He would relax for a few seconds and then struggling more strongly and it became an effort to keep him still,' Constable McMaster said in his inquest statement.

The officers kept repeating to Parkinson to stay still and that the ambulance was coming.

When Constable McMaster had to momentarily release his grip of Parkinson's left wrist, the offender, still growling and struggling violently, grabbed the officer's right hand so hard, another policeman had to help release it.

Parkinson was finally still once the ambulance arrived.

In Constable McMaster's view, Parkinson appeared to be dead. Ambulance officers performed CPR to no avail.

It had been a traumatic scene for the Simpson family, their neighbours and the emergency responders.

During a search of Parkinson's Cortina, Constable Hall, who passed away in 2020, found a 25-centimetre knife on the driver's seat.

Rachel Grahame's father was quoted in *The Age* newspaper: 'He (Parkinson) is lucky he is dead because I would have killed him.'

I got in contact with Steve Dolman in November 2021. He's retired and had a box of newspaper clippings from the time, which his mother had saved.

I asked Steve about how he and his partner found the house where Parkinson was.

'Yeah, we heard it on another channel … I thought if this comes our way, we'll be prepared for it, and I knew the area fairly well. So, we sort of meandered our way to where I thought it might end up … that area was a new estate. And that's where he was. So, using a bit of gut feeling, and stopping and talking to people, we managed to follow his track, and caught up with him. The (police) radio was pretty busy, and we couldn't get through on the air straight off. So, I just went straight in,' Steve explained.

I then asked confronted him with when he approached the Simpson's house.

'He (Parkinson) came through a passageway, running, with the shovel up in the air. So, I was going to be the next victim. But I decided, I wasn't going to be.'

Steve is matter-of-fact about what happened when he was forced to shoot a rapidly approaching Parkinson.

'He was shot once, and he went down, and I went out to get my partner who was running up the driveway, and I yelled "I've shot him, get an ambulance …." I turned around after John had gone out to call an ambulance, and he was coming towards me with the shovel up in the air again. And he was above me on this patio. And I thought: there's only one thing I can do here … didn't have much of a chance. And that's when I shot him a second time.'

I wondered aloud if having to shoot someone caused any trauma for Steve.

He continued, 'We went back to the car, and then we were taken into the Homicide Squad at Russell Street. So, we finished up there. I forget what time of day it was, but it was one or 2 a.m. And then [I] started work the next day,' Steve explained.

Steve then advised me that back then, officers weren't offered counselling.

As for Steve's understanding of why Parkinson committed those acts of extreme violence on that day, he said, 'He was off his medication, and he should have been more strictly monitored.'

* * *

The unfathomable afternoon of violence by Parkinson was an almost unheard-of occurrence in Australia back in the 1970s. There would be shooting massacres to come (Hoddle Street, Queen Street and Port Arthur), but 40 years ago, when Parkinson terrorised pockets of the south-eastern suburbs, it was like something that happened 'somewhere else'. And the perpetrator was a young man training to take care of people and save lives.

No one who knew Parkinson could believe what had happened. In disbelief, medical student mates of Parkinson spoke to reporters.

Steve Clarke, one of Parkinson's flatmates, said, 'He was just a normal type of guy, very quiet. He was not a violent person and had several friends.'

Another flatmate and fellow medical student, Michael Dowd, said that Parkinson was 'someone who was always there to go and talk to when you were feeling down'. The flatmates said that Parkinson seemed to enjoy university and was especially comfortable in his fourth year where there were opportunities for real patient contact.

There was early speculation by his friends that Parkinson's rampage could have been triggered by a skiing accident a few months earlier. Parkinson had gone on a five-day trip to Mt Buller where he fell while skiing. Another medical student friend who was also on the trip, said Parkinson was hit on the head with an overhead tow bar. 'He had his head stitched and then said he wanted to go home,' Mr Weinrich commented.

* * *

The inquests into the deaths of Martin Parkinson and Rachel Grahame took place in November 1974. The coroner found Senior Constable Dolman had been justified in the fatal shooting of Parkinson.

The inquests also revealed Parkinson had a psychiatric history. The young man had been admitted to Melbourne's Larundel Hospital in 1972. A psychiatrist who'd treated him, Dr John Gordon Brown, gave evidence at the inquest that Parkinson claimed he was getting telepathic messages.

It was also revealed that Parkinson was under a court-ordered probation at the time of his suburban rampage. He'd appeared at the Melbourne County Court on an attempted rape charge in November 1973. He was accused of attacking a woman he knew in Mitcham (an eastern suburb neighbouring Nunawading where Parkinson attended high school) in 1972. He had gone to the house of the woman, knocked her to the ground and lay on top of her.

Prior to that, in July 1972, Parkinson had sought medical help from a psychiatrist at Monash University and told the doctor he was feeling anxious and depressed. Parkinson had been diagnosed with schizophrenia, and under encouragement from the doctor, he entered a psychiatric unit as a voluntary patient.

But Parkinson only stayed for one day before leaving the hospital. It was one month later that he assaulted the woman.

As a condition of parole, Parkinson was sent to Larundel Hospital again where he was treated for the schizophrenia with electroshock treatment and medication. By all accounts, he responded well, and he was released after ten weeks. He was to stay on a course of antipsychotic medication and see his doctor monthly, which would then be scaled back to every three months.

Parkinson complied with these conditions and was able to resume his medical studies and got the job as a ward assistant at Cabrini Hospital. The judge in the attempted rape case considered Parkinson's medical studies and future prospects when sentencing him.

Judge Dethridge said at the 1973 court hearing, 'You apparently look like passing your third year, and I would be loath to impose a sentence that might have a prejudicial effect on you in the future.'

The judge went on to say he believed Parkinson's behaviour was due to a 'psychiatric reason', and he had no evidence at that time to indicate he would offend again.

For Parkinson, the judge's mercy meant he could continue with his plans to become a doctor. Had he been convicted of the charge it was likely his medical career would have been over.

At the time, the case raised questions about whether people with serious mental illness, such as schizophrenia, should be able to continue their studies for a profession like medicine. These questions were, of course, posed in the climate of the 1970s, and the understanding of mental illness and its treatment is more evolved today.

Parkinson's psychiatrist at Larundel, Dr John Brown, said, 'If you make laws saying that having got this illness they can't practice in their chosen professions, you are putting psychiatry a long way back.'

Dr Brown had written to Monash University, which was deciding whether to allow Parkinson back into his medical degree, and noted that the young man's outlook was 'reasonable' but that it would be 'difficult to predict accurately' whether he would relapse.

Dr Brown noted that Parkinson had stuck to his medication and visited him as an outpatient. However, when the rampage happened, Dr Brown said Parkinson had not made his most recent scheduled appointment and appeared to have stopped his medication.

At the 27 November 1974 inquest into the murder of Rachel Grahame and the shooting death of Parkinson, Sister Renee Kittelson told the coroner that changes had been made to the way medical students were employed as nursing assistants, and she agreed that the hospital should have known about Parkinson's court-ordered probation. Had she known, she would not have employed him.

She said that from time to time she employed medical students, mostly from Monash University, and had checked the reference of one man who came to her for employment at Christmastime 1973. The subsequent medical students who were employed, including Parkinson, heard about this work from their peers, so it was taken on trust that they would be of similar calibre.

In Sister Kittelson's statement to the coroner, she said, 'I never had any complaints from either patients or staff members about Martin, except that he was a bit slow. He was a friendly person who would talk to the patients when he had nothing to do, but he was inclined to be a quiet person.'

The actions of Parkinson on 7 September, 1974 were shocking and left many people traumatised and bewildered. The descriptions of the pale, haunted Parkinson dressed in white and stalking the streets are truly the stuff of suburban nightmares.

CAMPAIGN
OF TERROR

It was a Friday night in Melbourne, 10 February 1984, and 41-year-old Nanette Ellis was planning to go out after work with the girls from the office.

Nanette was the advertising manager for the *Free Press Leader*, a Belgrave-based newspaper that was part of the Leader Community Newspapers group in Melbourne. The team was a small and tight-knit group, made up of editorial and advertising, who produced the paper for the residents of villages in the region known as the Dandenongs – one of the most picturesque areas in Australia. Nanette was a hard worker, well respected and loved by her colleagues.

A strikingly beautiful woman, Nanette had been a single mum to her two sons Greg, 16, and Craig, 18, for several years, since she and her husband divorced. She was paying off her house in Manuka Drive, Boronia – an outer-eastern suburb not far from her workplace – and had devoted herself to raising her boys. Apart from a regular aerobics class she did with a friend and a few drinks out with her workmates, Nanette lived a very quiet, modest life. Her looks were so arresting that Nanette was often asked to model for advertisers and had appeared in several fashion and lifestyle photo shoots for newspaper features.

But things had been quite unsettling for Nanette in recent weeks. On four consecutive mornings, her car had been pelted with rocks as she drove along Monbulk Road on her way to work. The first time it happened on 31 January 1984, Nanette wasn't even fully aware that a rock had been thrown at her 1976 Corolla sedan, but it had lodged under the bonnet, piercing the radiator, which caused the engine to boil. She called Craig, who met her, and then organised a tow truck.

The next day, a rock was thrown at her car as she travelled to work between 8 a.m. and 9 a.m., and this time it shattered her windscreen. The rock throwing happened again the next two mornings at the same time. Was someone targeting Nanette?

What happened next left Nanette and her sons in no doubt that someone was victimising her. Sometime during the evening of Saturday, 4 February, Nanette's car, which was parked in her driveway, was vandalised. Paint – a water-based fawn colour – was tipped over the roof, cascading down the boot bonnet and driver's door.

Nanette discovered the damage at around midnight. It was frightening for this hardworking suburban mother who 'didn't have an enemy in the world', according to her son Craig. Was it kids making mischief by vandalising cars? There had been a few reports of car vandalism in the neighbourhood that weekend. Or was it someone who had more sinister motives?

Then, unbelievably, Nanette's car was targeted again. On Monday evening, 6 February, someone slashed her car's tires, ripped off a numberplate and aerial and bent back the windscreen wipers. The police patrolled Nanette's neighbourhood and escorted Nanette to work and back home for the next few days. Nanette's boys kept an eye out too.

But suddenly, the vandalism stopped. Nanette and her family hoped that they had seen the end of this spate of attacks.

On 10 February, a police car escorted Nanette from work until she was clear of Burwood Highway – the main arterial between the office and her home. Nanette arrived home at 5.15 p.m. to get ready to go out with her girlfriends from the office. She was being picked up at 6 p.m., and that morning she had laid out her clothes for the evening – a red shirt and black pants.

Craig had been home during the day restoring an old Holden he had been working on for ages; he was on holidays from his job as a chef at a nearby reception centre. Nanette had called him that day to check-in, and Craig had asked her if everything was all right.

'She told me she thought everything was fine now,' Craig said.

He had planned to go to the drive-in with some friends and had left the house around 4.30 p.m. His brother Greg had come home from school a bit earlier and then jumped the back fence to spend time with his friend, who was a neighbour.

Greg Ellis arrived home, using the front door, just after 6 p.m. He remembered the time well because he'd finished watching the TV show *Perfect Match*, which finished at 6 p.m., at his friend's house.

The radio was on, and Greg noticed the Valentine's Day cards on the table that his mum had bought for him. Greg had recently been on a student exchange to Japan and wanted to send cards to his new friends. Valentine's Day was a big thing in Japan for friends to exchange cards.

As he walked through the house looking for his mum, Greg noticed blood – a lot of blood – and clumps of blonde hair in the hallway.

Greg found his mother on the concrete ramp at the end of the house, just outside the laundry. Nanette was dead, having been the victim of a frenzied knife attack.

The brutal murder had taken place sometime between 5.15 p.m. and 6 p.m. when Greg came home – a window of just 45 minutes, meaning her killer could have been watching Nanette and the house.

Nanette's murder devastated her family and her colleagues at the *Free Press Leader,* who knew of the intimidation that she had been subjected to in the week before her death. Colleagues at the *Knox Sherbrooke News,* the newspaper that covered the Boronia area, wrote a heartfelt front-page tribute to their friend: 'We won't forget Nanette'.

'Nanette Ellis had class and always kept her problems to herself. That's why no one other than her mates at the *Free Press* really knew the terror she suffered in her last days of life.'

Police made a public plea at the time for anyone who was in the Monbulk Road, Tecoma area near Morris Road and Wattle Avenue to think about their movements between 8 a.m. and 9 a.m. on 31 January and 1–3 February when Nanette was targeted by the rock-throwing incidents. The details about the vandalism to her car – the paint throwing and slashed tires – were initially kept back from the public.

Police also canvassed the streets around her home hoping to find information on any suspicious activity people had seen on the day of the killing.

Victoria Police Homicide Detective Senior Constable Kyle Simpson is the officer in charge of the cold case reinvestigation. I spoke to Simpson in 2012 when I was writing *Murder in Suburbia* where this chapter first appeared. Simpson said the reinvestigation into Nanette's murder began in 2010, as a result of the Homicide Squad's review of unsolved cases dating back to the 1950s.

'I was allocated the case and commenced looking at it from the point of view "was there an identified suspect?" and if so, "what had been done?"' Simpson said.

'One of the most striking things I noticed was there was no identified suspect at all.'

Simpson explained the process for investigating cold cases. 'Each of us within the Homicide Squad is allocated a number of cold cases. Each member's allocation will be in varying states. Some files will be what we call a "paper review" where we simply go through what is there. Others will be at a more active investigation phase.'

Simpson said there were key points that determined whether a cold case would be reinvestigated. 'We make a review to ensure there are avenues of inquiry that haven't been explored. Should we be able to explore those avenues and get a result, the brief would need to be "prosecution-ready", so in other words, we'd have sufficient witnesses still available and willing to give evidence and we have enough exhibits available to prove our case. If we fall over on either of those, the reality is it (the cold case) is probably not worth pursuing.'

When Simpson looked at Nanette's file, he saw the initial 1984 investigation by the Homicide Squad was extensive. 'The team, led by (former detective) Jack Jacobs interviewed an enormous amount of people. There are in excess of 800 individual information reports, which give an idea of the vastness of the investigation. They followed every rabbit down every hole and got nowhere.'

A 1985 coroner's inquest into the murder delivered an open finding but found that Nanette had died from a haemorrhage caused by stab wounds.

But Simpson says fresh eyes and contemporary investigation techniques gave Nanette's family hope for a result. He said there were several investigation tools, such as improved forensic analysis and cognitive interviewing of witnesses, that could be used to review a cold case.

In the initial investigation, much of the publicity focused on the incidents that seemed to point to Nanette being targeted by someone. Simpson said it still was not clear whether the incidents were linked.

'Whether the throwing of the rocks is linked to the vandalism, we can't say with any degree of certainty. However, we are aware that there were a number of other people who had their vehicles damaged by rock throwing.'

He also said, 'While we are not dismissing a link, we are saying it's strange her car is damaged driving to and from work, is then subsequently vandalised and then she is murdered. Whether there's a link between them or not, we cannot establish that at this stage.'

Could a woman have murdered Nanette Ellis?

Simpson said that theory had been a line of inquiry. 'We never rule anything out.'

He said that within the crime scene, there were no visible indicators that Nanette had been sexually assaulted. 'That doesn't mean one didn't occur, but there were no visible signs of a sexual assault'.

'The reason why Nanette Ellis was targeted is still obscure. We can't find a reason why she was targeted at this current point. That doesn't mean that one won't eventuate. When I looked at the case and spent a fair bit of time within the statements and the information, it was apparent that Nanette wasn't engaging in what I'd describe as "high-risk" behaviour. When we speak about high-risk behaviour, we mean things like engaging with known criminals, drug use, risk-taking behaviour. She wasn't doing anything like that. There was nothing apparent in her lifestyle that gave me cause to be concerned.'

Simpson said the serial rapist and killer Peter Dupas had been ruled out as a suspect. Police investigated Dupas for Nanette's murder because of the way she was killed.

Dupas is serving three life sentences with no possibility of parole for the murders of three women, whom he killed in separate incidents. He is also the prime suspect in the unsolved murders of three other women.

The homicide team used the 30th anniversary of the murder to put Nanette's case back in the public's mind. 'It was a particularly brutal attack.'

'One of the reasons cold cases are so important to us as investigators is because a lot of these families have lived these tragedies for five, ten, 15, 20 years,' Simpson said. 'This family has lived this for 30 years. It's one thing knowing who has committed a murder or having reasonable suspicions as to who has done it and living with the fact that we don't have enough evidence for a viable prosecution. It's a whole different ballgame when the investigators don't have a suspect. After 30 years, these guys deserve answers.'

I first met Craig Ellis in August 2012 at his apartment in inner-city Melbourne. I had been corresponding with the family and the investigating detective Kyle Simpson since 2010. Nanette's case was one that intrigued me because we had worked for the same company, albeit more than 20 years apart. I felt a particular desire to know more and report on her case because I also live in the City of Knox (the council area in which Boronia is located), and by 2012, I was the reporter for the *Free Press Leader*, the paper for which Nanette was the advertising manager at the time of her murder.

Craig, 48, had not spoken publicly about his mother's murder for over 25 years. He was interviewed a few times when there were renewed public appeals – in 1985, there was a A$50 000 reward offered for information, and in 1987, the case was featured on the Channel 7 program *Australia's Most Wanted*.

'I've had advice that maybe it's time to not be so secretive about it,' Craig said.

'Talking about what happened to Mum is something that is not easy for me to do. As a young person, you can block it out to a certain extent because you are full of energy and you have new things going on in your life, but there's always that pain there. I always felt it [Nanette's murder] was a real affliction on me, or a handicap, that it had happened to me. I used to be treated a bit differently because of what happened. Now there are only a few friends who know what happened to my mother.'

He remembers Nanette as a truly lovely woman and mother.

'Nanette, even though she was very attractive, was very modest and not pretentious,' Craig recalled.

Nanette was a big supporter of Amnesty International and wrote letters to try to help free people who were in jail in other countries for petty crime. Craig recollected that there was an Amnesty International sticker on the left-hand rear window of her car. Nanette was also very creative and loved art, painting and sketching.

Craig said he had been tormented for years over thoughts that he could have saved his mother.

'I nearly came back home that afternoon because I smoked at the time and I'd forgotten my cigarettes. I had a carton at home, but I thought, "I'll get a pack at the milk bar",' Craig said. 'I nearly came back … and it would have meant it would have been in that time frame of when she was killed. So, whether I came back and it would have delayed the killer, or I could have been killed myself. I just think if there were two of us, one would have survived to tell the story.'

Craig said his mother fought with all her might against the killer.

'She absolutely put up a big fight. Mum really did fight hard to defend herself. Apparently, she'd fallen in the hallway, and then the murderer had stabbed her while she was down. She still had the strength to drag herself up again and get out through the laundry.

'We were told Mum had suffered an irrecoverable stab wound to the neck, which severed or pierced the carotid artery. That was quite distressing to learn. She still got outside the house. Had she not sustained that wound to the carotid artery, she could have survived.'

Craig has often wondered if he knows the killer. Will he be shocked when he finds out who murdered his mum? The brothers – Greg has lived in Japan for many years with his family – are more hopeful than ever that the killer will be brought to justice. They have faith and trust in the determined and thorough investigation by Senior Constable Simpson.

'I've wracked my brain for years over who could have done this,' Craig said.

'It wasn't a robbery or a sexually motivated crime. Mum was targeted. I am open-minded about the rock-throwing incidents, but the vandalism to the car was personal.'

He also expressed, 'I am angry with the person who did it. I want to see justice and I want to see some sort of compensation to our family for what we have suffered. Whatever that is, we will pursue it. It's been such a huge thing to carry all these years.'

Craig has two adult daughters and said he feels the loss of his mother more intensely than ever before.

'As I get older, the enormity and horrendous nature of what happened to my mother has really hit home because I imagine what it would be like for my daughters to lose me now and think how lucky they are to have both their parents. Everyone in the family has been affected – they've not had a grandmother; we've not had a mother. There have been a lot of people affected. My late grandmother for instance, Nanette's mother Mavis, had to carry that for 28 years until her death and never found out what happened to her daughter.'

Five years after their mother died, the boys found out they had a sister. Their grandmother told them that in 1989, Nanette had a baby when she was 18 and the little girl was adopted.

Janet O'Donnell is that girl.

Though she always knew she was adopted, Janet's relationship with her adoptive family was difficult. She grew up only a few suburbs away from Nanette, who unbeknown to her was raising her own family with her husband Max Ellis. Max died in 2013. He was officially eliminated as a suspect in the immediate investigation after his ex-wife's murder.

'The stories of why and where I was from were never discussed. But I always had a very difficult time in this family, so I was always an angry child that was frustrated I was never told about my biological family,' Janet said.

Janet said Craig tracked her down in 1989, not long after he first discovered her existence.

'The cruel part was that I was 28 then and was estranged from my adopted family. If they had told me about Nanette, I would have had a chance to meet her, as I only grew up a few suburbs away. So, the fact that I finally connected with Craig and Greg, and then found out about her horrific murder, I felt that once again I was cheated, and so was Nanette.'

Janet said when she was younger, she battled with many personal demons and was just not able to comprehend the enormity of Nanette's murder. It has taken her several years to heal.

'I was having a lot of personal problems in my own life at the time I met Craig and was unable to handle the news of Nanette's death. I met my partner and we moved away to live in Darwin, so really, I was not in a good space emotionally to handle it at all. I think I became numb, in denial, and blocked it out with alcohol, which I used a lot to deal with emotional pain in my younger years. Being adopted had a very negative impact on my life. I was a very troubled and mentally ill child, adolescent and young adult,' Janet recalled.

'I honestly believe we, the three kids, have come together, so easily and effortlessly now for an important reason. I strongly believe Nanette's killer is soon to be brought to justice,' Janet said. 'I am a very spiritual person. Nanette, my mum, has always been a bit of a guardian angel for me – someone to call on when life becomes tough. Nanette was taken away from me when I was a baby and taken away from the boys when they were teenagers. I will be there for the boys when her killer is convicted. I want that so much, more for the boys than myself.'

Craig said the family needed their day in court.

'It would make such a difference to me, even to find out what the motive for her killing was,' Craig said.

'Nanette was a good mum, and we feel her loss so much.'

Craig's daughter, Samantha, has taken up a role in keeping her grandmother's unsolved murder in the public eye, including creating a Facebook page 'Justice for Nanette Ellis'.

In 2017, Samantha and Craig were guests on the podcast that I co-host with Meshel Laurie, called *Australian True Crime*.

Even though Samantha never knew Nanette, the ripple effect of what happened on that early evening in 1984 is always present.

'In an earlier time in my life, it was something I didn't really understand. I knew about it; however, I didn't understand the intensity or the reality of it,' Samantha told us in that interview. 'So, I think now as an adult it really hits home. I always wondered why Mum and Dad, well particularly Dad, were quite protective over me and worried when I would walk the streets either alone or with a small group of friends. And even now as an adult, being in my own home, I don't feel safe at times because I know what's happened,' she said.

On the 30th anniversary of Nanette's murder in 2014, Victoria Police announced a A$500 000 reward for information that led to the apprehension and conviction of the person responsible for her death.

Homicide Squad Detective Senior Sergeant Stuart Bailey said at the press conference announcing the reward, 'While over the years, Homicide Squad investigators have processed more than 800 pieces of information, we still don't have any suspects or a motive for Ms Ellis's murder.'

As Nanette's murder approaches 40 years unsolved, her family holds hope that police will find the person responsible for her brutal death.

Nanette Ellis, 41, was stabbed to death in her Boronia home, in Melbourne's outer east, on 10 February 1984. Her murder is still unsolved. Picture used with permission of Craig Ellis.

THE ROYAL PARK TRAGEDY

A shocking and strange case of murder intrigued Victorians in 1914. A young Melbourne schoolteacher was found shot dead in the grounds of inner-city Melbourne's Royal Park on 14 September. Patricia Angela Bickett, 23, had been shot three times, and it didn't take police long to find the culprit.

As Patricia lay dying in Royal Park, the largest open space in Melbourne, a witness saw the man who had fired at her fall to the ground and try to shoot himself.

The witness told police that it then appeared that the man was kissing the woman he had just shot. The witness had been passing through the park on his way home and started to chase the gunman but could not catch him.

At 4 a.m. the next morning, a nervous, desperate-looking man seeking food approached a young watchman on board the small coastal steamer *Prophet,* docked on the Yarra River. The watchman, who was finishing up his shift, gave the man some food and saw the visitor on his way at 7 a.m. Returning to the steamer later that evening at 5 p.m., the watchmen found the man hiding.

The man, who had a thick 'European' accent, said, 'I will give you all the money I possess if you will take me to Newcastle.'

The young watchman, again showing kindness to the man, let him have some more food and sleep overnight on the boat. At 7 a.m. the next morning, the watchman called the police at Russell Street to come and investigate the strange man hiding out on the vessel.

Four officers went down to the scene and found the weakened man, who had a bullet graze to his cheek and his face blackened with gunpowder. The police had a fair idea who the mystery man was already. A manhunt had been underway for the killer of Patricia for two days.

'Is your name Antonio Soro?' one of the detectives asked the man.

The nervous man answered, 'Yes, I am sorry. I don't know why I did it. God knows.'

Later at the City Watch House, when asked if he had shot Patricia Bickett, Antonio Soro, who had come to Australia from Italy in 1909, said, 'Yes, I am sorry.' He then gave a most dramatic explanation for the crime when questioned further by detectives.

Soro told the police that the shooting was a suicide pact that had gone wrong. 'We agreed to die together ... it is her [Patricia's] mother's fault,' Soro said.

Soro claimed that he and Patricia had been sweethearts caught in a love triangle. According to Soro, Patricia's mother Maria had set up an engagement between her daughter and an engineer named John Graham. But the Italian insisted to detectives that the young schoolteacher had wanted to marry him, not the engineer.

'The girl wanted to marry me,' Soro told the detectives. 'She gave me money to buy a revolver.'

He said Patricia had begged him to run away with her because she could no longer live with her mother. 'She asked me to shoot her, and I did, and then I tried to shoot myself,' Soro said in his statement to police. With his shooting attempt unsuccessful, Soro said he raced back to Patricia's Brougham Street, North Melbourne home to tell her mother of the tragedy, but that there were so many people at the house he panicked and ran away.

Committed to stand trial for murder, Soro reportedly sobbed in the court and was so hysterical that he was remanded in custody for a week to undergo medical treatment.

The newspapers dubbed the death of Patricia the 'Royal Park Sensation' and the 'Royal Park Tragedy'.

On 22 September, over 500 school students from North Melbourne's Boundary Road State School, where Patricia had taught, attended her funeral. 'The tears of many of the scholars showed the affection she had won,' the *Horsham Times* reported.

Antonio Soro studied engineering in Sardinia, Italy, and had come to the attention of the automotive industry and politicians with his invention – an air compressor that he hoped was worth millions in patents. In fact, when he was found in Perth, Soro had papers in his possession that showed the invention had been patented in at least 17 countries. A syndicate of people was interested in making money from the invention and was supporting the young engineer. Frank Patterson, an engineer from the inner-Melbourne suburb of Burnley said he had seen a working model of Soro's invention and thought it 'most valuable'. Before he became known as a murderer, Soro was referred to in newspaper reports as 'the Ballarat inventor,' and his one-horsepower wind turbine invention had some hype behind it.

One of the friends that Soro had made in Ballarat was James Bickett – the musician brother of schoolteacher Patricia. The Bickett family had a property in Ballarat, and Soro had stayed with them, getting to know Patricia well.

The murder of Patricia was not the first time 28-year-old Soro had come to the attention of police.

On 2 July 1912, Soro had been found in a disoriented and dishevelled state outside a North Fremantle house; North Fremantle is a small suburb of Perth. Soro, who described himself as an inventor, told the resident that he and a companion had flown an airplane from Ballarat, Victoria, but had lost their way. Soro said that when the petrol in the craft had run out, he had leapt from the plane into the sea and swam ashore.

The newspapers soon picked up on this intriguing tale of an Italian inventor who had fallen into the sea. Investigators had their doubts though, and Soro's aeronautical tale was soon proven to be a lie. There was no dramatic leap from a plane – Soro had actually been reported missing from Ballarat on 27 June, less than a week before he was discovered in Perth.

The truth was that Soro had caught the steamer *Kapunda* from Port Adelaide to Fremantle under an assumed name: Signor Gatrono Marini. Signor Marini, aka Soro, had told the clerk at the booking office that he had arrived that day by train from

Melbourne. Soro was charged with being of 'unsound mind' (as it was referred to back then) and hospitalised while investigators made inquiries.

The story got stranger. On 23 June 1912, a few days before he went missing from Ballarat, Soro had accused an Italian couple of stealing his invention. The matter went to the Ballarat Supreme Court almost two years later in February 1914. Giovanni Guiliano and his wife Annette were charged with theft. Soro said the pair had stolen an essential part of the machinery, which he could not reproduce, and had refused to give it back unless the inventor transferred some of the patents to them. A jury found them not guilty. The judge, Mr Justice Hodges, labelled the case 'nonsense and jumble to begin with' and remarked that he had been unable to follow it.

Later that year, Soro would be in court again, but this time it would be for murder.

During the October 1914 inquest into Patricia Bickett's death, witnesses, including her mother, described the events that led up to Patricia's death. Mrs Bickett said that Soro, who was a boarder at their North Melbourne house, had never asked her permission to 'keep company' with her daughter and disputed Soro's claims that the pair were in love. Mrs Bickett detailed an incident a few days before 'the tragedy' (as newspapers had labelled it) when her daughter's fiancé Mr Graham had visited and left late in the evening, at around 10.30 p.m.

Also giving evidence at the inquest, Mr Graham said that as he left the house, there had been a scene at the doorstep when Soro came between Patricia and him. Mr Graham said Soro had been overemotional and shouted, 'You insult Miss Bickett! You are no friend of her father's!' Mr Graham said he was going to hit Soro, but Patricia intervened and ushered him away. Mr Graham said he thought Soro was jealous.

Mrs Bickett had witnessed the incident and told Soro he was no longer welcome in their home as a boarder. She told the court that she did not think that there was any special relationship between Patricia and the Italian engineer.

Soro's defence was that Patricia had asked him to shoot her, and he had given detectives two letters – in Italian – written by him that sought to explain the incident. One of the letters, addressed to 'my dearest mother' said: 'I was directed to do this by my girl ... she said buy a pistol and let us kill each other.' The letters were somewhat incoherent, possibly due to the translation, but also from Soro's state of mind – he had been diagnosed by doctors to be highly neurotic, depressed and excitable.

During Soro's trial in Melbourne, in late October 1914, following the coroner's inquest, the Crown prosecutor Mr Wolinarski said that Soro's crime was pre-meditated and well arranged, contrary to the almost unbelievable story Soro had told of a suicide pact. The prosecution presented the theory that while in Royal Park, Soro had tried to convince Patricia to leave Mr Graham and run away with him. When she refused, Soro shot her in a fit of jealousy. Mr Wolinarski said Soro's story that Patricia asked him to shoot her was an attempt to destroy the deceased's good name and character.

Although the defence suggested that Patricia had been killed in a 'fit of insanity', the jury disagreed and found that he was sane enough to know right from wrong. When a verdict of guilty was returned, Soro reportedly trembled and sobbed violently;

however, he remained silent when asked by the judge if he had anything to say.

On 22 October, 1914, Soro was sentenced to death.

On 16 November 1914, Soro's death sentence was commuted to life imprisonment. The Italian had escaped the gallows but would spend the remainder of his natural life in prison.

In 1918, having served three and a half years of his sentence, Soro was released and repatriated to Italy. The Italian Government needed Soro, a reservist, to return and fight for his country. The Italian Government and Soro's family had been quietly making appeals for his release, and under Australian law at the time, a foreign prisoner who had served at least two years could be released and deported.

Italian man Antonio Soro, who claimed he was an inventor, was found guilty of the 1914 murder of young schoolteacher Patricia Bickett at Royal Park, Melbourne. Source: 1914 'PATRICIA BICKETT'S DEATH.',
Truth (Melbourne ed.) (Vic. : 1914 - 1918), *10 October, p. 6. (Via Trove)*

BEYOND BELIEF

The Salvation Army–run house in Melton, an outer-western suburb of Melbourne, was meant to be a safe haven for families like ten-year-old Steven and his mum.

The pair had moved to the house in early 1993, and life was settled and comfortable. The 28-year-old mum was the 'lead tenant' in the house that also took in vulnerable teens. Getting by on a single mother's pension, Steven's mum welcomed the extra money that she was paid to take care of the other residents, and she was grateful to have a stable home for her son.

When Nathan John Avent, 23, arrived at the Smoult Avenue address unannounced on the morning of 11 July 1994, Steven's mum had no reason to worry. Avent had done some gardening and home maintenance chores at the house a few months before for his father, who oversaw the management of the Salvation Army's properties in Melbourne's west, and both of his parents were members of the church.

Avent lived in Hoppers Crossing, a western suburb 30 kilometres from Melbourne's CBD. Known as 'Hoppers' by locals, it became a suburb in the 1970s when land was subdivided, and affordable housing drove young families out west. It is in the council region of Wyndham, which is the fastest-growing municipality in Australia.

Avent and his young wife, 19, were expecting a baby and living with his parents – a situation that caused him frustration. Being young and with the responsibility of parenthood looming, Avent had become tense with the constraints of living with his parents and the lack of sexual contact with his wife, who was seven months pregnant.

On that day, 11 July 1994, Avent packed his bag and set off to the Melton address, stopping for fuel and to return some videos on the way. He had watched the movies *Driller Killer, Cannibal Apocalypse* and *The Best of Martial Arts* a few days before.

When Avent arrived at the Smoult Avenue house, he asked to see the backyard so that he could assess which plants he needed to buy. He was greeted by Steven, a friendly, engaging child who then called his mother, still in her pyjamas, to the door.

When she let the boyish-looking Avent into the house, she had no idea that the bag he carried was filled with a killing kit – two knives, rope, gloves, sticky tape and a tomahawk. Avent had parked his car half a kilometre away from the house – out of sight – so that he could pretend someone was picking him up. What happened in the house that morning was worse than most people could ever imagine – the stuff of violent horror films played out in the western suburbs of Melbourne.

After he had done his fake survey of the backyard, Avent asked if he could wait at the house to be picked up. Steven was playing games, and the pair watched a bit of television. Asking to use the home phone, Avent pretended to dial a number and then told Steven's mum that he was expecting his lift in 20 minutes. No doubt needing to get on with her morning, the woman said she needed to get ready for work and excused herself to have a shower.

Steven, who was playing a board game and facing the television, was oblivious to the danger approaching.

Standing behind the boy, Avent took the tomahawk from his bag and struck Steven on the back of the neck, which, according to the coroner, killed the child instantly by severing his spinal cord and carotid artery. Avent struck him several more times before taking the axe to the kitchen and rinsing it under the tap. He placed it back in his bag, took out a hunting knife and walked into the bathroom where Steven's mother was still in the shower.

Confronted with the knife, Steven's mum was forced from the shower and to her bed where Avent told her lie down. Terrified and desperate to know if her son was all right, she complied with Avent's demands. She was forced onto her stomach and he tied her hands together and began to strangle her. But then he suddenly stopped. He had 'a change of heart', as a judge later remarked during his sentencing of Avent.

'I can't do this,' Avent said midway through strangling Steven's mother. Avent allowed her off the bed, and she wrapped herself in a doona. Having escaped death for the moment, Steven's mum asked where her son was. According to court documents, Avent bluntly told her, 'You don't understand. It's too late, your son is dead.'

Confused and distraught, she asked Avent why there was no blood on the knife, and he coldly told her he had used an axe. *Avent had used an axe to kill a child* – the most brutal act imaginable.

'Call the police,' Avent told her.

She ran for her life out the door and to a neighbour's house.

In a move that was at complete odds with the violence that had just occurred, Avent, sobbing and hysterical, called his mother. 'Mum, I've hit someone … with an axe.'

The case sickened the community.

In police interviews, Avent, often described as 'baby-faced' in news reports, said that on the morning of the murder he 'started thinking that today I would try to kill somebody'. While Steven's mum had gone to have a shower, Avent told detectives, 'I thought maybe I'd change my mind, but I didn't …. I sat for a few minutes thinking if I should really do it, then before I knew it I was doing it.'

Up until that day, Avent had only had a brief encounter with crime, when he lost his job at a Target store in Sunshine, another western suburb of Melbourne, in 1993, for stealing A$300. His older brother also worked at the store but had been promoted, a fact that was frustrating to Avent. After his dismissal, he could only find casual work, through his father, and this is what led him to meet Steven and his mum.

He pleaded guilty to murder and false imprisonment on 11 May 1995 in front of Justice Bernard Teague at the Supreme Court of Victoria.

Avent's actions indicated that he was a disturbed young man, but the psychiatrist who assessed him, Dr Leslie Walton, said the killer displayed no personality disorder. His family told the courts that Avent was passive, and school reports said that he was a pleasant and cooperative student. Avent was immature though, and this was reinforced by observations from the medical profession and his own mother.

At the plea hearing, Dr Walton said that Avent told him that he was motivated to rape, rather than kill. Avent had told police that sex was sinful, and Dr Walton said the killer was embarrassed by his crime of sexual violence. Dr Walton also said that Avent had a simplistic approach to life and was depressed at the time of the murder.

Avent's defence tried to pin his murderous actions on the violent horror films he had watched in the days before he murdered Steven. His lawyer Aaron Schwartz said 'fantasy and reality' had merged for his client, who would use the videos to escape from the problems of his life. Prosecutor Paul Coghlan said in court that Avent had told police that he had violent urges because he watched too many videos. Mr Justice Teague said he found no basis for any finding that Avent's viewing of violent videos played any part in his actions.

It seemed like it was a moment of cold-blooded madness. Mr Justice Teague noted Avent's remorse for the crime. Another psychiatrist, Dr Karl Golumbeck, told the court that Avent 'anticipates a life of good works under the auspices of the Salvation Army upon his release from prison'.

Mr Justice Teague made the landmark Australian legal decision to allow Avent's sentence to be televised. The videotaped footage was to be made available for television news, and networks had to show at least two minutes of the delivery of his sentence.

On Thursday, 18 May 1995, a single camera from Channel Seven was in the courtroom to record the sentence, with the videotape made available to other commercial networks. The camera was only to be focused on Mr Justice Teague during the sentencing. If people were expecting an OJ Simpson–style televised treatment, they were to be disappointed. The decision was debated in the media with the then president of the Victorian Council for Civil Liberties Robert Richter, QC, saying he hoped it would demystify sentencing for the public. Both the then Premier of Victoria, Jeff Kennett, and the federal Attorney-General, Michael Lavarch, were critical of Mr Justice Teague's decision.

Mr Kennett said, 'Justice is not entertainment. This totally ignores the crime that has been committed.'

Mr Lavarch said the decision made him 'uneasy'.

Steven's mother's evidence and victim impact statement was described by Mr Justice Teague as 'compelling', and he said that he had 'deeply reflected' on its contents.

To Avent, Mr Justice Teague said:

You told police you deeply regretted what you had done and that you hoped for forgiveness .... I allow for the circumstances that in prison you will need protection. As in the community, so in jail, a special loathing is extended to those whose victim is a young child .... You indicated to expert witnesses that when you packed your bag, your plan was to rape [Steven's mother] and that Steven was an unexpected obstacle to your plans who had to be got out of the way. On the one hand I find the clearest signs of careful planning for violence in the days and hours before the murder, then there was the careful surveying of the scene, then there was the extreme brutality to take the life of a 10-year-old boy. There followed a cold-blooded cleaning of one weapon and the selection of another, and then there was a chilling armed attack on a defenceless woman in her bedroom. On the other hand, I am faced with your having come from an impeccable home situation with devoted parents and a caring wife … and no history whatsoever of previous violence. Added to that there was, when you were poised to kill again, a change of heart and mind comparable to that of St Paul. [In the Bible, St Paul, one of Jesus Christ's most loyal disciples, was once a persecutor of Christians before he had a revelation on the road to Damascus. St Paul was then known as Saul, and after the resurrected Jesus appeared to him he went blind for three days before his sight was restored and he converted to Christianity.]

Avent was sentenced to life for the murder of Steven and six years for the false imprisonment of Steven's mother. The non-parole period was set at 21 years.

Because the cameras in court were fixed on the image of Mr Justice Teague, the millions of viewers around Australia did not see Steven's shattered mother crying out, 'You'll never be in there long enough, Nathan. Never long enough! Die in there!'

A veteran *Herald Sun* reporter, the late John Hamilton, described a poignant moment later, when a female police sergeant told the packed courtroom, many of whom were family and friends of the victims, 'You can all leave now.'

'She was crying too,' wrote Hamilton.

Avent was quickly ushered out of the courtroom.

Avent appealed his sentence, saying that the media glare on his case meant that he was given a harsher jail term. The Victorian Court of Appeal rejected that it was influenced by the presence of a video camera in court, but the judges agreed that his sentence was 'manifestly excessive', given that there was no pre-mediated murderous intent. His sentence was reduced to 25 years with a minimum of 18 years.

Meanwhile, Steven's mother and father, his sister and extended family were left with the trauma of Avent's actions. Steven's mother's victim impact statement is heartbreaking to read. It was published in the *Herald Sun* on 19 May 1995, the day after Avent was sentenced for the first time:

> Everything in my life has been totally shattered; emptiness continually hounds me day after day; and what followed on from that unforgettable day, I can only describe as a living nightmare .... When unpacking some of my clothing [after she and her daughter had moved from the Smoult Avenue address] I came across his black jumper, which he always used to wear. It smelt like him and I cuddled it and cried and cried. This was all I had left .... I feel so alone in my grief ... sometimes I think the offender should have finished the job he came to do, and killed me. Instead he left me here to suffer the heartache .... I cannot erase from my mind what the offender did to Steven while I was innocently showering that day, I never saw what happened, but I sometimes have vivid pictures of what my thought processes decided what happened .... I have a lock and

chain installed on my bathroom door, and while showering I check this constantly, making sure no one is coming in …. I have lost all trust. When someone comes to my door, I don't open it, but hide and stay quiet until the person is gone. I often have a knife by my side ready to defend myself …. I feel my soul is slowly shrivelling up, and one day there will be nothing left inside of me, just an empty human shell, and then I'll die …. What of Steven's loss? Who will talk on behalf of his losses? His right to live on this Earth, his right to live a rich, full and joyous life, shared by his family and friends? There was a human being behind that name, a 10-year-old boy, a little boy who lived, breathed, laughed and cried. The offender did not have the right to end Steven's life.

Avent was released from jail in 2012, after serving his minimum sentence.

MURDER ON A LONELY ROAD

In the early hours of Friday, 24 November 1944, the bodies of two men were found shot to death, in Templestowe, an outer-north-east suburb of Melbourne. Nowadays it is an expensive, bushy residential locale. Back in 1944, the area had a scattered population and was full of fruit orchards. In the 1940s, to take a trip to Templestowe would have been considered 'going bush'.

Initial newspaper reports labelled the killings 'Tragedy on Lonely Road'. The lonely spot in question was Manningham Road, and a cyclist on his way to work discovered the scene.

The body of 22-year-old labourer Roy Pugh was found 'huddled' in the back seat of a taxi with a bullet wound in the middle of his forehead. Mr Pugh hailed from Collingwood, a gritty, inner-Melbourne suburb, so the dead man was a long way from home.

The other dead man, taxi driver Harry Nicholls, 43, was found five metres from the taxi and had multiple bullet wounds.

Police quickly established that Mr Pugh was known to them and had a criminal record. It was noted in newspaper articles that police believed his death was the result of an underworld dispute.

Mr Pugh had been convicted for a number of offences in his short life, the most recent for wounding with intent. He had received a two-year sentence and 'ten strokes of the birch', according to a report published in *The Advocate*.

A birch is similar to a cane, and the punishment, known as 'birching' – essentially whipping or flogging someone across the buttocks – was used in Australia into the 1960s. An article in *The Argus,* dated 23 September 1886, titled 'Birching at Pentridge' explained the practice to readers as 'the whipping of offenders against decency under 21 years of age' and 'an invention for the cure of the worst larrikin'. Newspapers such as *The Argus* and *The Advertiser* regularly ran stories about court-ordered birchings, mostly for juvenile offenders.

There were two others in the taxi that evening – a young woman, Dorothy Grace Maxwell, 23, and Ronald Eastwood, 19. It didn't take police long to pick up the pair and take them in for questioning at the Russell Street police headquarters.

Initially, Eastwood claimed that he and Pugh had been pushed into a taxi at gunpoint by men he didn't know, and he had been able to jump from the taxi. When police told him they had reason to believe that he had been in the car when Pugh was shot, he tried to blame a known criminal for the killings. However, the man he chose to blame was in jail at the time of the shootings.

From the statements given by Eastwood and Miss Maxwell, police pieced together the events they believed occurred that evening.

Eastwood and Mr Pugh were childhood friends and had been drinking together at the Retreat Hotel in Nicholson Street, Abbotsford, on the afternoon of 23 November.

Deciding to keep the good times rolling, the pair intended to carry on to a party when Mr Pugh, a married man, remembered he had a date to meet his girlfriend, Miss Maxwell, who was known to them as 'Maxie'.

Pugh phoned for a taxi from a telephone booth in Collingwood, and then both the men and Miss Maxwell were picked up from an inner-city house where Miss Maxwell had been staying.

Police believed the taxi driver, Mr Nicholls, was persuaded to drive out to the north-east under the false premise that he was transporting a patient to hospital. Mr Nicholls was on an emergency call-out roster that night. The husband and father of an eight-year-old son received the despatch to pick up some people in Fitzroy. Pugh had stated when calling for the taxi that he needed to take his wife to hospital.

The men instructed the driver to go to the Fairfield Infectious Diseases Hospital, and when Miss Maxwell first entered the taxi, she was told by Pugh, 'You're supposed to have diphtheria.'

As Mr Nicholls headed towards the hospital, Eastwood pulled the gun on the driver with the intention of taking the taxi.

'Put it away, there's too much traffic,' Pugh allegedly told Eastwood, and the pair started to argue.

Miss Maxwell told police that Eastwood, who was in the front seat, turned around and a shot was fired at Mr Pugh.

By this stage, the taxi was on Heidelberg Road, which is, and also was in 1944, a major arterial, hence Mr Pugh's concern that another car or passer-by would see them trying to hijack the taxi.

Eastwood claimed that when Mr Pugh had called for the taxi when they were in Collingwood, he had pulled out a gun and proposed that they hold up the driver. Eastwood ended up with the gun because he couldn't drive, and they had agreed that Mr Pugh would take over the taxi once they had menaced the driver. He also said that his friend had grabbed for the gun and that had caused the shooting.

However, Miss Maxwell told detectives that the pair had been friendly the whole time and that even when Eastwood fired the gun, he was calm and collected.

Miss Maxwell, terrified after seeing her boyfriend shot, leapt out of the taxi as it was moving slowly along the road. She said a cyclist gave her a lift back to Carlton.

According to Eastwood, he then told Mr Nicholls to 'follow the road'.

The driver kept on driving. 'He did not speak anymore. He was very silent,'

Eastwood's statement said. He claimed they drove out past Heidelberg, and when the car slowed, Mr Nicholls tried to jump out. Eastwood attempted to stop him, and Mr Nicholls was shot and killed. Eastwood's statement was read out at the coroner's inquest into the deaths on 8 December 1944, and the details were published in the Saturday edition of *The Argus* the next day:

> The car was almost stopped, and he tried to jump out the side. I had been doing a bit of thinking on the way out about what I was going to do. I intended to put him out and drive the car as far as it would go. He jumped out before it was stopped and got almost on the road, and I lost my head and the gun was pointing in his direction, and I

pulled the trigger and the gun went off. I just pulled the trigger as fast as I could go, and the gun went off several times. The taxi driver fell back against me in the front seat. The gun was then empty.

The post-mortem examination of Mr Nicholls found that he had been shot at least four times in the back; one of the bullets had penetrated his lung.

Eastwood told police he 'half-dragged and half-carried' the driver's body to where it was eventually found the next morning.

Walking along the dark, lonely road, Eastwood asked directions to Heidelberg Station, and got off the train at Victoria Park in the city. He had dumped the gun but never revealed its whereabouts to police.

In the morning, Eastwood, a waterside worker, went to work as usual and was arrested later that day at a billiards club in Johnston Street, Fitzroy.

It turns out that Miss Maxwell may have had a lucky escape in more ways than one because Eastwood told police when being questioned that he and Pugh both intended to 'have a go at Maxie' after they had driven her into the bush. Eastwood described Miss Maxwell as 'Pugh's 'sheila' to the police officer.

When the time came for Eastwood to stand trial for murder, the story was somewhat of a sensation for the newspapers. One report in *The Argus* described that Eastwood was frequently 'overcome with emotion' while he was in the witness box. 'He swayed and seemed likely to collapse,' the 23 February 1945 report said.

When sentencing Eastwood, Mr Justice Martin dismissed the attempts by the defence to suggest the accused was not to be blamed for carrying a loaded revolver around.

His defence lawyer said Eastwood was a product of the 'firearms age' and that he could not be wholly responsible for what occurred.

Mr Justice Martin said, 'The young man of today has many privileges which his father did not have, but being allowed to roam at will with a loaded revolver is not one of them.'

Eastwood was acquitted of murder but charged with two counts of manslaughter, and on 28 February 1945, he was sentenced to 18 years' imprisonment.

Meanwhile, the community rallied around the slain taxi driver's family. *The Argus* reported that a group of anonymous Australian soldiers in Papua New Guinea were so moved by the tragedy where Graeme Nicholls, now aged nine, had lost his taxi-driver father that they sent him a parcel of handmade gifts.

Graeme's teacher at Bentleigh East primary school, Miss Marjorie Macdermid, wrote to the newspaper so that they could publish a thank you. The newspaper printed the article 'Kindly Soldiers Remember Fatherless Boy' on 15 March 1945.

Recently this lad, Graeme, aged nine, was the delighted recipient of a parcel from New Guinea. On opening it he found a very original moneybox, made from two coconuts beautifully polished and carved. The box contained five/ (shillings), some New Guinea coins, and Christmas and New Year greetings from anonymous sympathisers. These kindly soldiers, themselves enduring the hardships and hazards of a New Guinea campaign yet found time to interest themselves in bringing happiness to a small boy so cruelly deprived of a father. Perhaps from your columns they may learn of Graeme's appreciation.

THE ASSASSINATION OF JANE THURGOOD-DOVE

John Magill wants to live to be over 100 years of age so that he can see the men involved in his daughter's brutal murder brought to justice.

Mr Magill's youngest daughter, Jane Thurgood-Dove, 35, was executed in the driveway of her suburban Melbourne home – in front of her three children – after she had picked them up from school on 6 November 1997.

Until that moment, Jane was an ordinary mum and wife. She shared a weatherboard home with her husband Mark in a quiet street just minutes from where she grew up in Niddrie, 13 kilometres north-west of Melbourne's CBD. You couldn't get more typically suburban than the Thurgood-Doves. They quietly and lovingly went about their daily lives like hundreds of thousands of other Aussie families. Mark was a factory foreman, and Jane had stopped working when her first child was born, her days busy with the school run and the endless tasks that make up family life.

Police know a great deal about the crime after thousands of hours of investigations over the years, but they have not been able to bring the killers to justice ... yet.

The murder of the suburban wife and mother shocked Victorians, and to this day it remains one of the crimes that haunt police. Mention the name 'Jane Thurgood-Dove' and most Victorians who were old enough to remember the news coverage immediately recall the front pages of the newspapers that ran the photo of the naturally pretty woman, with blonde and caramel-highlighted hair and bright eyes. A much-published photo, taken earlier in 1997, showed Jane with her three children. Her son, ten when his mum died, smiles broadly for the camera. Her daughters, aged two and five, cuddle up close to their mum. The horror of the murder – a woman gunned down in front of her children – sickened the state and seemed to baffle police.

I first met the Magills at Niddrie Village Shopping Centre in April 2012, and as we headed towards the car park, they greeted at least five people along the way in the few minutes it took.

The family is well known and respected in the area. Mr Magill, in his late eighties, was a butcher and for many years managed a popular butcher shop in Moonee Ponds, a few suburbs away from Niddrie. He had only just retired in 1996, the year before Jane's murder.

'The community, the people we've known for years, closed in around us and protected us,' Mrs Magill, said.

I was invited to the Magills' home and we spent several hours speaking.

The couple raised their three daughters there – Jane was the baby of the family – and on the door frames of the kitchen there are pencil markings noting the heights of the girls over the years.

Sitting at their dining table – the same one that held countless family dinners over the years – I wondered about Jane's children, who are now adults. Their smiling faces beam out from photos on the walls and shelves.

Jane's murder was an organised hit gone wrong.

In the same street lived a convicted criminal and his wife, Peter and Carmel Kypri.

Police know that the wife, who was said to resemble Jane and drove a four-wheel drive, was the real target of the hit, which was a payback from underworld figures who had a grudge against her husband.

The couples did not know each other, and the Kypris moved away from the street not long after Jane's murder.

Mr Magill said he had been told that in the days after the murder neighbours told the police canvassing the area that the Kypris would have been the intended target of a shooting, not Mrs Thurgood-Dove.

At least four men were involved in the fatal shooting – the gunman, the driver of the getaway car, the person who stole the car and the organiser of the cold-blooded hit.

The gunman, described as 'pot-bellied', chased Jane around her four-wheel drive, as her three children looked on from inside the car. The gunman callously shot Jane when she tripped and fell, then he ran to a silver-blue Holden Commodore, which sped away. The burnt-out wreck of the car, stolen from inner-city

Carlton a few days prior, was found in nearby Farrell Street. It is believed that the men switched to a white Commodore.

The gunman undoubtedly stalked Mrs Thurgood-Dove in the days before her murder. Several witnesses had seen the car that carried the men to the murder the day before near the school attended by two of her three children. Mr Magill said he thinks the men were watching his daughter the night before her death – when she was at their home to celebrate his birthday.

The Magills said there is not a moment that goes by where Jane is not in their thoughts.

Mrs Magill recalled the horrific moment they found out that their daughter had died. The night before, the whole family had celebrated Mr Magill's birthday and they shared what would become their last goodnight kiss to their daughter as she left for her Muriel Street home, just minutes away. His birthday has ceased to have much meaning for Mr Magill since then, as each one reminds him of his precious daughter's murder and the fact that those involved are still unpunished.

Mrs Magill said she was pottering around the kitchen and preparing dinner when she heard the police helicopter flying loud and low. The couple went out to the street, as had other residents, to see what was going on. Little did the Magills know that the police activity was to do with their family just streets away.

'We'd had dinner and there was a knock at the door,' Mrs Magill said.

'John had answered the door and he said it sounded serious and we asked the police inside. They asked if we had a daughter Jane and then we were told she had been shot and had died,' she said.

'It was just like that, so blunt, though I can't imagine how you would ever deliver that sort of news to anyone.'

The couple are angry and frustrated and worried that justice will never be done.

'I've thought of nothing else but Jane's death and going for the person who is ultimately responsible for it,' Mr Magill said. 'That's why I want to live to well over one hundred. Under normal circumstances, situations like Jane's death doesn't happen with families like ours.'

Mrs Magill added, 'But it does – look what happened to us.'

Another murder, with some connections to Jane's, occurred in 2000 and showed that though rare, innocent people can get caught in the web of the underworld, with fatal consequences.

Keith Allan was a suburban solicitor who was murdered in 2000. Though his body had not been found, three men, including Keith's law clerk, Julian Clarke, were convicted in 2007 of his murder and sentenced to jail terms in excess of 20 years. Clarke had stolen at least A$420 000 from the law firm's trust account. Keith had eventually discovered the fraud, and Clarke organised to have his boss killed.

Peter Kypri's cousin, Costas Athanasi, was one of Keith's killers, and he is currently serving 25 years for his main role in organising the murder. Mr Allan had represented Kypri in a 1999 assault case.

Mrs Magill said Jane was a devoted mother and wife. 'She would help at her children's primary school doing reading with students, and they loved her,' Mrs Magill said. 'Jane was always thoughtful.'

Mrs Magill shared one memory of Jane's thoughtfulness: In mid-1997, the Magills embarked on a dream six-week tour of the United Kingdom and Europe. The couple arrived in Paris on

Mrs Magill's birthday, and waiting for her at the hotel reception was a card from Jane.

'Jane had contacted the tour operator and found out what hotel we would be staying in. That was her all over.'

Mr Magill pulled out a thick binder of news clipping on the murder and recalled the battles they have had to get the police to increase the reward for information that could lead to a breakthrough in the case. He has painstakingly kept a diary of events since 6 November 1997.

Mr Magill said he was always of the opinion that a large reward was a key factor in getting people to talk about who was involved in his daughter's assassination.

Mrs Magill said in the late 1990s, the then Victorian Premier, Jeff Kennett, rang them directly to offer his personal and government's support in whatever they needed.

She said when the couple mentioned that there seemed to be some issues with getting a reward approved, Mr Kennett told them he would see to it. Not long after, a reward of A$100 000 was offered. But Mr Magill always felt the money needed to be more to get serious intelligence.

There is now a A$1 million reward on offer for information that leads to a conviction. When the reward was first announced in 2003, police received a vital tip on the identity of the gunman.

That information was that the gunman was allegedly ex-Rebels Motorcycle Club member Steven John Mordy. He had died from heart disease, aged 39, in 2000 after years of abusing his body and mind with amphetamines and booze. His close associate, Jamie Reynolds, was believed to have stolen the getaway car. He is also thought to have been waiting at the spot where they torched the vehicle and then drove Mr Mordy and another man away. Police had been on the verge of questioning Mr Reynolds for his part in the murder when he drowned in a boating accident in 2004.

Such is the police's determination to solve Jane's murder that they have also offered immunity to a veteran criminal with bikie connections if he testifies against the person who ordered the execution. The man they want to speak to was the driver of the car that drove the killer to and from Muriel Street.

The Magills are angry about the length of time it took to definitely establish that the murder was a mistaken identity killing.

In the early years after Jane's death, police focused on a theory that a police officer was involved in her murder. The policeman – who lived just streets away from the Thurgood-Doves in Niddrie and was interviewed several times over the murder (he reportedly failed a lie detector test) – was for a time the prime suspect who police theorised had ordered a hit on Jane because of thwarted romantic feelings.

The man, who was known to the family and moved in some of the same circles, was reportedly obsessed with Jane.

Mrs Magill said she knew the policeman in question and had even met with him a few months after her daughter's death.

'He was infatuated with Jane, and he was probably in love with her. But she was happily married and had the kids,' Mrs Magill said. 'After I'd sat down with him to talk, I knew he had nothing to do with Jane's murder,' she said. 'I straight out asked him if he had anything to do with it. [The police] zeroed in too much on this man as the suspect.'

It was also reported that Jane had a 'dark secret'. When I brought this up for discussion, Mrs Magill shook her head and scoffed. 'That was absolute rubbish,' she said. She feels it was a diversion that stole precious police investigation time from finding the true culprits.

A teacher at the kindergarten the children had attended came forward to police with information that a year prior, Jane had said 'everybody has secrets, even me'.

'We didn't even know her, and she was speaking on our family's behalf,' Mrs Magill said. 'It was most probably a throwaway comment by Jane.'

Mrs Magill became a volunteer in the court system as a support worker after Jane's death. She wanted to help other families who were victims of crime and assist in navigating the confusing and painful twists and turns of the legal process.

Through their painful experience, the Magills have become friends with other parents of Victorian homicide victims, such as George and Christina Halvagis, whose daughter Mersina was stabbed to death as she was tending to her grandmother's grave at Fawkner Cemetery in October 1997. Serial killer Peter Dupas is serving three life sentences and is never to be released for the murders of Mersina, Nicole Patterson and Margaret Maher. They also got to know Roger and Joy Membrey through their shared pain of losing their daughters. The Membreys' daughter Elisabeth, then 22, vanished from her Ringwood home in 1994. Elisabeth's body has never been found. Shane Bond was found not guilty of her murder or manslaughter in 2012.

'I always say, you can do anything in Victoria because you won't be punished,' Mrs Magill said.

The Magills showed me a home video, filmed on Easter Sunday, 1997. It is a much-cherished memento of their life before Jane's cold-blooded assassination. Jane would be dead by the end of the year.

'That was when we were happy,' Mrs Magill commented to me as she lovingly watched her family laugh and talk and help Jane and her husband Mark's children find Easter eggs hidden around the house and backyard. It was such a picture of normal family life.

I couldn't stop thinking that the beautiful young mum I was watching in the video would be on the front pages of newspapers just months later, an innocent victim of Victoria's underworld.

In the video, Jane is revelling in her children's delight at their Easter egg hauls. There are playful scenes of Jane and one of her sisters re-enacting the Irish dancing phenomenon of the late 1990s Riverdance and of making paper hats for her kids.

Later on in the night, Mr Magill captured his three daughters dancing to the Crowded House song 'Don't Dream It's Over'. Jane is swaying to the song and then cheekily arching her back out of the frame of the video camera.

'For a long time after, if I heard that song anywhere it would reduce me to a tearful mess,' Mrs Magill said. 'Then a while ago I was in a clothes shop and thinking how much Jane would have liked some of the things in there and the song came on. That was my daughter who I carried and bore and protected for all those years.

'I'll never forget and I will never forgive.'

Driving me to the tram stop, Mr Magill said, 'People talk a lot about "moving on" but how do you do that after your child is murdered? Until people become a victim of the homicide of a loved one they will never, ever understand. We can never move on. He finally said, 'I can't die before I see justice for my Jane.'

THE SLEEPWALKING MURDER

Ivy Cogdon suffered from nightmares that were often so bad she believed them.

The 50-year-old mother from the Melbourne suburb Carnegie was prone to 'nervous complaints' – as anxiety and associated psychological conditions were referred to in the earlier half of last century – and she was under the care of several doctors.

On the night of 11 August 1950, Mrs Cogdon's night terrors were so real to her that she did the unthinkable. Her only child, Patricia, 19, was asleep when Mrs Cogdon entered her room with an axe in hand and smashed her daughter's skull. Poor Patricia was found in the early hours of the morning, dead in her bed, with the bloodstained axe near her body.

Mrs Cogdon was interviewed by police and charged with her daughter's murder on Saturday, 12 August. Detectives told newspapers that Mrs Cogdon had made 'certain admissions' during the interview.

It was a shocking case – a mother killing her own daughter in such a brutal way – but there was more sensation to come.

Mrs Cogdon's admissions would have seemed far-fetched to most people, and certainly did to the detectives. Mrs Cogdon told the interviewing detectives, 'I dreamt the war was all around the house. I head Pat screaming and rushed into her room; it was full of soldiers. I hit at them. I remember hitting the bed. Oh, Pat, I don't want to live now.'

Mrs Cogdon pleaded not guilty to her daughter's murder. Her defence was that she was sleepwalking at the time she killed Patricia and believed she was protecting her girl from Korean soldiers who had invaded their suburban home.

At the coroner's inquest into Miss Cogdon's death, Dr Henry Stephens, a Collins Street psychiatrist said he thought Mrs Cogdon was a somnambulist – a sleepwalker. Several other doctors, who had been treating her, told the court they believed Mrs Cogdon would not have known what she was doing at the time of the killing.

Her complex neurosis included severe nightmares, which were disclosed to the doctors who were treating her condition. According to medical experts who assessed her, Mrs Cogdon was a 'hysterical type' who could suffer blackouts and was prone to sleepwalk.

Mrs Cogdon's trial by jury began in December 1950 and made national – and international – headlines for her unusual defence.

Mrs Cogdon's sister, Florence Millar, said the day before the gruesome event, Mrs Cogdon told her she had awoken from a terrible nightmare about red spiders and found herself in her daughter's room brushing imagined creepy crawlies off the girl.

Mrs Cogdon told the court Pat awakened while she was trying to get rid of the 'red spiders' and said, 'What is the matter, Mummy? What are you doing?'

'I said I was just tucking her in,' Mrs Cogdon recalled tearfully. Her fear of red spiders was prompted by the knowledge that someone in Carnegie bred these spiders and sold them as pets. When Mrs Cogdon heard that these people let the spiders in their house as a hobby, she told the court she 'shuddered' at the mere thought.

During his cross-examination by the Crown, Edward Campbell, a psychologist and lecturer at Melbourne University, said that Mrs Cogdon had developed a 'tyrannical super-ego', which drove her to 'over-protect' her daughter.

The concept of the 'super-ego' was introduced to psychology in the 1930s by Sigmund Freud's psychoanalytic theory of personality. According to Freud, personality is composed of three elements: the id, the ego and the superego, which work together to create complex human behaviours. The id is driven by a human's unconscious survival needs, with Freud calling it the 'dark, inaccessible part of our personality', The ego is driven by reality, and the superego is driven by morality, and works to help us act in socially acceptable ways.

Dr Campbell said his tests had revealed that Mrs Cogdon had remarkably low tolerance to perceived problems or challenges, which meant she was likely to quickly overreact to common worries such as war.

Dr Campbell said Mrs Cogdon had recounted her nightmares to him, including one where three ghosts had stood at the end of her bed and told her they had 'come to take Pat'.

Her greatest fear was the Korean War and protecting her family from invading soldiers. The night she died, Patricia had mentioned to her mother that she might become a transport driver if the Korean conflict hit Australian shores (the Korean War lasted for three years from 1950 to 1953). Mrs Cogdon worried her beloved daughter would be 'polluted' by any invading soldiers.

Mrs Cogdon said she had lain awake worrying and Patricia had called out, 'Mummy, don't be silly worrying about war. It is not at your front door.'

Not long after, Pat would be dead.

Appearing extremely fragile on the dock, Mrs Cogdon collapsed at one point, dragging her nurse along with her. The nurse sat alongside the accused murderer to comfort her during the trial, which lasted less than two days. Her husband, Arthur Cogdon, quickly went to her aid, along with several doctors present who had given evidence during the trial.

The sleepwalking defence was backed up by Dr H Stephens, a psychiatrist who had rooms in Spring Street, in Melbourne's CBD. Under cross-examination, he said he had met with the accused 25 times since her arrest and found she suffered from hysteria and somnambulism, with associated amnesia.

Dr Stephens's evidence startled the court because he said Mrs Cogdon could have acted silently while getting the axe and hitting her daughter – whom she believed was a soldier sitting on Patricia's bed.

Crown prosecutor Mr M Cussen asked how the axe blows could have fallen on the same area of Patricia's head if Mrs Cogdon was in a sleepwalking state.

Dr Stephens replied, 'I do not think that was the target. I think the blows were aimed at a hallucinatory body or satyr, or some object which was trying "to pollute" her daughter.'

'Do you think it possible for a frail woman to wield a six-pound [2.7-kilogram] axe and bring it down twice with great force on the bed without waking herself up?' Mr Cussen queried.

Dr Stephens said he thought it was possible.

The three doctors who gave evidence also concluded that Mrs Cogdon was not insane and showed no psychotic traits in the numerous tests she underwent.

One of the doctors, Collins Street psychiatrist Dr J Hurt said he had examined the accused for seven hours and believed her hysteria manifested in sleepwalking. He recounted that Mrs Cogdon had told him she had done things such as turn on gas jets in the middle of the night and been found wandering in the street in her nightdress. Dr Hurt said he had witnessed a sleepwalker in action and disputed the popular belief that they walked with their arms outstretched to stop themselves bumping into objects. He told the court that sleepwalkers had been reported to step over and around obstacles in their path while they were in their somnambulistic state. But the doctor said he had never known of a sleepwalker to commit a violent act.

It was clear to the court that Mrs Cogdon was an *extreme* sleepwalker.

Mrs Cogdon's love for her daughter was not questioned. She admitted she was devoted to Patricia and loved her deeply. The pair had a close, loving relationship. The brutal death Pat suffered at her mother's hand was at complete odds with the evidence given by family about how much Mrs Cogdon almost worshipped her daughter.

On the strength of the medical evidence, the jury found Mrs Cogdon not guilty. She collapsed in the dock when the verdict was announced.

The case made legal history in Australia because it was the first time a person accused of murder had successfully used sleepwalking as a defence in the country.

* * *

Prior to Mrs Cogdon's case, there were very few other documented cases where sleepwalking was used as a defence.

In 1846, American man Albert Jackson Tirrell was acquitted of the murder of his lover Maria Bickford. Tirrell had visited the Boston brothel where the victim worked, slit her throat from ear to ear and then set three fires at the scene. He went into hiding after the crime. Tirrell's lawyer managed to convince a jury that his client had been sleepwalking when he killed Ms Bickford and was unaware of his violent actions. However, according to an US-based research organisation Sleep Forensics Associates, Tirrell's attempt at covering his tracks by lighting the fires and running away from the scene are not actions that are consistent with sleepwalking. Tirrell's sleepwalk defence would probably be unsuccessful if he were tried in a courtroom of today.

Following Mrs Cogdon's case, there have been other cases of the 'sleepwalking defence' or 'homicidal sleepwalking' worldwide.

In 1955, another Australian woman used sleepwalking as a defence for murder. Alice Lange, 47, was charged with murder after she shot her sheep farmer husband Theodore at their home in Wesburn, Victoria. Mr Lange was shot in the back of the head as he slept. Mrs Lange told police her husband was a 'terrible man'; however, her two adult children and members of the small rural community in the Yarra Valley said the family was well respected and happy. Mrs Lange had undergone shock treatment for depression a few years before.

Daughter Valda, 19, gave evidence that her mother had 'a faraway look' in her eyes on the morning of the shooting.

Mrs Lange told police that in the early hours of 16 August, she got out of bed and got a shotgun from her son Ronald's bedroom. In her statement she said, 'I went back to the bedroom and laid [the shotgun] on my pillow, with the barrel at my husband's head ... I waited for over a quarter of an hour before I could pull the trigger.'

Mrs Lange told police she had 'terrible thoughts' going through her mind prior to the murder.

'I wanted to obtain some more shock treatment. My husband said it was very expensive and suggested I should see a Chinese herbalist ... ,' Mrs Lange said (as reported by *The Age* on 27 September 1955).

Mrs Lange's counsel was high-profile criminal defence lawyer Frank Galbally, who presented the sleepwalking defence to a packed courtroom – the case had attracted much attention from newspapers.

Son Ronald told the court his mother was a sleepwalker and that on occasion she would get up in the middle of the night and do the ironing while still in a sleep state.

Mrs Lange was found not guilty on the grounds she was insane at the time of the killing, but she was kept at Pentridge Prison 'until the governor's pleasure be known' (that is, indefinitely).

The most well-documented case of the 'sleepwalking defence' is that of Canadian man Kenneth Parks. In 1987, Parks, who at the time was 23 and had a baby daughter, drove 22 kilometres to the home of his mother-in-law and stabbed her to death. He had also choked his father-in-law into unconsciousness. Parks then drove himself to a police station and said, 'I think I have killed some people ... my hands.' He had deep cuts to the tendons in his wrists that required surgery.

Parks, who had a good, close relationship with his in-laws and was described as a 'gentle giant', had no memory of the event. Initially specialists and law enforcement did not believe Parks' claims, but after exhaustive medical tests and an investigation, there seemed no other alternative explanation. In 1989, amid worldwide media attention, Parks was acquitted of murder and attempted murder. In 1992, the Supreme Court of Canada upheld the acquittal.

In 2005, a British man was acquitted of murdering his father because he was sleepwalking. Jules Lowe, then 32, was found not guilty on the grounds he was 'insane' when he battered his father to death in 2003. An expert found Mr Lowe was in a state of 'insane automatism' when he committed the violent act, meaning he could not be held responsible for his father's death. Automatism is the legal definition of 'acting involuntarily'. Mr Lowe was found not guilty by reason of insanity. He was sent to a psychiatric hospital and released after ten months.

Records show Mrs Cogdon died in 1952 at Mont Park, a mental hospital in Macleod, Melbourne, which closed in 1999.

Ivy Muriel Cogdon killed her 19-year-old daughter Patricia with an axe on 11 August 1950. Mrs Cogdon claimed she was in a sleepwalking state at the time. Source: 1950 'Somnambulism plea in murder trial SLEEPWALKING MOTHER SET FREE BY JURY', The Argus (Melbourne, Vic. : 1848 - 1957), 20 December, p. 3. (Via Trove)

TRUST
ABUSED

Lyle Allan lost his only sibling in the most horrific of circumstances.

Keith Allan, 53, was murdered sometime in the late evening of Sunday, 28 May 2000. He was the victim of a professional hit. The killers of the unassuming suburban lawyer have been found guilty and are currently serving lengthy jail sentences.

But that's not the end of the story for Lyle, who still can't mourn his brother properly. Keith's body has never been found, and the men responsible for the cold-blooded killing are keeping their mouths firmly shut on its whereabouts.

The world of homicide victims is one Lyle never dreamed he would ever be a part of, though he always worried that his little brother would wind up in trouble.

'I never thought Keith would be killed though,' Lyle told me when we met in July 2012.

Lyle said his brother's business acumen left a lot to be desired, but he was an honest, clean-living man.

'He was hopeless with money,' Lyle said. 'He was trusting, too trusting of people.'

Keith was a hard worker who didn't drink or smoke. His passion was harness racing but being quite a frugal man, he never bet big sums. He attended Northcote High School, and then went on to complete a law degree at Melbourne University. After graduating, Keith bought a solicitor's practice in Military Road, Avondale Heights. He opened a second practice in Springvale in 1996.

However, his poor business skills led to financial troubles, and Lyle had to bail his brother out in 1996 when the purchase of a stud farm went wrong. Lyle never hesitated in helping Keith, but it cost him dearly – over A$150 000.

After he helped his brother out of the stud farm mess, Lyle insisted that the home the pair shared in the suburb of Northcote – next door to their childhood home where their mum Mavis still lived – was transferred into his name.

Julian Clarke was born in 1956 in Marrickville, New South Wales, and grew up in Geelong. He worked in the public service for ten years before becoming a law clerk.

Clarke came to work at Keith's office from an employment agency in 1995, when the volume of conveyance work became too great for Keith and his small staff to handle.

Unlike his frugal boss, Clarke bet large sums on the races, and when Melbourne's Crown Casino first opened in 1994, he became a frequent gambler there.

Clarke became co-signatory of the firm's trust account and also did most of the office banking. Lyle said this was an example of his brother's poor business judgment, which tragically, would cost him his life.

Clarke began to improperly use money from the firm's trust account, in the hundreds of thousands, to fund his own lifestyle as well as his 'roll-over' system where he would give gamblers money from the trust to allow them to keep gambling at the casino. Clarke was a member of the Mahogany Room at the casino, which offers members high-stakes gaming.

Some of the money went to the Crown Casino credit line of Frank De Stefano, the disgraced former mayor of the City of Geelong. De Stefano plundered A$8.6 million from clients of his own accounting firm, and most of this money was spent at Crown. De Stefano was sentenced to a minimum seven years' jail in 2003 and was released in 2009.

The punters who 'borrowed' from Clarke were meant to pay the money back so the firm's trust account could be replenished. Clarke himself was a big punter and living the high life, which did not match up with his A$30 000 annual salary. With his boss oblivious to the day-to-day business keeping of the firm, Clarke could keep feeding his gambling habit and lifestyle.

Clarke feared he would be found out after Keith's legal practice came under the scrutiny of the Law Institute of Victoria. Having already stalled the institute's investigation and requests for him to provide the firm's ledgers, Clarke knew he was going to be found out over an inspector's request for records of certain payments. These were to be reviewed on 5 June 2000. So, Clarke plotted the murder of his boss to hide his gambling-related thefts. He thought that if Keith 'disappeared', then the blame would be able to be placed on Keith.

After a cheque was dishonoured and several settlement payments were not available, Keith realised that his firm was in serious trouble and he informed his staff of the situation during a lunch on Friday, 26 May, just two days before he was murdered.

Clarke enlisted the help of an associate, Costas Athanasi, whom he had met through Peter Kypri (also known as Kyprianou). Athanasi was a man with a network that included some people involved in crime. Kypri was the target of a thwarted abduction and murder plot in 1994, allegedly over a A$200 000 debt.

Kypri's wife is thought to have been the true target of an underworld hit that tragically took the life of Melbourne mother Jane Thurgood-Dove in 1997. The Kypris and Thurgood-Doves lived in the same street.

Clarke needed a killer, and Athanasi recruited Sudo Cavkic, whom he'd known since the mid-1980s. Clarke even paid for Athanasi's 'help', with A$70 000 taken from the law firm's trust account.

As part of his plan, Clarke arranged to meet Keith Allan at the practice's Avondale Heights office on the evening of Sunday, 28 May 2000. Before Keith arrived, Clarke composed a letter to his boss, which was part of his plan to get away with killing Keith, making it look like he'd disappeared on purpose:

Keith,

It is with great reluctance that I write this letter.

I cannot however go on with the charade that you have demanded of me.

Keith, I like you very much and there is nothing that I would not do to save your practice and the jobs of [the staff] and myself. I feel that this has not been better illustrated than my complicity in covering your tracks and the sham of trying to delay the investigation by the Law Institute these past 8 months.

It cannot go on any longer.

Unless you have adequate funds in trust to trade and by that I mean to cover all trust balances by 9.30 a.m. Monday, 29 May 2000, I will have no alternative to report the matter to the Law Institute unless you have already done so.

Please do not do anything rash. Rather stand firm as the investigation by the [Law Institute of Victoria] may not hold the horrors you fear.

Lastly, Keith, you have indicated to all and sundry your preparedness to take your own life. Put this thought out of reach, Keith.

Clarke had apparently told Keith that he might have someone who could help the firm out of its financial mess. CCTV footage shows the two men at a service station in East Keilor at 9.53 p.m. where they had driven separately. Police believe that Cavkic was already there waiting, and Keith was abducted at gunpoint and then murdered.

Lyle had been at dinner at Cramer's Hotel in Preston with Keith earlier in the evening, along with a few other friends and his brother's girlfriend, Cheryl.

Earlier in the day, Keith had told his big brother that the law firm was in trouble and he needed urgent access to A$100 000.

'I said goodbye to Keith as he left with Cheryl, and I thought he would come home after taking her home,' Lyle said.

'At 9.27 p.m., a man rang and wanted to speak to Keith. I rang Keith on his mobile, and he said he would ring him the next day. I did not ask Keith where he was, and I was derelict in doing so,' he said.

'I thought Keith was at Cheryl's place. That was the last conversation I had with him.'

Lyle tried to call Keith numerous times after 11.30 p.m., to see where he was. Lyle had expected his brother home already and was a bit worried.

'Only one and possibly two of those calls were answered, but Keith's phone hung up immediately after the response. There were no words spoken at the other end,' Lyle said. 'We got a call at 3 a.m. from the police to ask if Keith was at home. I checked his bedroom, and he wasn't there.' He then went on to say, 'From that time on, we were constantly in communication with the police.'

The reason for the call from police was that two officers had found Keith's Mercedes in Ayr Street, Laverton, at 2.20 a.m.

Keith's disappearance was starting to look like foul play very early on – virtually hours after he was murdered, thanks to the curiosity of two senior constables on an otherwise routine night shift. Senior Constables Michael Strongman and Travis McCarthy did what all good police should do – they followed their curiosity.

At 2 a.m., the duo spotted a white Jaguar with New South Wales registration plates drive past them, and they decided to follow it. The Jag, driven by Athanasi, headed into an unlit part of the street. The car pulled up near the blue Mercedes – Keith's car – driven by Cavkic.

When Cavkic was questioned about why he was in the Mercedes, he gave a fake name and address and said his friend 'Keith' had lent him the car. Cavkic said he'd met 'Keith' on a pub crawl at the Taylors Lakes Hotel. (Taylors Lakes is a suburb 23 kilometres north-west of Melbourne's CBD.) This story was proven to be a lie because Keith Allan was a lifelong teetotaller, and according to Lyle, he would never lend his car to anyone on a whim. There was also no CCTV footage at the Taylors Lakes Hotel to prove that Keith or Cavkic were at the hotel when it was alleged.

Chillingly, there were also two shovels with fresh soil inside the vehicle and a small petrol tin containing fluid. Police believed that the men had planned to burn Keith's Mercedes so there would be no link to Athanasi and therefore Clarke. Keith's mobile phone and wallet were in the car too. Cavkic also had a loaded pistol, and it was later revealed flecks of Keith's blood were found on his right trouser leg and sock.

'If it wasn't for those police officers, Julian Clarke's involvement may never have been revealed,' Lyle said.

Clarke had made sure he was well away from the scene and later that morning started to weave his story that Keith had gone missing on purpose to avoid the financial mess the firm was in. Clarke told one employee at the practice not to bother coming to work because Keith had gone missing overnight. Clarke also called Lyle to set the scene that Keith had landed the firm into 'the shit' and had fled the problem.

'When Clarke rang me early in the morning, he asked to speak to Keith. I told him Keith wasn't there. He then told me that Keith was in "the shit" and that his practice had more money going out than coming in. I was careful not to tell Clarke anything, and he didn't know the police had phoned us during the night. He told me that Ray, the newsagent near Keith's office, had told him that the police had been outside Keith's office about 5 a.m. in the morning. I told the police everything about that call,' Lyle said.

Mrs Allan had a heart attack two days after her son disappeared. On top of the trauma of knowing something terrible had happened to Keith, Lyle was at his mother's bedside as she lay seriously ill.

'All the police would say to me was that the likelihood that Keith was a missing person was very remote. Mum never knew that Keith had been murdered,' Lyle said.

The brothers had shared the care of their mum, but with Keith gone, it was all left to Lyle, which was stressful and left him little time to take care of himself.

'Keith and I got along very well, and we were close. He always took care of our parents too.'

The boys' father, Olliver Allan, had died in 1993. Mrs Allan died in 2002, just weeks before Clarke, Athanasi and Cavkic were charged with her son's murder.

Lyle is convinced it was the strain of Keith's disappearance that hastened her death. 'Mum might have lived a few more years had it not been for Keith's disappearance.'

Lyle said it was also very distressing to have Keith's character called into question in the media in the early months of his disappearance.

'He was being portrayed in a few articles as a high roller who had a double life, and then in the first trial, the defence claimed that he had disappeared on purpose,' Lyle recalled angrily.

'Clarke fed the line to police that Keith was in financial trouble when they were investigating what happened to him.'

The journey to jail for the three accused killers was a lengthy one.

At their first trial in 2004, they all pleaded not guilty. However, a jury found them guilty of Keith's murder, and each man was sentenced to more than 20 years' jail. But in 2005, the trio's sentences were thrown out on appeal and a retrial ordered.

The reason for the retrial was that it was determined that during the first criminal trial, the jury may have been in some confusion about the proof required for reasonable doubt. A juror had directed a question to the judge: 'What percentage is reasonable doubt?' The judge had explained that reasonable doubt was the highest test known to the law (meaning that the prosecutor must prove the defendant's guilt beyond a reasonable doubt). The Court of Appeal found that the judge should have told the jury that reasonable doubt was not a percentage and that consequently, a juror applying a percentage value to reasonable doubt could have meant a miscarriage of justice.

The second trial in 2006 resulted in a hung jury.

The third trial in 2007 resulted in a guilty verdict. Clarke was jailed for a minimum 23-and-a-half years, Athanasi a minimum of 19 years, and Cavkic a minimum of 21 years. The trial judge, Justice John Coldrey, said the killing was in the worst category of murder.

A 2009 appeal by the men was refused.

Lyle is bitter and weary about the way families of homicide victims are treated.

'The person accused of murder has every right, their defence is paid for and they get top counsel. It's up to the state to prove they are guilty. Victims get very little support. The State Government tries, but it's skewed in favour of the accused's rights. Enduring three criminal trials has been hell, and I was treated badly, almost humiliated, while being cross-examined. It has been so stressful.'

In a strange twist to the harrowing case, Lyle found himself living in the same block of units as a man whose disappearance made international headlines in the 1970s. In 2004, Lyle moved from Northcote to Toorak Road, East Hawthorn, a suburb in Melbourne's east.

One of his new neighbours told him the unit next door used to be occupied in 1974 by John Stonehouse, who was a junior minister under British Prime Minister Harold Wilson. Stonehouse faked his own death in Florida in November 1974 and ended up in Melbourne, Australia, to set up a new life with his mistress (who had also been his secretary). It was an eagle-eyed bank teller who alerted police to a possible fraud involving tens of thousands of dollars by Stonehouse, and he was put under surveillance. He was arrested on Christmas Eve, 1974, and was for a short time thought to be the notorious fugitive and murderer Lord Lucan. (Stonehouse had been a spy for the then-Czechoslovakia since the early 1960s. This was only revealed publicly after his death in 1988, but the Thatcher Government had learned of it in 1979.)

Finding this intriguing, Lyle mentioned the loose connection to the prosecution solicitor who was preparing for the 2004 trial.

'I told an Office of Public Prosecutions solicitor this, and they told me I must keep my mouth shut,' Lyle recalled.

'Stonehouse faked his disappearance, and it was ammunition that the defence would use if they knew. And they did use other cases of persons who had faked their disappearances,' he said.

The scars of his brother's untimely and violent end have made life a struggle for Lyle.

He said his life has been irrevocably changed since Keith's death; he has post-traumatic stress disorder and had a stroke in 2016.

Lyle found support from people whose loved ones have been victims of homicide, including Janine Greening, whose 73-year-old mother was sexually assaulted and choked to death in 2000 by two teenagers, whose identities are still subject to a suppression order. Janine is one of the founders of the Victoria Homicide Victims Support Group (VHVSG), which was formed in 2005 to assist the families and friends of homicide victims. He and Janine became great friends.

'Lyle is an inspiration to all of us in the group,' Janine said.

'He has always managed to keep his sense of humour and maintains hope that someone will one day tell the truth about where his brother is. He has enriched the lives of our group, but it is unfortunate he has had to meet us this way, like it is for all of us that such tragic circumstances have brought us together.'

Janine and other members of the support group sat through the second and third trial of Keith's killers.

'Lyle's strength was amazing,' Janine said. 'He had no immediate family anymore to support him, and we all admired his strength and character in not giving up on getting justice for his brother.'

While Lyle knows he can't find his brother (and the killers aren't talking), he is putting his last sliver of hope in information from the public.

A family member or associate of the killers may know where Keith's body has been buried. It is thought his body may be somewhere in Victoria's Macedon Ranges because Cavkic's mobile phone records showed him to be in the Mt Macedon area on the night Keith was murdered.

'There's nothing I can do though to find Keith,' Lyle said. 'I am at the mercy of the men in jail for his murder, and I doubt the body will ever be found. To reveal where Keith is would be an admission of their guilt.'

Keith (left) and Lyle Allan with their beloved mum Mavis.
(Picture used with permission of Lyle Allan.)

THE TREASURE HOUSE MURDERS

The murder of a reclusive Melbourne mother and daughter in 1956 dominated newspaper headlines at the time and is still unsolved to this day.

On 14 December, the bodies of Mary Boanas, 83, and her daughter Rose Fisher, 52, were found in their Brunswick Street, North Fitzroy, home by a relative who had come to check on the pair.

Mrs Boanas was found dead in her bed from an apparent head injury. Her daughter was found facedown on the kitchen floor with a coat placed over her. She had severe head injuries, and it appeared she had been startled from behind as she prepared a meal for her bedridden mother. One newspaper gave a greatly detailed report and said the meal being prepared was sheep brains, which were found in the sink.

The mother and daughter were, according to relatives, distrustful of people and institutions and kept their money in their home. There was around £1500 worth of notes found in the house, equivalent to around A$50 000 in today's money. The house was also filled with expensive art, vases and jewellery.

When police were searching the house, they found it furnished with ornately carved wooden furniture, brass and porcelain vases and intricately carved Chinese figures. The police also found diamond brooches, rings and other gold jewellery, worth thousands of pounds, hidden around the house. The house, a double-storey terrace in the inner-city suburb of Fitzroy, nowadays an expensive area populated by hipsters, students and professionals, was described in newspaper reports as being beautifully kept, with a stunning garden that was hidden behind a 1.8-metre hedge. The women had rented out space in the house to boarders over the years, and police started to concentrate their efforts on speaking to anyone who had stayed there.

Police believed someone who knew their habits — and the fact that they had many expensive items in the house — must have murdered the women.

Victoria Police Homicide boss, Detective Inspector C Petty said that although police didn't have any definite leads, they did want to hear from anyone who had seen a car parked outside the house next door between 11 a.m. and 2 p.m. on the Friday, which is when they strongly believed the murders took place.

The murder weapon was also missing. A cobbler's hammer from the house was thought to be the weapon that had been used to bash the women to death. The police were told that Mrs Fisher did her own shoe repairs.

The horrific scene, dubbed by newspapers as the 'treasure house', was discovered by Mrs Boanas' sister Rose Moss. Mrs Moss had arrived at the address at 4.50 p.m. on Saturday, 15

December and found that the milk and a carton of eggs that another sister had left the day before was still on the doorstep. She had tried to visit the day before but her calls and knocks on the door were unanswered.

The women's next-door neighbour described them as 'charming, old-world-type ladies, who kept to themselves' and remarked that they were both so frail that they wouldn't have stood a chance against their attacker.

The women weren't always so reclusive. They had lived for most of their lives in Beijing, China, where Mrs Fisher's husband owned a newspaper. The women fled to Australia in 1936, before the Sino-Japanese War (1937–1945). Mrs Fisher's husband remained in China but was killed during the conflict.

Family told police, and the newspapers that were rabidly following the case, that the women became distrustful and fearful of people after their experiences in Beijing.

The search for the pair's 'slayer' was likened to the scale of investigations into the murder of 14-year-old Shirley Collins in 1953, and the serious assault of a woman named Gloria Bentham.

The murder of Miss Collins remains one of Victoria's most notorious unsolved crimes. Miss Collins's body, which was beaten with a beer bottle and lump of concrete, was found in the driveway of an unoccupied holiday house in Mt Martha on 12 September 1953. Three days prior, Miss Collins had set off from her suburban Reservoir home to attend her first teenage party, walking with her mother to the bus stop. The bus would take her to Richmond West Station in Melbourne's inner-east, where it is believed she was abducted.

In 2012, the *Sunday Herald Sun* reported that a man, who police have not yet named, gave a deathbed confession to killing Miss Collins and gave quite specific details of what occurred. This man also confessed to the murder of 20-year-old typist Elizabeth Williams in 1949. John Bryan Kerr, a radio announcer, had been convicted of Miss Williams' murder and sentenced to death, though this had later been commuted to 20 years' imprisonment.

The case of Gloria Bentham was sensationalised in newspapers around Australia. Miss Bentham, 22, was found naked, beaten and critically injured on the bank of the Yarra River at Burnley, Melbourne, on 11 March 1956.

A truck driver, Henry William Armsden, 19, was convicted of her attempted murder and sentenced to 13 years' jail.

In the lead-up to his arrest, it seemed the whole of Australia was transfixed by reports of Miss Bentham's progress as she recovered in hospital. Headlines such as 'She's getting better: flowers give joy to Gloria' gave readers up-to-date news on the young woman's recovery.

Miss Bentham was out with a girlfriend and two American sailors on the night she was attacked.

Armsden pleaded guilty in court, and newspapers reported proceedings painstakingly, even making note that during medical and police evidence, 'Armsden sat with his head down reading a cheap soft covered novel'.

Soon after the conviction, three media outlets, *The Argus,* the *Sun News-Pictorial* and radio station 3AW, were all convicted of contempt and fined £200, £200 and £100 respectively. The editors of the newspapers and the production manager of the radio station were also fined individually. The fines and convictions resulted from a picture of Armsden that was published in the newspapers.

3AW was cited for contempt because of a segment called 'While Melbourne Sleeps' where a detective was interviewed about events leading up to Armsden's arrest. It was successfully claimed by the Crown that the material published and broadcast could prejudice a fair trial. *The Argus* had put a white cross through Armsden's face in their edition, but the *Sun News-Pictorial* had not covered his image.

Meanwhile, police set about interviewing people who had connections to the 'treasure house', namely lodgers. One man spoken to was Ukrainian-born moulder Paul Bent, 28, who had boarded several times with the women.

He remained on the detectives' radar, and in June 1957, he was arrested in Newtown, Sydney, and charged with the murders.

A witness told police that Bent had visited her to sell her some goods and mentioned that he was buying a hotel in Sydney. When the witness, a housemaid, asked him where he had acquired so much money, he told her that he was now a real estate agent.

Bent would have had knowledge of the women's habits and their wealth, and police were convinced he was the murderer.

Bent appeared in the Supreme Court in August 1957. An associate, migrant Michael Olijnyk, told the court that Bent had asked him to do 'a job', which was to rob the women. Mr Olijnyk claimed that Bent told him, 'I know where there's a place where there is £500, maybe more.'

Mr Olijnyk said that afterwards, when he read the news that two ladies had been killed, he contacted the police.

Another man, Miloslav Kucera, took the witness stand and said he and another man had gone with Bent to a house in Fitzroy, where Bent had told them there would be a lot of money.

Mr Kucera told the court that Bent wanted him and the other man to scare two 'old women' who lived at the house and take money. Mr Kucera, who at the time of giving evidence was serving a two-year jail sentence for housebreaking, said he told Bent he was not interested.

According to newspaper reports, it took the jury just four minutes to find Bent not guilty of one count of murder; the other charge was dropped by the Crown.

However, that wasn't the end of Bent's court appearances.

On 11 March 1958, he was found guilty of stealing a transistor radio from a house in Nicholson Street, North Fitzroy, just minutes away from the 'treasure house'. The theft in question happened on 13 December 1956, the day it is believed Mrs Boanas and Mrs Fisher were murdered.

Bent, who had been locked up for over four months while awaiting trial for the murders of the women, was this time freed by the judge on the proviso that he adhered to strict parole conditions for three years.

The murders captured the attention of Melbourne but faded quickly from memory.

The killer has never been brought to justice.

After the publication of my first book, *Murder in Suburbia*, which this case was featured in, I received a fascinating email from a relation of Mary Boanas and Rose Fisher. They told me they were there on the day her relatives were murdered.

They were visiting 'Aunty Min and Rose' with their mother and three siblings:

I was then the 11-year-old standing outside their front door whilst the murderer was still inside the house. They (Mary and Rose) had partly raised me on their return from China, when we had a family guesthouse in Healesville. They later bought the house in Fitzroy. Aunty Min was my grandmother's sister, and Rose was her daughter.

As was the custom of the day, they took in male borders, not because they needed the money but because it was considered safer to have a male person living in the house; they were wrong. It was one of these men that murdered them for their money. They did not trust banks and kept their money wrapped in socks and underwear in their drawers.

Our Mother took us for a pre-Christmas visit as she did every year. If they were not home, they would leave their front door key for me to enter the house and wait for them. The key was hidden in the vine twisted around one of the pillars on the front verandah. However, this particular day it was not there, very strange I thought.

As it was a hot day, my mother took us (four children) to get ice creams as we were sure they would return soon, they were looking forward to our visit. We returned, but there was still no answer; we did not know at that time they were dying in pools of blood not far inside the door.

On returning home, my mother phoned one of her aunts who had a spare key, and Aunty Rose said she would go and check on them. That was when she made the gruesome discovery. I believe our Holden car was pictured in the news article of the day ....

THE MURDER OF DOROTHY DAVIES

Obsession turned to cold-blooded murder on a winter's night in Sydney's Woollahra in 1944.

The eastern suburb of Woollahra is one of the premiere postcodes in Sydney. It is an affluent area, just five kilometres from the CBD and not far from world-famous Bondi Beach.

In the 1940s, Woollahra had an eclectic scene, filled with artists, professionals and boarding houses.

Dorothy Jean Davies, 22, shared a flat in the area with a woman who worked for the Transport Department. Miss Davies worked as a delivery truck assistant at the Sydney Towel Supply, but she had also previously worked for the Transport Department as a tram conductor.

In August 1944, Miss Davies told Enid Poche, one of her three sisters, that she was 'going around' with Richard William Underwood, thirty. Underwood was a married tram conductor who used to work with Miss Davies.

Mrs Poche told Miss Davies to be careful, as Miss Davies was also engaged to a solider named Colin Dennerley, who was due back soon on leave from the army. Mrs Poche asked her little sister if she thought she was being fair to Colin by going around with another man. Miss Davies replied, 'No, perhaps not, but what can I do?' It was the last time Mrs Poche saw her sister.

Three days later, on 25 August 1944, Dorothy Jean Davies was dead.

Miss Davies was found dead on Edgecliff Road, Woollahra, not far from her home at around 8.30 p.m. Medical student Kenneth Rice found Miss Davies lying on the footpath groaning and rocking from side to side. She had been shot in the chest at close range and died soon after from her injuries.

At 11.15 p.m. that night, the police arrived at Underwood's home in Sydney's Waverley, not far from Woollahra. They told him that Miss Davies had been shot, to which he replied, 'Is she dead?' When told that Miss Davis had died, Underwood said, 'I half expected something like this,' and proceeded to weave a story of his own making for detectives.

At first, Underwood told Paddington Detective Sergeant Aubrey Keating that he had arranged to meet Miss Davies at 8 p.m. but she hadn't arrived. But then, acting nervous, he quickly changed his story and told police that while he didn't shoot Miss Davies, he was with her.

'I was there when she was shot. I will explain it to you,' Underwood said. He said he met Miss Davies at Wynard, near the CBD, and was walking her home when a man rushed up and shot her. Underwood said that Miss Davies fell to the footpath as her attacker ran away and that he knelt down on his knees to try and lift the dying young woman.

'That is how I got blood on my clothing,' he told Keating.

This tale quickly unravelled, and Underwood finally said to Keating, 'You win, I shot her.' He then claimed it was accidental when the pistol he was showing Miss Davies 'went off'. When asked where the murder weapon was, Underwood told police that he had thrown it over a bridge into the water.

The true motive for Miss Davies' death became clear when detectives kept pressing Underwood, who admitted he was jealous of her soldier fiancé. As with so many affairs, the relationship between Miss Davies and Underwood was complicated. While she had declared her passion for Underwood, Miss Davies still wore an engagement ring from Mr Dennerley. And while Underwood had told Miss Davies that he was divorced from his wife, Olga, he was in fact, only separated.

Newspapers at the time lapped up the sensational nature of the crime with headlines such as 'Former connie "terrified" of suitor' and 'Shot girl who loved him; left her writhing on ground'. One report on her murder in Fairfield newspaper *The Biz* described Miss Davies as 'a tall, attractive brunette'.

It was a letter that sealed Underwood's fate and exposed his motive for murder. While police were searching his home on the night of Miss Davies' death, Underwood ripped up a 'Dear John' letter Miss Davies had written to him.

In the letter addressed to 'Dearest Rick' (and pieced back together by the detectives), Miss Davies said she could not continue with the relationship. Extracts were published in newspapers during his murder trial in November 1944, and they revealed a tormented young woman: 'You must surely know that every tiny moment with you hurts like the devil because I know I can never really be yours for always.' Miss Davies was ending her relationship with Underwood.

God, Rick, darling, will you ever realise how much I love you, and understand how unfair you are to me when you expect me to just keep on going on and on as we have been. I am afraid I just can't take it anymore. Now you know why I want to break it off .... I also hope you know now how much you really mean to me, so please help me – yours, Jean.

At a coronial inquest into Miss Davies' death, which came before the murder trial, the dead woman's three sisters all gave evidence in court about their sister's fear of 'another suitor'. Mrs Thelma Cowie said while she did not know Underwood, her sister had told her she was afraid of a man named Dick who worked on the trams.

'He had put it to her that he was divorced, but she found out different, that he was not divorced, but separated,' Mrs Cowie told the court.

Another sister, Edna Everingham, described a conversation she'd had where Miss Davies described Underwood as 'very persistent'. 'He told her that if he didn't get her, no one else would,' Mrs Everingham told the coroner.

There was one witness to the crime, law clerk Mr Roy Shostak, who said he was on a tram in Edgecliff Road at 8.29 p.m. and saw a man and woman on the footpath. He told the coroner he heard a sound 'like a cracker or a tyre blow out' then saw the woman scream and slump to the ground. Mr Shostak said he could not see the man's face, as his back was to the tram.

Underwood's guilt was compounded when a tram driver and friend of Underwood, Colin Campbell, said the accused had called at his home on the day of the shooting to get a Colt revolver, which he had left there.

Underwood was sentenced to death for the murder of Dorothy Davies, but this was commuted to life imprisonment on 7 March 1945.

Underwood's wife was granted a divorce in 1954. By that time, Underwood had served ten years in Sydney's Long Bay prison. Mrs Underwood, asking for the judge's discretion, said she had been living with another man since 1950 and was expecting a baby. The judge granted Mrs Underwood a decree nisi in 21 days, rather than the usual six months.

FATAL RIDE

Sydney taxi driver Wendy Bell was planning her exit from the job.

A woman who was unassuming and liked a beer and a good laugh with friends, 59-year-old Wendy had been paying off a little unit in Port Macquarie, New South Wales, and was ready to take life a bit easier. The taxi-driving game wasn't as enjoyable as it used to be. She had seen it change over the years.

Wendy had even stopped working nights because she felt unsafe. While she loved the job she had done on-and-off for years since university, especially the social aspect of chatting with the customers, Wendy wanted a change of pace and scenery.

On 4 May 1995, Wendy had been invited to go sailing with good friend, Graham Sealby, from the Manly 16ft Skiff Sailing Club. Wendy loved being out on the water. At the last minute, she cancelled, opting to drive her taxi that day. Her upcoming move would mark the end of a 12-year stretch driving for Manly-Warringah Cabs, and she wanted to make as much cash as she could to start her life on the New South Wales north coast.

Michael Shand Walker was waiting for a taxi that same day. Walker, a Scottish migrant, had planned his trip for a long time.

Walker was a published author – he once had a short story called *Fatal Distraction* published in the *Family Circle* magazine under the nom de plume Naomi Sands. When he climbed into Wendy's taxi late that morning, the events that followed could have been straight out of the plotline of a novel.

A father of two, Walker, then 42, was a conman who tried to make his fortune from insurance rip-offs. Walker had taken out four insurance policies on his life, worth a total $783 000, and he planned to cash in on these by faking his own death.

An innocent taxi driver was to be the main character of Walker's elaborate plot. He planned to hire a taxi driven by a male of similar height and build to himself and direct him to drive to Mona Vale Cemetery where he would murder the poor cabbie.

Walker had chosen Mona Vale Cemetery, in Sydney's north, because he knew of a dip in the road there, where a vehicle would not be visible to passers-by. He had even earmarked a gravestone to use for his ruse.

Walker planned to shoot the taxi driver, disfigure the body and face to make it hard to identify, and soak the body in a warm bath of salt water so that (or so he thought) a coroner would not be able to work out the time of death.

He then planned to put his jewellery and a medical bracelet that said he had a middle ear condition on the corpse. Walker had even plotted how he would dispose of the body: he would place the body in a surfboard bag, along with a briefcase of his personal papers. Dressed in similar clothes to the body, Walker would catch the last Manly ferry from Circular Quay and at some stage of the journey, dispose of the dead taxi driver overboard so that the body would be chopped up by propellers. A spare change of surfer-type clothes would be on hand for Walker to change into, but not before he imagined he would sit next to an elderly couple inside the ferry, complain of feeling sick and then go outside for some air. He figured that by leaving his briefcase inside the ferry and making sure he was first off when it docked, he could disappear and begin a new life.

Walker had sorted out his will and changed it so that the monies from his life insurance would be paid into an estate, and not to his estranged wife. An uncle in Scotland, George McBean, was to act as executor of Walker's will, though the man didn't know it yet. Uncle George would only find out about what his nephew had done on arrival in Australia.

Walker believed he had planned everything. One of the life insurance policies even paid out an extra A$100 000 if the policyholder died on public transport. He had stolen identity documents from a man staying in the same Sydney hotel, and before he left his home state of Queensland, Walker had bought a .38 Smith and Wesson revolver.

Waiting at the taxi rank on 4 May, Walker was planning a 'dry-run' of his murderous scheme. But nothing went right that day for Walker, and tragically for Wendy Bell a split-second change to his step-by-step plan cost her life.

Walker had planned to get in the taxi in front of Wendy's, but someone else got there first. It wasn't until he sat in the front seat of the next available taxi that he saw the driver was a woman.

In that moment, Walker decided to kill her anyway. Later testimony from a fellow prisoner, who turned police informer for the case, revealed Walker's split-second thinking. Walker told his fellow inmate, 'Well I fucked up, and it was supposed to be a man .... I thought, "What the hell, I'm here now. I may as well take her for a dummy ride".'

Walker made small talk with Wendy and asked her to take him to Mona Vale Cemetery to visit a relative's grave. Walker even asked her to stop at a florist on the way so that he could buy flowers for the grave. Meanwhile, the revolver was hidden in his briefcase. During the course of their chat, Wendy revealed that she didn't have any children or immediate family in Sydney. In Walker's mind, this was a green light for his crime – he made the assumption she wouldn't be missed.

On arrival at the cemetery, Walker took the gun out of his briefcase and concealed it behind the bunch of flowers. Although he was sitting beside her, Wendy wouldn't have been able to see what he was doing because the open briefcase hid his actions. Walking back to the taxi after his faux grieving, Walker planned to shoot the unassuming taxi driver at the secluded spot. However, in a momentary reprieve for Wendy, a funeral procession drove past, and Walker hopped back into the taxi instead.

Complaining he felt ill, he asked Wendy to drive him to a doctor. He even asked her to pull the taxi over so he could get out and be sick, and he pretended to vomit on the side of the road.

When Walker re-entered the taxi, he got in the back seat, saying to Wendy that he didn't want to breathe all over her.

Walker was becoming agitated because his plans were going awry. And Wendy, who was attuned to human behaviour after driving taxis for so many years, was beginning to get concerned.

She was driving Walker from one place to another, with no proposed end destination; the bill was already A$42 on the meter. Then something only Walker and Wendy would know prompted her to hit the taxi's internal alarm, which sent an alert to her base that she was in danger. Perhaps it was a discussion about how Walker would pay the taxi fare that led to her anxiety about where this taxi ride was headed.

Witnesses reported seeing the taxi driving erratically and heading towards Dee Why Police Station, no doubt in an attempt by Wendy to get help. Before they reached the police station, Walker shot Wendy in the back and tried to commandeer the vehicle. The taxi stopped abruptly when Wendy was shot, and in a panic, Walker jumped out of the vehicle. As he pushed Wendy from the driver's seat, her foot became wedged on the accelerator and the car took off again. Walker was trying to steer the car with his hand through the window but was being dragged alongside. At 12.22 p.m., the taxi smashed into a tree right outside the police station. Shocked onlookers surrounded Walker and held him for the seconds it took police to arrive.

Walker confessed on the spot to police that he'd killed Wendy, extending his fingers to imitate a gun.

Wendy's murder shocked the community. The crime rocked her taxi driver colleagues and devastated her friends. At her funeral, more than 100 taxis formed a funeral cortege, and colleagues had flown black ribbons on their car aerials the day after she was killed.

Wendy's murder was covered widely in the media. It was such a shocking act and the circumstances so strange and cold-blooded.

The *Sydney Morning Herald's Good Weekend* magazine ran a feature by Jane Cadzow in November 1995 called 'The Last Ride of Wendy Bell' and the Sydney-based magazine *Lesbians on the Loose* dedicated its June 1995 cover to Wendy with an article written by the then-editor Frances Rand. The photo used shows a smiling, relaxed Wendy in an outdoor chair with a beer and a cigarette. It seemed to be the quintessential image of Wendy.

Both Rand and Cadzow interviewed people who knew Wendy – friends from work, from the lesbian and gay community of whom Wendy was a part of, and old school friends.

Ted Kilby, the-then radio manager at Manly-Warringah Cabs, said, 'Everyone liked Wendy; she was a jolly sort of lady.'

Wendy lived a quiet life, but some of her friends were taken aback that at her standing-room-only funeral, not much was mentioned about who she really was – all the parts of her life that made her interesting and engaging, as well as special to them.

The then-chairman of Manly-Warringah Cabs, Frank Martin, spoke at Wendy's funeral at the Northern Suburbs Memorial Garden and Crematorium, describing her as 'pleasant and efficient; an asset to the industry'. Mr Martin was the only person who spoke at the Catholic funeral, beside the priest.

Friends said they were upset that they couldn't speak at the funeral about their friend – about her musical abilities (Wendy played cello, piano and violin), the fact that she was the 10th person to join Sydney's Clover Women's Club, a lesbian association, in 1972, and of her intelligence and determination. Wendy completed her higher school certificate as a mature age student and studied Russian at university.

A friend, Ros Campbell, told Cadzow for *Good Weekend* that Wendy 'nearly always took her Russian book with her in the cab'. Ros also recalled to Rand an eerie conversation she'd had with Wendy not long before her murder. Wendy had dropped Ros at the airport for a trip to New Zealand and said, 'Ros, I must get out of Sydney soon. If I don't, I'll be dead.'

Another major part of Wendy's life was a long-term relationship with a woman named Tina. The pair ran an Indian restaurant, with Tina, who was Anglo-Indian, at the front of house and Wendy doing the cooking. Tina died by suicide in the early 1980s, and it was Wendy who found her.

While in custody awaiting his trial, Walker escaped from Long Bay Correctional Centre and was on the run for several weeks. He made his escape on Friday, 3 May 1996, in a laundry truck, and it was only noticed he was gone when he failed to attend a late afternoon assembly.

A week after his escape, the most recent photo of Walker was published in newspapers in an attempt to locate him. Authorities feared Walker would try to harm himself or someone else. They also thought he may head to Queensland, and they were right. He was recaptured a few weeks later on the Gold Coast.

More controversy followed for Walker when in February 1998, he sacked his barrister after learning he had driven taxis 25 years ago to make extra cash while studying law. The trial was postponed for a few days while Legal Aid organised alternative defence for him.

Walker's estranged wife, Robyn, gave evidence at his committal hearing that he had plotted to kill on at least one other occasion. Mrs Walker told the court that in 1993, her husband suggested the pair take out life insurance policies. It was Mrs Walker's death he planned to fake with a sensational plan to blow up a plane and make it look as though the pilot's body was hers. He had concocted a scheme to take a 'lovers' holiday to a secluded spot at Stradbroke Island. According to Mrs Walker, the pair did a 'trial run' of the plan in 1994, and her husband packed a picnic hamper complete with a semi-automatic gun and soft drink bottles filled with petrol.

It was just the two of them – the pilot had wandered away to sit on the beach while his chartered passengers enjoyed an hour's romantic time together. Mrs Walker said her husband became agitated when he noticed a tent at the spot and realised they were not alone. She said she convinced him to put away his gun and that he was acting 'crazy'.

Mrs Walker said that even on the return home, her husband was talking about another scheme involving a helicopter pilot. She told the court that it was at this point that their relationship fell apart and she left, taking their two children with her.

During his trial, Walker's defence said the death of Wendy was caused by his state of mind – he suffered from depression, Meniere's disease (a condition of the inner ear) and an addiction to prescription drugs. Walker also claimed the gun discharged 'by accident' and that he did not even know how to properly handle a firearm.

When asked by prosecutor Mark Tedeschi to explain the safety measure on the gun, Walker appeared to recoil from the weapon he had been handed and told Mr Tedeschi, 'I don't want to touch that.' Walker would not even look at the gun. He denied he had fired the gun three times in the taxi. Mr Tedeschi said that something 'much more sinister' must have occurred to make Wendy drive her taxi at speed to try and get help at Dee Why Police Station. He said that she must have felt sheer terror in the moments before she died.

Walker was found guilty of murder by a jury. At his sentencing hearing, he told the judge, 'I'm not a taxi-driver-stalking monster.'

Walker was sentenced to a maximum of 19 years in prison.

On 23 March 2000, Walker appealed against his sentence. His lawyers submitted that certain information from a police informer – a fellow prisoner – should not have been admitted into evidence. Walker also wanted the jury's verdict to be deemed unreasonable (based on some of the evidence from the police informant) and set aside. The appeal was dismissed.

Walker's maximum 19-year sentence expired in 2016. His 14-year minimum non-parole period ended in September 2011.

He was transferred to a Scottish prison in March 2011 in an approved international prisoner transfer under Australia's International Transfer of Prisoners Act 1997.

I enquired about Walker's transfer to the Scottish Prison Service via email in 2012, when I was first writing about this case. The email reply confirmed Walker's transfer; however, due to the country's data protection laws, the service could not say which prison he was transferred to or whether he has been paroled.

LESBIANS ON THE LOOSE

JUNE 1995 • ISSUE 66 • VOL 6 NO 6   FREE

SLAIN TAXI DRIVER

Wendy Anne Bell, 59, was murdered on May 4, 1995. Lesbians and gay men are mourning the death of their friend who survived the shotgun suicide of her lover to die at the hands of a gunman one week short of her retirement. The last words Wendy spoke to her best friend were, "If I don't get out of Sydney soon I'll be dead."

Sydney Taxi Driver Wendy Bell was murdered by Michael Shand Walker in 1995. Walker wanted to fake his own death and use the body of a taxi driver to carry out his plan. (Image from LOTL.com, used with permission from LOTL magazine.)

THE LAKEMBA
MURDERS

The Dart family were the epitome of the industrious, respectable working class that populated Australia post-war. William Dart was a well-respected master plumber, who had his own small business with son Ronald. Dorothy 'Dorrie' Dart, 49, looked after the running of the comfortable Lakemba brick and weatherboard suburban cottage and raised the couple's children, now grown up. The couple's daughter, Dorothy Jean, still lived at home but was soon to be married.

Lakemba had always been a solid working-class area and became a popular settling place for immigrants over the decades since the 1950s from countries including Greece, Italy, Lebanon and Bangladesh. The suburb, 15 minutes south-west from Sydney's CBD, is now home to one of the largest mosques in Australia and is known as one of the most diverse communities in Australia with an incredible food scene.

Dorothy Jean, 20, and Norman Kahler announced their engagement on 27 December 1949. They were both looking forward to a happy future together. However, the life of this average suburban family was violently torn apart one week after the joyous news of the engagement.

On the evening of Tuesday, 3 January 1950, Mrs Dart was found battered to death and her daughter barely clinging to life in their Garrong Road home. Both women had severe head injuries, and Mrs Dart had been scalped in the frenzied attack.

Police had been called by neighbours who heard piercing screams from the house at 8.15 p.m.

When police arrived, they forced open the front door to find a nightmare scene. Mrs Dart was dead in the hallway. The walls, floors and furniture were spattered with blood. A trail of blood led them to young Dorothy who was unconscious in the kitchen, with gaping head wounds.

She was rushed to the nearby Canterbury District Hospital but died a few hours later at 11 p.m.

Police immediately began the search for the murder weapon, believed to be a lead pipe or some similar heavy instrument.

Mr Dart Sr was away on a fishing trip at Lake Burrill, and son Ronald, who was married and lived nearby, was told of the tragedy and came to the scene immediately.

Dorothy Jean's fiancé was inconsolable when told of her death. Police interviewed Norman at his home and he was completely bewildered as to why anyone would want to harm his wife-to-be and her mother.

'Dorothy had no enemies as far as I know. She was a sweet-tempered girl,' Norman told police. 'I can't understand why anyone would want to harm her. The whole thing seems like a nightmare. Her mother had the same disposition,' he said. 'The man must have been a maniac.'

In the days following the horrific crime, detectives were convinced that the viciousness of the attack meant that the killer had a personal grudge against the women and would have been known to them.

They focused on talking to men who were known to Dorothy Jean and thought that a rejected suitor could have been the killer. It had been reported that Dorthy Jean's engagement ring had been smashed to pieces, along with her hand, in the wild attack, but a post-mortem had shown her fingers were not broken.

Detectives tried to piece together the women's movements before the killer arrived at the house. It appeared that Mrs Dart was reading a newspaper in the lounge and her daughter was knitting items for her wedding trousseau in the kitchen.

The Darts' next-door neighbour told police that after hearing screams from the house, he looked over and saw a man who appeared to be bending over and 'prodding something' on the floor.

Several other neighbours reported seeing a man leave via the front door but then run around the side of the house and escape over the fence.

The only solid clue, besides witness statements, that police found in the days following was a bloodstained dark-blue polka-dot scarf discovered in the Darts' backyard. It appeared the killer must have dropped it as he made his escape.

The press had dubbed the killer a 'maniac', and Sydney was shocked by the brutality of the murders of the unassuming women. If everyday people like them had been killed then surely it could happen to anyone?

Three days after the murders, a man presented himself, in the company of his parents, to Campsie Police Station. The man was

Kevin John Irwin, 23, a moulder who lived on the same street as the Darts. (A moulder is a tradesperson who constructs moulds for use in casting metal products.)

On Saturday, 7 January 1950, the police charged Irwin with murder. That same day, over 1000 people attended the funeral of the Dart women. *The Sydney Morning Herald* reported that 500 people stood in sweltering heat outside St Andrew's Church of England during the service. There were another 500 inside the church. Mother and daughter were buried together. In a show of respect, all stores in the shopping precinct surrounding the church were closed.

Irwin was refused bail and remanded in custody. An inquest into the deaths was conducted in February 1950.

Irwin's father John gave evidence at the inquest that on the night of the murders, his son came home after 11 p.m. with his trousers damp, which was odd because he had left the house at 7.15 p.m. to go to the movies. Mr Irwin said his son told him he had changed his mind and gone to Manly to the beach and slipped in the water.

Mr Irwin even told the hearing his son had asked him, 'What's going on up at Darts?'

A Lakemba resident, Geoffrey Furnell, also gave evidence and said that he was walking along Garrong Road at 8.15 p.m. on the evening of 3 January, on his way to his home in nearby Railway Parade, when he saw a woman struggling with a man on the front lawn of the Dart residence. Mr Furnell said he saw the man hit the woman with a cylindrical object the size of a rolling pin.

He went on to recall that the man dragged the woman back to the verandah, where there was a short struggle, and then he carried her into the house. The witness heard some more thumping noises and then he saw a man come to the window, press his face to the glass and then disappear.

Bloody heel prints had been found on the verandah and in the kitchen of the murder scene, and the spotted scarf found in the backyard was confirmed by Mr Irwin to be similar to one he had recently owned. The heel of shoes handed to police, from the Irwin house, matched the bloodied heel impressions.

A crown of a wristwatch winder was also found amid the bloody scene in the kitchen. A detective from the scientific branch of the Sydney Criminal Investigation Bureau said that police gathered items from Irwin's home, including the clothes Irwin had worn on the night of the murders and a wristwatch. The detective confirmed that the winder matched the wristwatch that belonged to the accused.

Crown witness Sydney psychiatrist Dr John George assessed Irwin of having the developmental age of a 13-year-old. However, Dr George said he believed the accused knew what he was doing at the time of the murders.

Irwin's defence made a plea to the court that their client was of 'unsound mind' when he killed the Dart women and vigorously tried to have him declared insane due to his intellectual disability.

A work colleague of Irwin's testified that Irwin, a moulder, had been able to perform tasks with a fair amount of skill. Newspapers reported that Irwin was extremely nervous when in the dock, and he paused often before tentatively giving one-word answers to questions.

Irwin made a confession to police, which he now said he did not recall, nor did he have any memory of what occurred at the

Darts' home. When he was first questioned by police, Irwin had denied that he had anything to do with the murders and said the blood found on his clothes was from a brawl he had been involved in the same night. He admitted he owned a pair of golf shoes the same as the style and make that matched the heel impressions at the murder scene.

The policeman giving evidence, Detective Sergeant Jack, told the court that Irwin had reportedly asked to see the officer by himself. Jack said, 'He put his arm on the table, leant his head on his arm and burst out crying, saying, "I will tell you all about it. I killed them. I hit them on the head with a piece of pipe I took from the backyard".'

Jack recounted how Irwin had told him he went to the Darts' place to use the telephone, and Dorothy Jean had told him she was engaged. Irwin then alleged the women started talking about 'my sister's dead baby'.

'I thought Mrs Dart was grinning at me and making fun of me and my sister,' Irwin reportedly told the detective.

Jack told the court that Irwin recounted that he had excused himself and gone outside the Darts' house and picked up a piece of pipe, which he had hidden under his coat.

Irwin said that when he re-entered the house, he asked Mrs Dart what she was grinning about and then struck the unsuspecting woman on the head. When Mrs Dart was first struck, her daughter ran to help, and Irwin savagely beat her on the head too.

In line with what witnesses observed, Mrs Dart ran along the hallway, out the front door and onto the verandah, but Irwin struck her again and dragged the terrorised woman back inside.

Jack said that at the conclusion of his confession, Irwin told him, 'I know I'll spend the rest of my life in jail for this, but don't let them hang me. I don't want to die yet.'

Irwin was found guilty of murder and sentenced to death. His sentence was later commuted to life.

Electoral roll records accessed on ancestry.com.au show a Kevin John Irwin (occupation moulder) resided in Ashfield, an inner-west suburb of Sydney in 1972, 1977 and 1980. The only other electoral roll record for a man of the same name and occupation was in 1949, and his address was 21 Garrong Road, Lakemba. These records would suggest Irwin spent at least 20 years in jail for the murders of the Dart women.

On the one-year anniversary of the murders, Dorothy Jean's fiancé, Norman Kahler, and his mother put a memoriam notice in *The Sydney Morning Herald*: 'Cherished memories of Mrs Dorothy Dart and daughter, Dorothy Jean. They departed this life January 3, 1950. Always loved and sadly missed by Mrs Kahler and Norman.'

The Dart family home in Garrong Road, Lakemba where mother and daughter Dorothy and Dorothy Jean Dart were murdered. Source: 1950, The Sun (Sydney, NSW : 1910 - 1954), 4 January, p. 1. (Via Trove)

Dorothy Jean Dart, 20, was murdered, along with her mother Dorothy Dart in 1950 in their Lakemba, Sydney home by Kevin John Irwin. Source: Inquest Story Of Face At Window (1950, February 12). Truth (Sydney, NSW : 1894 - 1954), p. 12. (Via Trove)

CHILD MURDERS IN THE 1970S

In the 1970s, there were a number of Australian murder cases where teenagers and offenders barely out of their teens murdered other children.

The families of the children murdered probably never imagined such tragedy could visit their lives. Their children were just doing what other Aussie kids of the 70s were doing – enjoying a carefree childhood. In the 1970s, few parents would have thought twice about letting their children move freely around their neighbourhoods.

Edward and Audrey Thrussell had moved from England to Sydney and settled in North Ryde with their three daughters. They had come to Australia for a better life away from the bleak economic and social climate of 1970s Britain.

On 9 January 1978, 16-year-old Julie Anne Thrussell, their eldest daughter, set off from her Cressy Road home at 9.20 a.m. to buy a pair of jeans at Grace Bros department store.

The first-year apprentice chef used the public path that deviated through a nature reserve – a distance of around 200 metres – that led to a bus stop that would take her to the store. She was enjoying her job at the Sebel Town House in Elizabeth Bay and all the independence that came with earning her own money and learning new skills. Julie had even studied a cake-icing course at night school and was looking forward to a career in commercial kitchens.

Julie was due to go to work at 3.30 p.m. that day; however, the teen never made it to her shift. In fact, Julie never made it home that morning from the shops.

A man who was in the area visiting his in-laws that day found Julie's body on fire in bushland. Julie was only half a kilometre from home. Police believed her killer had hidden in bushland and hit Julie on the head with a rock. She had then been dragged off the path, raped, doused with petrol, and burnt alive.

Mr Thrussell had to undergo the horrifying ordeal of identifying his daughter's body. The following day, still no doubt in shock, Mr Thrussell gave a doorstep interview to newspapers, while inside the house, neighbours and friends consoled Mrs Thrussell and the couple's daughters aged 15 and 12.

'What are we going to do about this maniac? I don't think he is going to stop here?' Mr Thrussell asked reporters. He appealed to the public for help in finding his eldest daughter's killer.

Mr Thrussell was a salesman who had been working towards building the 'Australian dream' for his family. 'I thought the kids would have a good chance in Australia,' Mr Thrussell said. However, the Thrussells had been jolted violently from their hopes of a safe, happy suburban life in Australia.

It was a devastatingly brutal crime, and police had to work fast to find the killer before he struck again.

The path Julie took on her last moments of life ran alongside the Field of Mars Cemetery. Two days after her death, a 19-year-old gravedigger's assistant was arrested for her rape and murder. Christopher Douglas Dennis, who didn't live far from the Thrussells, appeared in the Ryde Court of Petty Sessions in handcuffs, flanked by six detectives.

Dennis was remanded in custody but managed to escape authorities for a few hours on 23 March 1978, when he broke away from a prison warder while being escorted to a medical examination in Sydney's CBD. Police scoured trains and all seven theatres of the Hoyts Cinema before Dennis was found on a bus in William Street, a main CBD thoroughfare. The then New South Wales Premier, Neville Wran, demanded an immediate report from corrective services about the incident.

Dennis was sentenced to life imprisonment for the murder of Julie Thrussell.

In 1980, the Thrussells received A$20000 in criminal injury compensation from the New South Wales Government. It was the maximum sum payable at the time – A$10000 for each parent.

In October 1992, it was reported that Dennis would be eligible for release in mid-July 1993, with the New South Wales Court of Criminal Appeal recommending he be under supervision for the remainder of his life. In early 1992, a bid by Dennis for a minimum term under the New South Wales 'truth in sentencing' legislation was knocked back, with the judge saying he could not be sure that Dennis would not 'present a danger to female members of the community' on release.

He was released on parole in 1995.

* * *

Two other families also found themselves the victims of an unspeakably brutal crime in 1978.

When Julie Atanasov and Magda Trajkov, both eight years old, failed to return from a playdate at a friend's house in the southern Sydney neighbourhood of Bexley, their parents spent a distressing night searching for their little girls.

On Sunday, 12 November 1978, the girls had walked to the house of one of Magda's friends. The house was in Oriental Street, a five-minute walk from the Trajkovs' Harrow Road home.

But worse was to come for the families who had both left the former Yugoslavia for life in Australia.

The families had been friends for many years, and the girls would spend a weekend at each other's homes every few months. The Trajkovs had settled in Bexley, and the Atanasovs lived in Yagoona, a south-west suburb of the city. Mr Atanasov had established a successful car trailer business in nearby Bankstown and he and wife Bozna also had a four-year-old son. Mrs Atanasov and her children had returned just days before from a six-week visit to the former Yugoslavia to visit friends and relatives.

At 3 p.m., the girls left their playdate and started their route back to Magda's house. They stopped at the playground of the local primary school for a while.

A witness last saw the girls talking to a young man in the grounds of the school between 3.30 p.m. and 4 p.m. Then the girls vanished.

Police searched through the night for the girls. At 10 a.m. the following day, two Bankstown police officers found Julie and Magda in a nearby reserve. Sergeant John McInerney and Constable Ian Dawson heard the weak cries of a child and it led them to the devastating discovery of the friends lying on the bank of Bardwell Creek. The girls had been smashed on the back of their heads with a rock.

Julie was dead from a fractured skull, and Magda was barely clinging to life. As she was taken to hospital, brave Magda was able to give police a thorough description of the man who had attacked them. They were now looking for a male around 18 years old with light-ginger hair, a moustache and a light beard.

More than 100 police officers scoured the bush reserve and creek area.

The next day, detectives arrested and charged a 17-year-old Bexley teen with Julie's murder and the attempted murder of Magda.

The youth, whose identity was supressed, confessed to the crime and told detectives, 'I took the girls into the bush and tried to kill them by hitting them over the head with a rock.'

The youth was concerned about his father and did not want him present at the police interview. However, the youth's father came to see him in the police station and asked, 'Did you do it, son?'

When his son replied, 'Yes,' the father asked, 'How could you do such a terrible thing to those little girls?'

An 11-year-old girl came forward as a witness and said she had seen the girls holding hands and skipping in the Bexley school grounds on the afternoon of 12 November. The picture of childhood innocence was heartbreakingly sad because just moments later the girl said she saw a man pulling either Julie or Magda back towards the centre of the schoolyard with the other girl holding onto her friend's hand. The witness had not said anything to anyone when she got home because she thought the young man might have been one of the girls' brothers.

The crime struck a nerve with the community, who were sickened by the attacks on the little girls. Crimes like these feed into the fears of every parent who, at the back of their mind, is terrified that harm will come to their child.

At the youth's 26 February 1979 committal hearing, Constable Dawson told the court about the day he found the little girls. Dawson said he had entered the bushland near the creek reserve and seen 'the face of a child looking at me. It was covered in dry blood.' He also detailed how he saw the body of a second girl with a large pool of blood beneath her head.

Magda, the survivor of the horrific attacks, did not appear in court to give evidence. Her father presented the court with a doctor's certificate to excuse his daughter from the court proceeding.

Police surrounded the children's court building in Glebe during the hearing because around 30 people were protesting with placards and calling for the return of the death penalty.

The young man was committed to stand trial for murder and attempted murder. He pleaded guilty to both charges and received two life sentences on 1 June 1979.

Justice David Yeldham said, 'No words of mine could properly describe the enormity of the crime.'

The convicted killer died in December 1995 at age 34.

* * *

The year before, Justice Yeldham had also handed down two life sentences to another teen killer.

On 30 March 1978, an 18-year-old man gripped the dock railings and closed his eyes as Justice Yeldham told the former shop worker that he would spend a very long time in prison.

In 1976, the then-16-year-old had sexually assaulted and murdered 12-year-old Sydney boy Garry Barkemeyer. Months later, the teen, now 17, struck again and stabbed 12-year-old Wayne Nixon to death after sexually assaulting the boy. He was considered extremely dangerous by the judge and the doctors who gave evidence for the court case.

On a Friday afternoon, 9 July 1976, the offender (who was under 18 when he committed the murders so is not named here) lured Garry Barkemeyer into a hidden part of Glebe's Jubilee Park with the promise of a few dollars to help him stack boxes. Garry had been with an eight-year-old mate, and the two boys followed the teen's instructions and waited for him at some sheds under the railway line, which ran through the large park. The two playmates had been trying out a yo-yo Garry had just bought with his pocket money when they encountered the older boy, who was tall and had shoulder-length, brown hair. The teen arrived 30 minutes later and told the younger boy to wait while he and Garry stacked the boxes. The boy later told police the teen had told him he was too young to help.

Garry was led away along a secluded path and attacked by the teen, who fatally struck him on the head with a rock, breaking his skull. He came back and told the younger lad that Garry had already left.

Garry's mother, Hildegard, reported her son missing to police on Sunday afternoon. Mrs Barkemeyer was living at a women's refuge in Glebe with Garry and her five-year-old daughter. Garry had returned home from school, quickly changed and headed out with his friend.

It wasn't until the younger boy's mother heard that Garry had not gone to school on the following Monday that police had any real leads on his whereabouts. Garry's mate led police to the area where he had last seen his friend. It was here that police made the tragic discovery of Garry's body in the bushes near the railway line. Garry had died from massive head injuries and his clothes were in disarray, which led detectives to believe there was a sexual motive to the crime.

After Garry's murder, fear rippled through the area, with parents reluctant to let their children play on the streets and telling them to beware of any strangers.

In October 1976, a A$100 000 reward was offered for information that could lead to Garry's killer.

On 30 January 1977, Wayne Nixon was enjoying his last days of summer before he was to start high school. He was riding his new bike, to which he had strapped a transistor radio, and was relishing the freedom that comes with having a set of wheels and not a care in the world. He had set off from his Kingston Road home in the inner-city suburb of Camperdown to visit a friend who wasn't home.

A witness saw Wayne being given a 'double' on a bike by a youth fitting the teen killer's description, along nearby Cardigan Road. It was not certain whether it was Wayne's bike he was on, but it's unlikely that the youngster would have left his new transport that he'd been so excited about receiving for his birthday in the September of 1976.

Wayne's partially clothed body was found dumped in thick bush against a fence in Jubilee Park, Glebe, in the same area where Garry Barkemeyer had been murdered. Wayne had been sexually assaulted and stabbed multiple times, including in the heart. Wayne had several cuts on his hands, which indicated he'd tried to fight off his killer.

The park was 2.5 kilometres away from where Wayne had last been sighted. Wayne's mother Hazel told reporters that it was unlikely her son had gone by himself to Jubilee Park.

'He used to go there with his friends, but after the Barkemeyer murder, I told him to never go there on his own,' Mrs Nixon shared with *The Sydney Morning Herald*.

Wayne's stepbrother Robert, 32, thought his little brother must have trusted whoever killed him.

'To have gone off with this youth, he must have known him for a period of time somewhere,' Robert said.

Wayne's bicycle was found in the Paramatta River, behind a psychiatric hospital a few kilometres from where his body was found. Police interviewed staff and patients of the hospital, hoping for more clues to the identity of the child's killer. The transistor radio that had been tied to the bike was also found separately to the bicycle and handed to police.

Hundreds of anonymous leads were given to the Homicide Squad after the murders of the boys, which happened almost eight months apart. Most of the information was worthless, but there were a few calls to police that would prove valuable.

The Homicide Squad was led by Harry Tupman, a revered detective who had arrested Ronald Ryan, the last man hanged in Australia, and was part of the team that solved the 1960 kidnap and murder of Sydney boy Graeme Thorne. Graeme's father had won the 1960 £100 000 Opera House Lottery (worth more than A$3 million in today's money).

A combination of information given to police by two witnesses about the teen seen 'doubling' with Wayne just prior to his death, and phone calls on the evening of his murder were the key to catching the killer, though police didn't know it at the time.

Detectives had to track back through calls received to make the connection.

An exclusive *Daily Telegraph* article in March 1978, 'Trapped by a whodunnit twist' detailed how detectives caught the killer.

Detectives took another look at phone calls made to Glebe Police Station on the evening Wayne's body was found on 31 January.

There was a phone call at 5.10pm. The caller, who sounded young, told the officer at the desk 'there is a body near the railway line at Jubilee Oval'. The senior constable probed the caller for more information. 'Is the person drunk?', he asked the caller, thinking it could be someone passed out.

'No, he is dead,' the caller replied. 'It is a boy about 13, and he is covered in blood.'

The senior constable told the caller to wait at the scene before giving directions to colleagues to search the area around the railway line.

As described verbatim in *The Daily Telegraph* article, the caller phoned back at 6.15pm: 'I rang a while ago about the boy's body near the railway line. I am ringing from Johnston Street, Annandale, and I have seen a fellow in the street with blood on his shirt.'

The policeman said, 'Don't let him out of your sight.'

The caller then told the policeman that the man had got into a brown Holden Sedan and described the number plate and gave a name and address for the man with the 'bloodied shirt', which was Barry John Gay.

There was no one with that name at the address; however, the car was in the street. Police quickly ruled out the owner of the car as being involved in Wayne's murder.

When the Homicide Squad re-examined the phone calls, Detective Inspector Tupman told his squad to track down the person named by the mystery caller. They didn't know if this person existed, but DI Tupman wanted all efforts made to find them.

Tupman and one of his sergeants found a woman whose husband and son shared the same name given by the young man who called police on the day Wayne's body was discovered.

The woman's husband and son worked at a newsagents in Enmore, a suburb in inner-western Sydney. The men were interviewed by detectives who wanted to know why the mystery caller would implicate their names in the murder of a child. The pieces of the mystery started to come together when the manager of the newsagents, Ken Fizzell, rang detectives to tell them about a feud the previous year in 1976 that Barry John Senior and Barry John Junior had with a teenager, who also worked at the shop.

The teenager had a grudge with the family because of something that happened when his father went into hospital. The teen was living with his father and three siblings in Marrickville at the time, and Mr Gay and his family had offered to help by looking after the teen's little sister, who was 13 years old.

For reasons not explained in the article in *The Daily Telegraph*, the family couldn't continue to have the girl stay in the home, and this caused the teen great distress. He thought it was wrong to eject his sister from the Gay family home while his father was in hospital.

Barry John Junior caught wind that the teen was going around claiming that Barry's father was fiddling the tills at the newsagents. This resulted in a physical fight between Barry John Junior and the teen.

The name of this teen was revealed to detectives by the shop manager Mr Fizzell, and they wasted no time doing door-to-door investigations to locate the youth.

During the door knock, they located a young man who, at first, told them he couldn't help with any information, but he did say, as reported by *The Daily Telegraph*, 'This bastard's got us all worried. The sooner you get him, the better. I'm not kidding, I'm even scared to go to the shop over the road when it gets dark.'

The detectives' interests were piqued by this youth, and the next day they visited him at the supermarket where he now worked and asked the teen to escort them to the Glebe Police Station.

Detectives organised a line-up of young men similar in age and appearance to the youth they were questioning.

When one of the detectives, Detective Sergeant Angus McDonald, told the teen that he'd been identified from a line-up as the person who was on the bicycle with Wayne, he said, 'She's a liar; she doesn't know what she's talking about.'

A few moments of silence later, he reportedly broke down and confessed. 'Yes, it was me on the bike, and I killed him,' the teen told detectives. 'I stabbed him and that is all to it. I told lies because I never thought I would get caught'.

He was charged with the murders of Garry and Wayne.

A black-and-white mug shot of the murderer that was splashed on the front page of Sydney newspapers showed a young-looking 17-year-old staring at the camera. The term 'baby-faced' would be apt to describe him.

The teen's confession, detailed in his March 1978 trial and reported in newspapers, is distressing.

When describing the murder of Wayne Nixon to Detective Sergeant McDonald he said, 'I don't know how many times I stabbed him. I was trying to have sex with him, but he kept struggling.'

Detective Sergeant McDonald told the court he asked the teen what Wayne's last words were before he was murdered.

'Don't do it to me,' he recalled.

He was found guilty of both murders.

In sentencing the teenager on 30 March 1978 for the murders of Garry and Wayne, Justice David Yeldham said, 'This case is indeed a tragic one; tragic mainly because two innocent young lives have been taken, and two families have been plunged into grief. Tragic also because you were at the time of the first murder but 16 years old ... and when you killed the boy Nixon, you had just turned 17. You are now only 18 years old .... I have given long and anxious consideration to the penalty which I should impose on you. Because of your age at the time you committed these offences, the usual sentence of life imprisonment is not a mandatory one. This court's first duty in a case of this nature is to ensure the protection of other members of the community, whether young or old. You have already killed twice, and each murder was callous and completely unprovoked. I must ensure as best I can that you are not given the opportunity to do so again. I consider it probable that you will at least for a long time be a danger to others …. In addition, the enormity of the crimes that you committed upon two innocent young boys is such that I can find no mitigating circumstances which would justify me in extending to you the mercy which you did not show in any measure to your young victims …'

The young killer was sentenced to 'penal servitude' for life (life imprisonment), though this was not a mandatory life sentence, with Justice Yeldham saying that due to his young age, he must be given all opportunity to undergo intensive treatment while in jail and be allowed to continue his education. The convicted killer, who started his life sentence as an 18-year-old, was released from prison in 1993.

* * *

Author's note: In 2014, after the publication of *Murder in Suburbia*, where this case chapter originally appeared, I was contacted by a retired priest who had counselled the youth while he was awaiting trial. He sent me a thoughtful letter, noting the dedication of the book 'for the victims of homicide whose stories are featured in this book' and that he appreciated the 'writing about the lives of the victims and the families so devastated by the murders of Garry Barkemeyer and Wayne Nixon … Justice Yeldham spoke of their grief in his judgment'.

I was touched by the letter and that the retired priest had taken the time to write and tell me about his connection to these murders.

He told me he was contacted by a police officer assisting with the prosecution case, suggesting the young man might need some support (as preparation for the inevitability of conviction and a possible life sentence in prison).

The priest visited him several times, and he provided a report that was tendered to the court and read by Justice Yeldham. He appeared as a witness during the trial to confirm that the statements in that report were 'true and correct' to the best of his knowledge. The report detailed, as told to him by the youth, some of the circumstances of his life, including the death of his father in 1976, a few months after he murdered Garry Barkemeyer.

The priest said in his report that he tried to 'suspend his own judgments' on the offender's behaviour and not offer any opinions. The report was intended as a recollection of his conversations with the youth while he was held at the Metropolitan Boys' Shelter in Sydney, awaiting trial, in case it was of any use in sentencing and while the young man was incarcerated.

* * *

Earlier in the decade, New South Wales was shocked by a murder that was committed by two girls. Dubbed the 'bikini cord murder' and the 'babysitters murder' by newspapers, the killing of three-year-old Daniel Hay defied the belief of most people's imaginations.

On 19 December 1971, a 14-year-old girl and her 18-year-old friend, Deslie Pamela Raymond, were babysitting at the home of the younger girl's sister in Wyoming, near Gosford. The girls had four children under five years old in their charge that night:

the younger girl's sister's two children and her sister's friend's children, little Daniel and his older sister. The two couples had left the children with the teenage girls while they went to a Christmas party nearby.

Deslie Raymond was not known to the sister of the 14-year-old, but the adults had no reason not to trust the pair with babysitting the children.

During the night, the girls went into the room where three-year-old Daniel was sleeping and tied a cord from a bikini around his neck, and then each girl pulled an end. The little boy was strangled to death. As if that was not horrific enough, the girls then hit him on the head with a saucepan, which fractured his tiny skull, held a pillow over his face and stabbed him in the stomach to make sure he was dead.

Afterwards, the girls tried to cover up their crime by slitting a flywire screen on the window of the bedroom to give the impression that an intruder had killed the little boy.

At 10.25 p.m., the younger babysitter went to a neighbour and told her that someone had broken into the house and killed Daniel. But the girls' story fell apart and Raymond broke down and confessed, saying that it had been her young companion's idea to commit the murder.

It was alleged in court that in her record of interview, Raymond said the girls had been watching television when her 14-year-old friend said she wanted 'to kill Danny'.

'I was not really keen at first, but I guess she talked me into it,' Raymond said.

Raymond allegedly told police during the interview that she had tried to stab the boy with a knife from the kitchen.

The 14-year-old girl told police that it was Raymond who hit little Danny on the head with the saucepan and that she held his nose while the older girl tried to strangle him again.

It would have been hard for the police to hide their shock.

A psychiatrist employed to assess the 14-year-old advised that the girl would need psychiatric care for many years.

Their trial judge, Justice Begg, was explicit in his words about the crime during the May 1972 trials. When sentencing the 14-year-old to life imprisonment, Justice Begg said the girl had taken part in a 'foul and monstrous crime on an innocent and defenceless victim'.

Raymond was also sentenced to life.

In November 1972, the girls won an appeal against their sentences because it was found the trial judge did not instruct the jury that it was open to return a verdict of manslaughter rather than murder.

One of the three appeals court judges, Justice Jacobs, said although the teens' assertion that they didn't intend to kill little Daniel seemed 'far-fetched', it could have been taken into consideration when the first jury decided their verdict.

'It was obligatory on the trial judge to explain to the jury how the absence of an intent to kill and the absence of a realisation that the act or acts done was or were likely to cause death could reduce the crimes from murder to manslaughter," Justice Jacobs said.

A retrial began in December 1972. Again, both girls pleaded not guilty. The newspapers also included the detail that it was an all-male jury this time, and they reached their verdict of guilty after a 20-minute retirement.

From the dock during the two-day retrial, Raymond, by now 19, said, 'I did not intend to kill or harm that poor darling child. It is like a nightmare. I am not guilty, and I am terribly sorry.'

The younger girl, aged 15 at the retrial, also expressed her remorse. 'I am not guilty of this crime. I don't know what came over us .... I didn't mean to do it. I am just sorry. I didn't mean to hurt him. I am just sorry.'

The judge for their retrial, Justice McClemens, said the case was 'beyond experience' and one that could never be believed possible.

'I have never known a case like it in 31 years on the bench,' Justice McClemens said.

He also said that despite Raymond being four years older than her accomplice, he felt the younger girl had heavily influenced her.

It was reported that the younger girl had tried to take her own life the day after her sentencing.

In the days before New South Wales' Children's (Criminal Proceedings) Act 1987, juvenile offenders were named and their photographs printed in the press. Photos of the 'bikini cord murder' girls were used prominently at the time. When the youngest girl was found guilty, her face was plastered on the front page of newspapers. The photo of an angelic-looking, smiling blonde stared out from the cover of a daily tabloid.

On 28 December 1974, it was reported that the younger girl, then 17, was on the run from the Parramatta Girls' Training Centre. The girl and four other inmates had climbed a three-metre-high wall in the exercise yard the day before. A spokesman for the Department of Youth and Community Services told the media the girl had been a model prisoner and that it was a shame that she'd 'spoilt her record'. Police warned the public that the girl could be dangerous.

The girl was captured three days later at her parents' home.

A 1978 *Sydney Morning Herald* article reported that the younger girl, now 20, was being prepared for release and may have been transferred to a minimum-security prison.

They were both released from prison in 1997.

This crime shocked even the world-weariest in the legal profession.

The teen girl killers would now be aged in their 60s. Have they had their own children? Did they have their identities changed? *Why did they kill a child?*

EVIL GREED

Adelaide pensioner Vonne McGlynn had her daily rituals. The fiercely independent 82-year-old was a regular sight walking up and down Somerfield Avenue, Reynella, where she had lived on her own for many years. Her nearest neighbours knew her as well as the elderly woman would allow, and at the very least, it was the kind of street where people would nod and say hello to each other.

Reynella is a suburb located 20 kilometres south of Adelaide's CBD, in the north of the City of Onkaparinga. Somerfield Avenue is a long, tidy and friendly street, well located near schools, transport and a hub of fast food restaurants on the main road.

Ms McGlynn would often venture to the local McDonald's, around 1.5 kilometres from her home, and order her favourite breakfast: bacon and egg McMuffin. And Ms McGlynn was fastidious and very organised. Her home was neat and simple. She didn't go for frills, and her home decor hadn't changed much over the years. Her kitchen refrigerator, which had been a gift in 1958, was still in perfect working order. She was, by all accounts from family and friends, very happy in her cosy little three-bedroom home.

Despite her age, Ms McGlynn was in generally good health and very active. She was an avid traveller and would often book short breaks away, usually day trips. Whenever she did, Ms McGlynn would dutifully notify the Red Cross, who gave her a welfare call each morning, to advise them that she did not require the service. Though she lived alone, Ms McGlynn was not a lonely woman. Her emergency contacts, provided to the Red Cross, were her younger brother Donald Smallwood, who lived interstate, and her next-door neighbours Roger and Sharon Zadow.

The Zadows kept an eye on Ms McGlynn. They had lived next door for 17 years. Mrs Zadow would cook extra meals for her neighbour – curries were gratefully received – and when Ms McGlynn was away, they would put her bins out and collect any mail. And it was reciprocated, with Ms McGlynn walking the Zadows' dogs or feeding their chickens while the family was away.

In August 2008, Ms McGlynn broke her arm, and this caused her to have to accept more help than she would usually have liked – Meals On Wheels for a while and some assistance to shower. Mrs Zadow thought a toaster might make things easier for Ms McGlynn and bought her one so that that she could make quick and easy meals while she had her arm in plaster.

Mrs Zadow often drove Ms McGlynn to the doctor, and on one of these trips, the pensioner mentioned that a young woman had come around to her house, asking to be her carer. Ms McGlynn said the young woman had banged on the front door, saying she knew Ms McGlynn had broken her arm and was asking whether she wanted a carer. Very careful about who she let into her home, Ms McGlynn told the woman through the security-door screen that she did not need a carer, but that didn't stop the persistent stranger, who then went around knocking on the windows of the house and insisting that she be hired.

'You need a carer. I want to be your carer. You can pay me, and I can move in,' said the woman.

Former neighbour and good friend Therese Molloy also found out about this strange visit when she was chatting to Ms McGlynn in November 2008. It would be the last time they ever spoke. Ms Molloy urged her friend, who over the years had been a de facto grandmother to her three children, to tell the police.

While Ms McGlynn didn't know the identity of the woman, she told her friends and brother that she thought she was from 'down the street'. By all accounts, Ms McGlynn was annoyed and upset by the incident.

On the evening of 2 December, Ms McGlynn had a conversation with her brother and told him she had hurt her wrist after a fall, and it wasn't healing well. The next morning, between 7 a.m. and 9 a.m., she received her daily call from the Red Cross.

So when on 4 December 2008, the Red Cross call went unanswered, the volunteer phoned the local police station. The volunteer knew Ms McGlynn's habits and that it was highly unusual that she would go away without letting the service know.

The first police visit came around 10.30 a.m. that morning, and the officers looked around the property, spoke to neighbours but did not enter the house. A short time later, an officer gained entry to the house by breaking a rear window and entering through the laundry. The officer cut himself in the process and went to the bathroom to wash his hand. He noticed that the house seemed tidy, but there was a hole in the ceiling where a manhole cover would usually be.

Another officer arrived at 1 p.m. and left a card in the letterbox to say that police had called around and that they had damaged a window. There was no lack of officers checking on Vonne McGlynn's home, because at around 9.50 p.m. that same day, three uniformed police officers went to the house after a neighbour had reported that the front door had been left open.

There was still no sign of Ms McGlynn, but what would later become apparent when the police compared notes, was that someone else had accessed the property between 11.30 a.m. and 9 p.m., as the house had been left untidy, with rubbish bags strewn over the floors of the rooms.

Several more visits occurred between 5 December and 9 December.

When neighbour Mr Zadow mentioned to a police officer that there were tiles missing from Ms McGlynn's roof and that he wanted to replace them, the officer told Mr Zadow he could also board up the window that had been broken.

Still, there was no sign of Ms McGlynn, but someone had definitely been in her home.

Meanwhile, on 9 December, police received a call from the Morphett Vale ANZ bank branch. A woman had attempted to withdraw A$2000 from Ms McGlynn's account by using her bankcard. The woman had presented a power of attorney form to a bank teller who had seen reports of Ms McGlynn's disappearance.

The woman was Latvian-born Angelika Gavare, a mother-of-two in her early thirties, who lived in Christie Downs and had never banked at the Morphett Vale branch before. Gavare had moved to Australia in 2001 on a spousal visa. Christie Downs was another suburb in the City of Onkaparinga region.

The bank teller phoned the missing persons unit of South Australia Police to report the encounter. The police officer she spoke to, Constable Robyn Ferraro, then phoned Gavare to find out why she was trying to withdraw money from the missing woman's account.

Gavare told Constable Ferraro that she was a friend who helped Ms McGlynn and that she had been asked by the pensioner to withdraw money to do some improvements on the Somerfield Avenue house.

Gavare was interviewed several times in December, including the day she had attempted to use Ms McGlynn's bankcard.

The young mother told the police that she did not realise that Ms McGlynn was missing but that she had last seen her on 27 November and had been given the pensioner's bankcard.

Gavare painted a picture to police that she knew Ms McGlynn very well and described her as an 'independent and mentally ok' woman who walked to the shops a lot.

'All old ladies, they, you know, tell their stories,' Gavare told police when she said she would have cups of tea with Ms McGlynn and chat at the Somerfield address.

Gavare said she had visited Ms McGlynn around eight times in two years. This, however, was at complete odds with evidence from those closest to the pensioner, such as the neighbours, who, despite living next door for 17 years, told police that they has only ever set foot is Ms McGlynn's home around eight times in total.

Meanwhile, Ms McGlynn's brother and friends were desperately worried for the pensioner, fearing the worst.

On 23 December 2008, Ms McGlynn failed to show up for an organised tour to Portland, Victoria, which she had previously booked and paid for. As Ms McGlynn was careful with her money and let people know when she was away, not going on the trip was highly suspicious.

There were public appeals for information, and Mr Smallwood told *The Advertiser* newspaper that he thought his sister was dead.

'She wasn't wealthy, and I can't see any motive for anyone wanting to harm her. But she's not the type to just go missing,' Mr Smallwood told *The Advertiser*.

Police had their sights on Gavare. The story she told with such confidence and ease did not seem right at all to investigators. They had built a profile of Vonne McGlynn, and the story from Gavare about being given access to her accounts and home did not match the habits of the quiet and private pensioner.

When police visited Gavare's home in the weeks after Ms McGlynn was last seen, they found some of Ms McGlynn's possessions there, including her passport, house keys and purse. There were personal bills and photographs as well – some of them were of the Molloy's three children, who were like grandchildren to Ms McGlynn. And there was a toaster – the one that Mrs Zadow had bought for Ms McGlynn (she identified it for investigators). In fact, it was the discovery of the toaster and a nest of tables that led a police officer at the scene – Detective

Sergeant Matthew Fitzpatrick – to strongly suspect that Ms McGlynn had been murdered.

Police kept working away in the background. The house in Somerfield Avenue was now a crime scene and the spotlight was firmly on Angelika Gavare.

Gavare's link with Somerfield Avenue was her mother Inara Dombrovska, who also lived on Somerfield Avenue and knew Ms McGlynn by sight. Gavare had lived with her mother before moving to her own home in Christie Downs, so she knew the area well.

The very worst news for Ms McGlynn's brother and close friends came in late February.

Some of Ms McGlynn's remains – a leg and torso – were found in a place called Christie Creek, and the location was right near Gavare's Scottsglade Road home. The decomposed state of Ms McGlynn's remains meant that a cause of death could not be determined, but it was obvious that someone had dismembered her body with a saw-like instrument. One of the body parts recovered included an artificial hip joint and its serial number was matched to Ms McGlynn.

Police also found fragments of a statue, which they believed to be from Ms McGlynn's home, and a pram. The pram would become an important part of the case they were building around Gavare being the killer of the elderly woman.

Gavare was arrested and charged with the murder of Ms McGlynn.

What followed was a case that shocked South Australia and uncovered one of the most callous killers Australia has ever seen. The case ended up one of the most shocking and bizarre in South

Australian criminal history, and that is no mean feat, considering the state's world notoriety for violent and gruesome murders.

Gavare made an application for a trial in front of a judge only because she feared any jury would be influenced by a series of newspaper articles about other murders of three other elderly women in their homes – there had been the spate of violent killings on lone women. Her application was granted, and her trial began in front of Justice Trish Kelly in 2011.

The evidence that was so damning for Gavare came from those closest to her.

A key piece of evidence against Gavare was the pram found at the creek. Her sister, Agnes Dombrovska, saw a news report in late February 2009 about the police discovery of the pram. The dark-blue cloth design with teddy bear print looked very familiar to her.

Phoning the police, Ms Dombrovska told them it was similar to one she had used to take her children to a playground near her mother's Somerfield Avenue home. The pram kept at her mother's also had a missing screw, which caused a lower beam to dangle down. The pram found at the creek also had a missing screw.

Several witnesses reported seeing a young woman walking by the creek with a pram filled with oddly shaped garbage bags in the days after Ms McGlynn's disappearance.

Director of Public Prosecutions Stephen Pallaras, QC, said Gavare used the pram to move Ms McGlynn's body parts for disposal, as well as other items from the pensioner's home that Gavare did not want.

Ms Dombrovska also said she was disturbed by the reaction of her sister, the prime suspect by that stage, when pressed about the missing woman.

'She just laughed,' Ms Dombrovska said. 'She just laughed it off, and I found that a bit odd … it was not a laughing matter.'

And it was not only her sister to whom she had joked about the murder. An ex-boyfriend of Gavare's, Ejaz Ahmed, said he and the accused had used an electric chainsaw when they were renovating a bathroom at the time of Ms McGlynn's disappearance. Mr Ahmed said he asked Gavare if she had done something to the old woman, and she laughed and joked, saying, 'Yes.'

Mr Ahmed ceased contact with Gavare after her arrest and was upset that she had implicated him in Ms McGlynn's murder, including the grisly accusation that he had disposed of the pensioner's head and hands for her during a time when he was on a trip to Pakistan.

Gavare's mother testified against her daughter in court, which turned out to be one of the most dramatic moments of the trial.

Gavare had told her mother a story on Christmas Eve, just a few weeks after Ms McGlynn was last seen, about what happened to the elderly woman. Knowing her daughter had something to do with the disappearance, Mrs Dombrovska demanded her daughter tell her what happened otherwise they could not celebrate Christmas together.

It was then that Gavare told her mother she had had been watching Ms McGlynn for a while and had gained entry to the 'old woman's' house while she was on her regular breakfast trip to McDonald's. When Ms McGlynn returned home, Gavare told her mother that she made her 'unconscious' and searched through the house. Gavare left the pensioner in the house and then returned later that evening, where she claimed Ms McGlynn was now dead. Mrs Dombrovska said her daughter told her she then wrapped Ms McGlynn's body in plastic sheets and had taken her away where the police would never find her.

No doubt reeling from the words coming from her daughter's mouth, Mrs Dombrovska was further shocked when Gavare said she had faked the power of attorney form and intended to use it to sell Ms McGlynn's house.

Mrs Dombrovska also told police and the court that she saw a little wooden table with carved legs and a toaster on top when she was at her daughter's home on 6 December 2008 to celebrate Gavare's birthday. Gavare told her mother that she had bought the table in a garage sale. However, the table was, of course, from the house of Ms McGlynn.

Gavare's day on the stand came and brought with it another shock turn. She had elected to give evidence after the prosecution had finished their case presentation.

Gavare told the court that while she did forge power of attorney documents to get access to Ms McGlynn's assets, she did not murder her. Gavare did admit though that she lied to police. In a complete backflip from the original story, she told police about being asked to renovate Ms McGlynn's home, and she also pinned the pensioner's death on her ex-partner, Giuseppe Daniele, who was the father of her youngest child.

Gavare's story was that Mr Daniele killed Ms McGlynn in an accidental hit-and-run car crash before forcing her to help him to stage a robbery as a cover-up, which explained why she had the woman's personal items at her home.

'It occurred to me that I could use the situation for my profit,' Gavare said in front of Justice Kelly.

'I lied because I felt that since I started lying I could not stop lying, and I had to continue with the story I made up,' she said.

Gavare had also admitted she had a history of dishonesty, having been dismissed from her newsagency employment for stealing co-workers' ID and bankcards, as well as banking letters from a mailbox. She admitted that she had forged powers of attorney before.

Mr Daniele had been called to give evidence too and said his ex-girlfriend was a compulsive liar whom he had not seen for several years. He had an alibi for the timeframe of Ms McGlynn's alleged murder and said he was at a nephew's birthday party 30 kilometres away from Somerfield Avenue.

Gavare's defence grilled Mr Daniele and put to him that he had threatened the accused if she did not help him cover up Ms McGlynn's death. Mr Daniele said Gavare's story was laughable.

He told the defence lawyer Grant Algie, QC, that he had never threatened Ms Gavare or knocked on her door on the night it was alleged Ms McGlynn was killed.

'No, you're absolutely wrong .... I get a bad vibe when I speak to Angelika,' Mr Daniele said.

There was no love lost between the pair. Their short relationship, which resulted in the birth of their daughter in 2005, had ended badly and they were in the midst of a custody battle over the child. Mr Daniele's sister had also given evidence to back up his assertion that he had been at his nephew's 12th birthday party on the evening of 3 December. Justice Kelly remarked that she was satisfied beyond a reasonable doubt that he had nothing to do with the disappearance and death of the pensioner.

Gavare's story was not holding up to scrutiny. There was too much evidence pointing to the fact that she was the killer.

While there was no forensic evidence to link her with the murder at the Somerfield Avenue house, blood was found in the boot of Gavare's car that was a match to Ms McGlynn. A police officer also testified that when searching Gavare's backyard, he had detected a smell of 'rotting flesh' in her shed, which led him to search her car. The constable said the car boot was in pristine condition, unlike the rest of the vehicle, and appeared to have been vacuumed.

The prosecution alleged that the car had been used to transport Ms McGlynn from Somerfield Avenue to Gavare's Christie Downs home.

There was also the internet browser history on Gavare's home computer that showed she had searched for information on 4 December about ANZ accounts, which directly linked with paperwork she had in her possession belonging to Ms McGlynn.

The case transfixed South Australians who were kept up to date with the latest court reports from the city's media, including newspaper *The Advertiser*. One of the most sensational days of evidence came on 17 August when a former prison cellmate of Gavare's told the court that the accused had confessed to her and had found the murder 'a bit of a turn on'.

Amanda Jayne Patterson, who, in the end, was not deemed by Justice Kelly to be a very reliable witness, appeared for the prosecution and said Gavare had told her about the murder while they were in Adelaide Women's Prison together. Ms Patterson was also facing other charges for dishonesty at the time. Ms Patterson said Gavare told her she believed that if the police could not find the head or the hands of Ms McGlynn, there would be no case against her. Gavare's lawyer, Mr Algie, called Ms Patterson a liar and thief who could not be believed, which enraged the woman.

'I don't know how you sleep at night knowing you are defending a murderer!' Ms Patterson shouted in court.

On 30 August 2011, the Supreme Court found Gavare guilty of Ms McGlynn's murder. In her sentencing of Gavare on 4 November 2011, Justice Kelly said the killer had been motivated by 'nothing more than sheer greed' and said her crime was in the worst category. Sentencing Gavare to life imprisonment with a minimum sentence of 32 years, Justice Kelly called her a 'greedy, narcissistic and deceitful woman'.

'There is no evidence of any remorse or contrition. You have not even had the decency to give some small solace to the family and friends of Ms McGlynn by revealing how and where you disposed of the head and hands of this most unfortunate woman.'

Justice Kelly also noted that Gavare's actions meant that her daughters would grow up without their mother and that they too were victims of the horrific crime.

On 4 May 2012, an appeal against her sentence was dismissed in the South Australian Court of Criminal Appeal.

To date, Gavare has not revealed where she disposed of the head and hands of Vonne McGlynn.

In an interview for a News Corp Australia podcast called *On Guard – Stories from Inside Australia's Toughest Prisons*, former prison officer Jennifer Kaschau shared about her time working at Adelaide Women's Prison. One of the prisoners she managed was Angelika Gavare.

'I had a conversation with a prisoner who had been released and had spent time in the same protection unit as her [Gavare], and she said that she sat there one night and told them all about how … "there's nothing like the blood splashing up on the walls"… was quite animated about discussing what she'd done to this old lady, how she cut her up in the bathroom of her own house,' Jennifer Kaschau recalled.

'And she said "they will never find the head and the hands"… so that to me questions …was there another person involved that they've just missed or she's maybe, protected?'

The former prison officer said Gavare was 'cold'.

'She's not someone that you would ever approach by yourself. You'd have someone right next you, just in case, because we just did not trust what she was capable of,' Jennifer told podcast host Amelia Saw.

She also shared, 'She was scary.'

THE KILLING
'BOUND TO HAPPEN'

It was a Saturday night on 1 April 1967, and Margaret Anne Pavarno was working alone at the TAB betting shop she managed in Mont Albert, an eastern suburb of Melbourne.

TAB 'Totaliser Agency Board' branches were a place where people could put a bet on the horse or greyhound racing, though nowadays the operations are mainly online, and physical outlets are disappearing each year. Horserace betting was regulated in 1961 in Victoria. The State Government owned and operated the TAB, and it generated taxes from agency licences with money put back into the racing industry. SP Bookmakers, 'bookies', still took bets on the racecourses, but now people could pop into their local TAB shop and place a bet.

The TAB in Victoria was privatised by the Kennett State Government in 1994, creating a publicly owned company: TABCORP Holdings Limited. The move was intended to protect the state's racing industry, which, according to Racing Victoria, generates A$3.2 billion to the state's economy. Victoria was the first State Government in Australia to sell a betting business.

In a 2014 article in *The West Australian* at the time when the state was considering selling its betting business, Jeff Kennett, who was the Premier of Victoria from 1992–1999, was quoted: 'If, when we sold the Victorian TAB, we knew what was going to happen with corporate bookmaking, we wouldn't have done it,' Mr Kennett said.

Corporate bookmakers now have a huge presence in the gambling industry, with punters offered an array of choices where they can place bets, mostly online and using apps. These companies don't have to put money back into the industries they profit from.

Margaret, 36, was the manager of the Mont Albert branch, located at 4 Churchill Street in the suburb's shopping village.

It was a job that came with risk. Saturday was a big day for TAB agencies, and the day's takings were not collected until the following Monday. That meant crooks knew that the outlets would be flushed with cash that would be stored away in safes.

TAB agencies had been targets of armed robberies since the agency started operations in 1961. In fact, the 1960s were a hectic time for armed robberies, and the previous year there'd been eight hold-ups at TABs. And by April 1967, there'd been five. TABs were seen as easy targets by greedy and desperate criminals. But no killings had occurred yet, though police feared it was only a matter of time.

There were even two policemen who were sentenced for the late-night May 1967 armed hold-up of a TAB in Bendigo, a large rural city in Victoria, that netted more than A$2000 (around A$26 000 nowadays). A third unknown man was also involved in the armed robbery. The hooded trio threatened staff with guns as they demanded money, with one female employee later giving evidence that she 'almost keeled over' with fright. The assistant manager on the night even said he was 'in fear of his life' during the three-minute crime.

Alfred Wright, 41, who at the time of the hold-up was a senior constable at Highett Police Station (a south-east Melbourne suburb), was sentenced to ten years' hard labour.

Wright's lawyer was Frank Galbally, a legendary name in law in Victoria. Mr Galbally told the court before sentencing in September 1967 that his client should be treated the same as any other person who committed a similar offence, even though as a policeman, he was held to a higher community standard in the eyes of the public.

'What can we deduce from the fact that many lawyers and policemen have fallen by the wayside,' Mr Galbally said. 'Nothing but that they are human beings .... Mr Wright has been married happily for 21 years and reared a family. Now all is lost because of one stupid act.'

The jury agreed and recommended that Wright's previous character and record be taken into account when sentenced.

The other policeman who took part in the hold up, Allan Brown, disappeared while awaiting trial in 1967 and surrendered to police seven months later. Brown was also a senior constable at the time of the hold-up and stationed at West Brunswick Police Station.

Brown had ended up at a country property of some acquaintances and stayed there for the duration of his disappearance. He was also represented by Frank Galbally, who told the court his client has been experiencing serious mental health symptoms in the four years leading up to the Bendigo

TAB hold-up. Brown's first wife had been tragically killed by a hit-run driver, and his mental health, understandably, declined.

Brown was admitted to a psychiatric hospital soon after he was recommitted for trial in 1968.

Brown appeared in court in June 1968 and denied he was involved in the armed hold-up, telling the judge he failed to appear for trial the previous year because he 'couldn't bear the thought of being framed'. It had been alleged in court that Brown had admitted being involved in the crime while being interviewed.

He was convicted and sentenced to ten years' jail and told the court 'I was convicted on the evidence of perjured liars'.

In November 1966, two employees of a TAB branch in Essendon, in Melbourne's inner north-west, narrowly escaped being shot when an armed bandit attempting to jump the counter accidentally fired a sawn-off, double-barrelled shotgun into a wall partition. Manager Jesse Palmer and employee Edna Jeffs were less than one metre away.

The bandit apologised to the women, saying, 'I'm sorry, I didn't mean to do that', then ordered them to go into the back room. There were four other workers in the room – three women and a man, and they were told to line up against the wall. The manager was forced to fill an office drawer with money from the agency's safe – A\$5015 (worth around A\$68 000 today, according to the Reserve Bank of Australia's online inflation calculator).

On Saturday night, 1 April 1967, a Mont Albert resident, a waterside worker – referred to as Mr X (more about why later in this chapter) – wanted to place 'four double bets on the trots at the showgrounds'. After putting his children to bed, he left his home to walk to the Churchill Street TAB agency. It was a less than ten-minute walk, and Mr X left home just before 8.50 p.m. He arrived at the agency a few minutes before 9 p.m.

When he entered through the door, he saw Margaret Pavarno, followed by a man, entering the door to the staff area at the rear of the building.

Mr X moved to the counter to place his bets (he didn't realise until later that the cut-off for the races he wanted to punt on was 8.55 p.m.). He could see Margaret, who he knew by sight but not by name, and she was staring at him, silently mouthing words he couldn't decipher. He later told police that it could have been 'help me'.

The staff area was partitioned off, with five windows – perspex with four rows of three large holes – so agents and customers could talk to each other.

The back door of the agency was in his view, and he saw the man open the bolts on the door, then open it inward and peer outside.

The bandit, who'd been rifling through the office searching for money while pointing his pistol in her direction, then moved towards Margaret and said, 'Come on, hurry up and open that safe.'

Terrified, Margaret said, 'I don't know the combination.'

The bandit then turned his attention to the man who was on the other side of the office in the customer section of the branch. 'You stay where you are too,' he threatened, pointing the pistol at him.

Mr X noticed the man had a stocking over his head. However, Mr X, seeking to diffuse the situation said, 'Open the bloody door and I'll give you a hand.' He walked over to enter the office and was momentarily out of view of the gunman and Margaret.

Mr X said he heard the man say to Margaret, 'Come on, come on, open the safe,' and she told him, again, that she didn't know the combination.

Mr X then decided to escape and left the branch to run to the phone box opposite to call triple zero, the emergency services line. While doing so, he heard a shot and a woman's screams.

Printer Robert Wilmot had arrived at Churchill Street at 9 p.m. to check in on his business, which was next door to the TAB branch. He had a clear view into the betting shop and saw a man facing Margaret, pointing a small pistol at her. Robert also saw Mr X standing in the shop. Then, he saw the gunman back away towards the rear door, waving the gun at Margaret as he made his way out of the premises. Robert got back in his car and drove the short distance to the milk bar further up Churchill Street to phone the police.

Government clerk Barry Grant had awoken from a nap at 8.30 p.m. on 1 April, after an afternoon at the movies with a friend, and decided to head to the Mont Albert TAB to put a bet on a race. Barry knew he had to make it to the TAB by 9 p.m. to get his bet in on time, and at 8.50 p.m., he half-ran and walked the less than two kilometres from his Surrey Hills home to Churchill Street. He arrived at 8.58 p.m. Before he made it to the shop, he later recalled he heard a high-pitched scream.

There was no one else in the shop waiting to put a bet on, so Barry was confident he'd made it in time to place his. Before he could check the number of the horse he was keen on, he heard a groan from behind the counter and saw Margaret leaning near the shop's telephone. She had a red stain on the top part of her body.

'Help me, I've been shot,' she pleaded.

Barry ran to the phone box outside. It was one of two, and in the second one was Mr X, who Barry recognised from around the neighbourhood. Mr X had already called an ambulance, so the two men went to have a look at the laneway next to the TAB and were joined by another man, Frank Fecske, who'd also popped into the shop and seen Margaret, bleeding to death. Then she collapsed. The men tried to assist Margaret, with Frank trying to help her breathe by pressing on her back.

By the time police arrived, Margaret was dead.

Police searching the area the next morning found an inside out women's stocking with one end cut that had some dark hairs sticking inside, with the root still attached. The killer had pulled it off in haste during his getaway. It was found on the footpath on Mont Albert Road, near the intersection of Stanhope Street. The gunman would have exited the TAB via Mason Lane, which runs from Churchill Street to Mont Albert Road. The back door of the building leads onto this lane.

The killer bandit escaped with A$166 (now worth A$2000), and a woman was dead.

From the forensic investigation of the fired bullet and cartridge, as well as Margaret's shirt, singlet and bra, it was thought the muzzle of the pistol was less than two centimetres from her body.

The police were looking for a six-foot man (182 centimetres), with dark hair, who may have had a limp. Door-to-door enquiries didn't turn up much information, and despite much media coverage, the case went cold fast.

Safety at TAB agencies was, however, a hot topic after Margaret's killing.

The Age newspaper ran a headline on 4 April 1967: 'T.A.B. "Victim broke rules"', quoting a letter that TAB General Manager R.Y. Davis sent to all staff and agents about the robbery and tragic outcome.

'There were three unfortunate aspects of the hold-up. They were: the agent's refusal to open the safe; the fact that the agent was alone on the premises; the time taken by police to get to the agency.'

Another article: 'Crime and the T.A.B' in *The Age* published two days after the murder quoted an 'experienced' detective's views on how the TAB should improve safety and deter robberies. 'The first thing the TAB should not do is hire female managers or grant agency licences to women. The job needs a man at the grille and someone who looks like he can't be bluffed ...'.

On a Saturday afternoon on 23 September 1967, a woman employee of the Camberwell TAB was grabbed by an armed bandit as he made his escape with A$6500 (equivalent to A$84 000 today).

'I'll shoot her if you move,' he threatened the staff and one customer.

The branch was 300 metres from the Camberwell Police Station, but by the time officers arrived, he'd made his escape in a stolen getaway car with no numberplates. One of the employees, a woman, returning to the branch, saw what was happening and ran to the police station to alert them.

Newspapers reported that staff were so shocked after the raid (they'd been threatened with a rifle) that it took some time for them to communicate to police what had happened. Thoughts of what had happened to Margaret months earlier must have been on their minds.

The inquest into Margaret's murdered happened in April 1968. Mr X, the man who'd seen the killer, was still terrified, so much so the Coroner Harry Pascoe agreed to supress his identity.

Mr X spoke to a reporter for a 12 August article in *The Age*: 'Mr X waits for a killer to call'.

'I'll never forget that stockinged face, the flattened nose, and those white blobs of his eyes as the man turned towards me ...,' Mr X said. 'If I had stayed instead of running out to the telephone booth outside, I'm sure he would have killed me too.'

He also said, 'That murderer's eyes have burned into my brain. I know he'll recognise me if he sees me again.'

Mr X revealed to the reporter that only a few people knew he had witnessed the murder, and he was so fearful he'd requested to do day shifts at work. 'I dare not walk home alone at night. That man knows I am the only one alive who saw him.'

The coroner found that Margaret was murdered by 'a person unknown'.

Margaret's murder was featured as a case on an Australian television program in 1970 called *Wanted*, which was broadcast on GTV-9 (now known as the Nine Network). Viewers were urged to call the GTV-9 studio or Russell Street Police Station if they had any information on the Victorian crimes featured on the program.

The case faded into obscurity, and Victoria Police's Media Unit confirmed to me in a 2020 email that it was still unsolved.

It's unlikely Margaret's murder will ever be solved. Did the man who murdered her ever unburden himself to anyone? Is he still alive?

The site of Mont Albert TAB is currently the base for the Railfan Shop run by the Association of Railway Enthusiasts (Australia), and most people who walk along Churchill Street or visit that shop would not know of the tragic, unsolved murder there of a woman more than 50 years ago. The Association was formed in 1961 and has been based at Mont Albert since 2012, after more than 20 years in Melbourne's Central Business District.

I visited the shop on 24 December 2021 and volunteer Harry Jackson was kind enough to show me the back of the premises. The kitchen, back door, and window (with metal security bars) are still the same as when Margaret Pavarno worked there in 1967. (I compared these with photos I had seen in the inquest file for Margaret's murder at the Public Records Office Victoria.)

* * *

Author note: I accessed much of the information for this chapter from the inquest file into Margaret Pavarno's death. When I arrived at the Public Records Office Victoria in North Melbourne, the staff member who handed me the files I'd ordered to look through said, 'You realise there's crime scene photos in these? Just wanted to let you know.' (Many of these kinds of files will have a warning in the front of the folders.)

I nodded.

As I leafed through the file, I saw the crime scene photos of a deceased Margaret lying on the floor of the TAB office. It was jarring to see, and I felt sad thinking about the murder of this young woman who was survived by her mother and sister. (Margaret's father had died many years before her murder.) I would love to have known more about Margaret, not just about the shocking circumstances of her final moments and death. Who were her friends? What did she like to do?

Mrs Pavarno died in 1976, and Margaret's sister in 2012, never seeing the killer brought to justice.

The access path via Mason Lane to the rear door of the TAB site.
The armed robber who killed Margaret Pavarno exited this way
on the evening of 1 April 1967. (Supplied by author.)

The site where Margaret Pavarno was killed while working at the TAB outlet on Churchill Street Mont Albert. The building is now occupied by the Association of Railway Enthusiasts. (Supplied by author.)

The kitchen and rear window of 4 Churchill Street Mont Albert. The bars on the window and the kitchen are the same as when Margaret was working at the TAB more than 55 years ago. (Supplied by author.)

THE BURWOOD
TRIPLE MURDERS

An innocent classified advertisement in a Melbourne newspaper by students seeking a housemate led to some of the most cold-blooded murders the state of Victoria has ever seen. The perpetrator was a man named Ashley Mervyn Coulston.

Not many Victorians who were old enough at the time will forget the crime known as the 'Burwood Triple Murders'. On 29 July 1992, the lives of three young people – student teachers Kerryn Henstridge and Anne Smerdon, both 22 years old, and Anne's brother-in-law Peter Dempsey, 27 – were ended in a bloody execution in their share house in Summit Road, Burwood.

Anne and Kerryn knew each other from university. For the girls, both from country Victoria (Anne was from Kyabram and Kerryn from Hamilton) the Summit Road house was just minutes away from Deakin University where Kerryn was doing the fourth year of her Bachelor of Education. Peter, a Telecom engineer who lived in the large rural town of Shepparton, was visiting at the house that night. He regularly stayed at the house while attending training courses for his work. The third regular tenant, a man in his twenties, also from Hamilton, was away visiting his family.

On the evening of 29 July 1992, the girls were expecting a caller to interview as a possible housemate replacement for Kerryn, who was due to move back to Hamilton the next day. She had the opportunity to return to her hometown with her mother that night but had elected to stay until a tenant was found and the bond sorted out. Her mother, Jeanet, was staying with a family friend a few doors away in Summit Road.

Several people had answered the advertisement, including a 'Duncan', who had said he had recently moved from interstate and had asked, 'I'm 40 years old, is that a problem?' There was even a note by the telephone, written by Kerryn on the night of the murders: 'Anne, Duncan is coming over tonight. Don't worry, someone will be home. Kerryn.'

It is quite possible that this 'Duncan' could have been Coulston, but what is known is that more than one stranger was expected at Summit Road that Wednesday evening. One potential housemate, a young man, turned up at 8 p.m. to look at the place. He told police that he left after ten minutes, with the women telling him they would be in touch about the room. This is the last time the three were seen alive.

It is almost certain that Coulston had read and telephoned in response to the advertisement. Using a Melway street directory (Coulston's thumbprint was later found on the page that included Summit Road), he drove for over an hour from his Westernport Marina home in Hastings, more than 60 kilometres away, to

Burwood, arriving at the house after 8.30 p.m.

No one except Coulston, then aged 35, and his victims know what happened that night before their unfathomable and brutal execution. To this day, Coulston has never uttered a word about the crimes. He answered 'no comment' during the police interviews about the murders and stood mute during his trial.

Coulston went to the Burwood house with a bag containing a .22 rifle, a silencer, ammunition and plastic cable ties. He bound, gagged and covered the heads of the three occupants, each in separate areas of the house, and then shot them at close range.

It was Kerryn Henstridge's mother who found Kerryn, Anne and Peter dead the next morning. Kerryn was supposed to meet her mother at the family friend's home, in the same street, where her mother was staying. When she didn't arrive, Mrs Henstridge became worried and went to the share house. When there was no answer when she knocked at the door, Mrs Henstridge climbed through a window and discovered her daughter's body facedown on the floor. For anyone, let alone a parent, the thought of what Mrs Henstridge discovered that morning is unimaginable.

News of the triple murders hit the media, and the photos of the three smiling, young victims with all the promise in the world made the front pages of both the *Herald Sun* and *The Age*. The crime shocked Victorians. For one, it was a chilling, cold-blooded execution that seemed to be out of a movie, rather than the quiet suburban streets of Burwood.

Secondly, there seemed to be no motive for the killings. Police were baffled and worked around the clock for a breakthrough in the case. The victims were young country people with no records or association with the criminal world. The killer took around A$200 from the house, but police did not believe that robbery was the motive. Another motive explored was that someone was infatuated with one of the girls.

There was also the possibility that the house was picked at random (this turned out to be the chilling truth), but with no solid leads in the weeks after the murders, police turned to the media to appeal for any information that could crack the case. Almost daily there were newspaper reports, and the public followed the case closely. The fact that there was a cold-blooded killer who had targeted a home at random filled many with dread, and there were real fears from the police that the killer could strike again.

The Homicide Squad questioned more than 400 people who advertised for a housemate in the week before the murders and wanted to know if anyone who answered the ads had seemed suspicious or had acted strangely. High-profile crimes tend to attract people who want attention, and false leads provided by a man who contacted investigators several times frustrated them. It wasted precious resources and time, and the man was charged with giving false information to police. A police caravan was set up outside the house in the hope that people could give them some fresh leads, and the devastated families of the three victims gave heart-wrenching pleas for help.

The wife of victim Peter Dempsey, Liz, begged the public for help. Married just three years to her sweetheart, Liz said, 'Life's just been ruined.' She lost her husband and sister in the evil act. Peter Dempsey's father, Frank, said the term 'animal' was too good for the killer.

The breakthrough for police came five weeks after the murders.

At 8.45 p.m. on 1 September 1992, married couple Richard and Anne Shalagin arrived at their car parked at Government House Drive opposite the National Gallery in St Kilda Road, where they had attended a function. As they got in the car to drive back to their Coburg home, the couple were surprised by a balaclava-clad man who terrifyingly and silently pointed a gun at them. The couple assumed that the lone gunman wanted money and thrust a few A$50 notes at him in the hope that he would disappear. He grabbed the money but did not leave as the frightened couple had hoped.

The gunman forced the Shalagins from the car at rifle-point and motioned for them to go to a darker area under a large tree. He told Anne to lie facedown on the ground, kicking her even as she complied. Taking a long, cream plastic cable tie, the man was about to bind Anne's hands. Richard Shalagin, who would later tell the Supreme Court of Victoria that he had no doubt he and his wife would die if they further obeyed the assailant's instructions, quickly noticed that the man had put his rifle down, and he seized his chance to instinctively leap and attack. Richard grabbed the man in a bear hug and snatched at the gun, yelling at his wife to 'run!' Richard was bitten on the hand by the man as he held him from behind. Anne ran away, screaming, and Richard broke away from his attacker and followed his wife. Hearts thumping and adrenaline racing, the Shalagins literally ran for their lives towards busy St Kilda Road.

The couple's understandably hysterical screams were noticed by two security guards, Paul Sycam and Graeme Loader, who radioed for police help. According to court reports, Mrs Shalagin warned two nearby people, 'Don't go, he's got a gun. He's tried to shoot us.' The security guards approached the man, who pulled a knife on the pair. Mr Sycam later told the court that he then saw the man crouch down and hold a sawn-off firearm at waist level. The armed assailant shot at the two men five times. Mr Sycam said he heard the first shot zing past the right side of his head. He then described how he felt a shot to his hip and despite this ran after the shooter.

After the publication of *Murder in Suburbia*, where this chapter first appeared, I was contacted by a retired policewoman who'd read the book. In the original chapter, I'd written that it was Mr Sycam, the security officer, who had been the one to catch Coulston, and then police had arrived at the scene and arrested him. What this woman told me was chilling about her encounter with the killer and, understandably, she was frustrated that over the years, and in my book, the exact details of Coulston's arrest were not clear.

I had got the information from newspaper articles where it had been reported that Mr Sycam overpowered Coulston. I had attempted to talk again to the woman to report her recollections of what happened that night. From our initial conversation, it was clear that from what she told me, she could have easily been killed by Coulston and was extraordinarily brave in disarming him. She said Coulston said nothing during their encounter, and he had the firearm aimed directly at her. Unfortunately, I never heard back. However, I wanted to acknowledge her in as much detail as I have because of her role in catching Coulston. She wrote in an email to me dated 16 February 2017: 'I was the arresting officer of Ashley Mervin (sic) Coulston (Burwood triple murderer). In your book, it states that the security officer completed the arrest prior to me attending the scene. This is incorrect, as I arrested Coulston on my own ....'

Ashley Mervyn Coulston was found to be in possession of 'chilling accessories' in his bag that night – a sawn-off shotgun with a homemade silencer made from an oil filter, a knife, a balaclava, high-velocity .22 cartridges, handcuffs, thumb cuffs and plastic cable ties. Ballistic tests had revealed that the shotgun used to threaten the Shalagins was the same one used to murder Kerryn, Peter and Anne in Burwood.

It was the gun that held the key to nailing Coulston for the murders.

Forensics conducted by Victoria Police showed that the bullets recovered from two of the Burwood victims had been discharged from the firearm found in Coulston's possession (a third bullet was too badly damaged to be examined). A forensic scientist found a high-velocity blood spatter on the dressing gown found over Anne Smerdon's head that matched the bloodstains on the oil filter, which had been fashioned into a silencer for the rifle.

A few days after his 'no comment' interview about the Burwood murders, Coulston spoke to a police officer, in the presence of his solicitor, about the rifle. Coulston told police that in the week before the murders, a sailing friend named 'Rod Davis' had asked for a loan of the rifle and asked him to shorten the barrel. Coulston said the gun was returned to his car boot. The man whom Coulston alleged had borrowed his weapon was an America's Cup yachtsman Roderick Davis, who was called to give evidence at Coulston's trial. Davis testified that he had been competing for New Zealand at the Barcelona Olympics when the three people were murdered and that he did not know Coulston.

Coulston maintained his story that he was visiting his partner Jan McLeod at Frankston Hospital on the night of 29 July. Ms McLeod backed up Coulston's story in court and said that he had not left her side between 8 p.m. and 9.15 p.m. that night, despite witnesses seeing him at 7.50 p.m. and 10.30 p.m. at the marina in Hastings where they lived on her yacht.

Police were left frustrated by Coulston's refusal to answer questions about what happened at Summit Road. Here was a man who seemed of normal intelligence, who on the face of it, functioned in society and was in a relationship, yet he had committed this random act of extreme violence. Coulston just didn't make sense, and they had to rely on his family history and expert analysis to try and find out what made him tick.

* * *

Coulston had come to the attention of the public before these shocking murders. In 1988, he made headlines but for entirely different reasons. It was Australia's Bicentenary year, and Coulston wanted to make his mark on history. His contribution was to attempt to sail the smallest boat across the Tasman to New Zealand. He painstakingly spent almost a year designing and building a 2.5-metre-long aluminium yacht, roughly the size of a spa bath, with the moniker *G'day 88*. It was a daring feat by anyone's standards, and while he was thwarted on his first attempt by a cyclone (he embarked from Sydney on January 26 and was rescued by a tanker 46 days later), his second attempt at making a piece of history was a success when he sailed the tiny sailboat to Brisbane from New Zealand, landing on shore on 6 January 1989. His adventure was celebrated in an *Australian Geographic* spread and newspaper reports, and he was dubbed 'Captain Bathtub'.

Like the young people he murdered, Coulston was from the country and lived on a dairy farm in the town of Tangambalanga in Victoria's Kiewa Valley. Born in 1956, he had a brother and two sisters and grew up in a loving family, despite his mother's chronic ill health that meant she had long spells in hospital. It was also reported by old school friends that Coulston was dyslexic and struggled at school. Described as shy, secretive and a loner, Coulston ran into troubles in his early teens, starting with robbing the local butter factory when he was 13 and burgling other buildings in the town.

It was a shocking incident when Coulston was 14 that gave a warning he was a dangerous person. On 19 April 1971, after two weeks of stalking two young female teachers, he broke into their house beside the tiny Kiewa School and abducted the women, both aged 22. As with his future crimes, Coulston armed himself with a .22 rifle. At gunpoint, he forced the two terrified women to drive him interstate into New South Wales, towards Sydney.

At 5 a.m. the next day, the trio stopped at a Gundagai roadhouse to get some food. The teachers started screaming for help, which alerted a truck driver to their plight and they were rescued. Coulston was found guilty of abduction, armed robbery and being 'armed with felonious intent' and sentenced to three months at a boys' juvenile detention home in Melbourne.

When he was released later in 1971, Coulston moved back to the family farm and then moved with his family to a new farm in northern New South Wales. Coulston's father retired the following year, and in the early 1980s, the family moved to Queensland, where Mr Coulston felt the weather would be better for his ill wife.

In his mid-twenties, Coulston moved back to New South Wales and had several jobs, including one at Hertz Rent-a-Car. An unnamed man told the *Sunday Herald Sun* that Coulston had to leave his Hertz job after a female colleague made complaints to the management. The woman provided evidence to police for Coulston's later committal hearing and told officers that after she had declined Coulston's invitations for dates, she noticed that he had been following her as she went to and from work.

Coulston had become more interested in sailing, the hobby that would bring him some national recognition. Sailing also introduced him to Jan McLeod, a woman more than 15 years his senior, and the pair struck up a relationship and eventually moved in together in Ms McLeod's yacht, moored at Hastings in Melbourne.

Coulston's trial began in late August 1993 at Victoria's Supreme Court and ran for almost a month. At Coulston's eight-day committal hearing at Melbourne Magistrates' Court in January 1993, the court was told of his abduction of the two teachers in 1971 and of the incident at Hertz with his female colleague. It was also noted that the Hertz employee, one of the teachers Coulston abducted and Anne Smerdon all had shoulder-length blonde hair in common. It was not proven whether this had anything to do with Coulston's motives, but it was a discussion point.

Coulston was tried for the Burwood murders and 11 other charges over the incident in St Kilda Road, including attempted murder of the security guards, the armed robbery of the Shalagins and resisting arrest. He pleaded not guilty to all charges.

The case was tried in front of Justice Bernard Teague. Prosecutor Ross Ray said in court that it was difficult 'to conceive of a more frightening, random or more cold-blooded execution of three innocent victims ... who are not known to the prisoner'. A Pentridge prisoner gave evidence that in several conversations he had with Coulston, he admitted to 'killing the kids' and had said that his biggest mistake was not getting rid of the gun. The prisoner, a convicted armed robber, said he told Coulston that his biggest mistake was the murder, to which Coulston replied, 'Yeah, I'm sorry.'

Coulston's partner Jan McLeod told the court that he was with her at Frankston Hospital, where she'd had throat surgery, until 9.15 p.m. on the night of the killings.

Justice Teague made many poignant statements in his sentencing remarks. When handing down the three life sentences with a minimum of 30 years on 21 September 1993, Justice Teague remarked, 'You appeared from out of the night. You invaded a typical suburban home. You executed three victims. You disappeared into the night ... the seasons of your life left to you will scarce allow for more feats of fame or notoriety. But you have made for the beloved of the three you killed an enduring winter. And for the three, there are no more seasons.'

Ms McLeod vowed to do whatever it took to clear her partner's name, describing Coulston as the 'dearest man I have ever known'. She told a newspaper that Coulston was in good spirits when she visited him because 'he knows we'll be out here fighting' for his release.

In 1995, Coulston was granted a retrial with the three murder convictions quashed on appeal. Coulston's lawyers made the successful appeal based on evidence at his first trial that related to the armed robbery that led to his arrest. The Supreme Court found that some of the evidence relating to the attack on the Shalagins was inadmissible during the first joint trial for the Burwood murders and the offences at St Kilda Road. The appeal judges said the suggestion of a similarity between the two incidents 'might well have a beguiling appeal to the jury'.

In the first trial, Coulston was acquitted of the attempted murder of the security guards but guilty of the armed robbery of the Shalagins, false imprisonment, intentionally causing injury, assault and using a firearm to resist arrest. The Supreme Court set a two-year minimum sentence for the St Kilda Road charges and said Coulston should have been granted a separate trial on these charges.

During the second trial that ran through August and early September 1995, Coulston's lawyers attacked the credibility of the officer who had performed the ballistics testing on the gun. Victoria Police Leading Senior Constable Ray Vincent was a ballistics expert and on duty both nights of Coulston's crimes. When he attended the St Kilda Road scene, he noticed the plastic ties and recalled that they were the same brand left by the killer at the Summit Road murder scene. When the bullets from the firearm were compared to bullets found at the Burwood scene, they were found to be a match.

Supreme Court judge Mr Justice Norman O'Bryan made specific reference to the attack Coulston's defence made on the professional reputation of Senior Constable Vincent, the main prosecution witness, during the second trial. Coulston's defence alleged that Vincent had substituted three different bullets for the ones taken from the Burwood victims, so that he could say in court that the weapon found on the accused at St Kilda Road was the murder weapon. The defence used private forensic investigator Bob Barnes as their expert witness. Mr Barnes had been dismissed from the Victorian Forensic Science Centre for 'scientific misconduct' in 1993, though the defence did not know this at the time. The accusations that bullets had been substituted were never proved by defence and were not taken seriously.

Coulston was again found guilty of the three murders in Burwood, and Mr Justice O'Bryan said 'the wicked nature' of his offences gave the court the power to give him a life sentence with no minimum. Coulston would be imprisoned for the term of his natural life.

He also noted that Coulston 'stood mute' during this second trial, as he did in his first. Justice O'Bryan said it was his belief that Coulston's fear of self-incrimination was the reason and that he had 'forfeited forever' his right to live outside the confines of prison. 'I am of the opinion that you should never be released,' Mr Justice O'Bryan said.

Coulston would not give up though and challenged his sentence with a second appeal in 1996, which failed at the

Court of Appeal. An application to the High Court for special leave to appeal against his conviction also failed in late 1996. He had exhausted his last legal avenue, and the families of the three murdered in Burwood did not have to endure more painful court appearances.

Outside the High Court on 13 December 1996, Rob Henstridge, Kerryn's father, said the families would be forever hurt over the lack of explanation or apparent motive Coulston had for the murders. The pain for them would go on, their lives forever changed by Coulston's cold-blooded actions.

'There is no explanation and we're never likely to hear one. We just don't know and we'll never know and that's what really hurts,' Mr Henstridge said.

Coulston baffled even Australia's best criminal psychologists and criminal profilers. Melbourne-based forensic psychologist Ian Joblin told *Herald Sun* journalist Russell Robinson that the Burwood triple killer perplexed him. In a 2005 interview with Robinson, Dr Joblin, who spent hours assessing Coulston, said he couldn't find a motive for the killings. 'In terms of trying to resolve the conflict between [Coulston's] presentation and the offending, it's the most perplexing one,' Dr Joblin said.

Dr Joblin has assessed some of Australia's most notorious criminals, including Matthew Wales, who murdered his mother and stepfather in a crime that scandalised Melbourne's high society, as well as convicted triple-murderer and rapist Peter Dupas (one of Coulston's 'never to be released' prison mates) and Port Arthur mass murderer Martin Bryant.

Coulston kept trying to prove his innocence. In a 1998 incident that forced the State Government of Victoria to reexamine its Freedom of Information (FOI) law, Coulston was able to obtain the names of 51 nurses who worked at Frankston Hospital in 1992, so that he could establish his alibi for the night of the triple murder and get the case reopened. Coulston and his partner Ms McLeod had always maintained that he was visiting her in hospital at the time the killer struck at Burwood.

The hospital's management initially knocked back two FOI requests by Coulston, but the killer appealed to the Victorian Civil and Administrative Tribunal (VCAT) who upheld his appeal. The Australian Nursing Federation and the then Premier Jeff Kennett slammed the actions of the hospital and said it had been incompetent in not protecting the privacy of its staff. Newspapers grabbed hold of the story, and readers were shocked to read that the hospital had no legal representation at the first appeal hearing and that Coulston had represented himself via video link to plead his case for access to the names. The fact that Coulston's legal challenges were being paid for by the taxpayer was also infuriating for Victorians. Premier Kennett received a letter from Coulston in early 1999, in which the prisoner assured him that he would not misuse the names of the nurses.

Premier Kennett used the incident as the means to change the Victorian FOI laws to ensure that public sector workers' names would not be released if there was a threat to a person's safety.

Chillingly, one newspaper even reported that Coulston was believed to have used the laws and applied to the State Corner for access to homicide files in the Mr Cruel case. The still unsolved Mr Cruel case involved the abduction and sexual assault of at least three schoolgirls from Melbourne's eastern suburbs. One girl, 13-year-old Karmein Chan, was found murdered – shot execution-style in the head – one year after she was abducted from her parents' Templestowe home. The identity of Mr Cruel is one of Australia's most notorious and haunting crime mysteries, and at one stage, police considered that Coulston might have been the perpetrator.

Coulston was also investigated at one time over the murder of Sarah MacDiarmid, 23, who was kidnapped from Kananook Station in Melbourne in 1990. Her body has never been found, and the case remains unsolved. Eventually, no evidence was found to link Coulston to Sarah.

(Author's note: Melbourne-based author and podcaster Vikki Petraitis released a podcast in 2021 called *Searching for Sarah MacDiarmid*, which I highly recommend people listen to.)

Is it possible that the three young victims in Burwood were the only people Coulston has murdered? Of course, it is most likely that the night Coulston was caught by police he had intended to murder the couple in the gardens near St Kilda Road, but could he have kept his dark desires suppressed between the abduction of his teachers in 1971 and the 1992 Burwood murders? Some investigators think not.

Coulston is in the frame for a series of unsolved rapes and at least one murder along eastern Australia. A man known as 'the Balaclava Killer and Rapist' began a reign of terror on the Gold Coast, Queensland, and Tweed Heads, New South Wales in the summer of 1979–80.

Coulston was living with his family in Kyogle, New South Wales, close to the Queensland border. A masked man at Tweed Heads abducted an English man, Geoffrey Parkinson, 33, with a female friend on 2 February 1980. Geoffrey grappled with the masked man and was shot dead with a .22 rifle.

Coulston is also suspected of being 'the Sutherland Rapist', who attacked women in the 1980s in Sydney's southern suburbs. This rapist wore a balaclava and carried a sawn-off firearm, just like the Balaclava Killer. Coulston was living in Sydney in the 1980s up to 1988, when he attempted his sail to New Zealand. These crimes are still unsolved; however, in 2020, it was reported by the *Daily Telegraph* that a DNA sample from an old exhibit from an unsolved rape in New South Wales in the 1980s was found to be a match with Coulston.

Coulston's crimes were planned meticulously yet his victims were chosen at random. His motives can only be speculated, as he has remained silent all these years, but many believe he killed for thrills.

Coulston is now one of just a handful of prisoners in Victoria who are serving life sentences with no minimum – his crimes deemed so heinous that he will die in jail. He joins murderers and rapists who will never be released, including Peter Dupas, who was convicted of murdering three women – Nicole Patterson, Margaret Maher and Mersina Halvagis as she tended to her grandmother's grave at Fawkner Cemetery in 1997.

In 2015, Dupas was named by the Victorian State Coroner as the person responsible for the murder of 95-year-old Kathleen Downes in 1997, but this was not revealed until 2020. Dupas had long been the suspect for Mrs Downes' killing. A 2019 trial for the murder collapsed because the key witness against Dupas, former lawyer Andrew Fraser, was too unwell with cancer to testify. Fraser was a key witness against Dupas in his trial for the murder of Mersina Halvagis. Fraser had spent time in jail for drug trafficking and shared a cell with Dupas.

Coulston is also in jail with another lifer, Leslie Camilleri, who with his accomplice Lindsay Beckett, abducted, raped and murdered two children – best friends Lauren Barry, 14 and Nichole Collins, 16 – in Bega in 1997. In 2013, Camilleri was sentenced for the murder of 13-year-old Prue Bird in Melbourne in 1992.

Ashley Mervyn Coulston is the stuff of nightmares, but tragically for his victims and their loved ones, he is all too real.

AUTHOR'S NOTE

The background and information about the murder of Denise Ann Howes came from The Redford Township Police Department in Michigan through a Freedom of information request.

Other resources I used in the writing of this book are the National Library of Australia's invaluable database Trove, newspapers.com, Austlii.edu.au, Coroners Court Victoria's website, The Public Records Office Victoria, The State Library of Victoria's newspaper collection, findagrave.com and ancestry.com.au.

ABOUT THE AUTHOR

Emily Webb is a journalist, true crime author and co-host of the popular *Australian True Crime* podcast.

She lives in suburbia with her husband and two children. Emily is the author of *Angels of Death: Doctors and Nurses who Kill* and *Suburban True Crime* (previously published as *Murder in Suburbia* and *Suburban Nightmare*). She also hosts and produces a podcast called *Killer Content: Inside the crime writer's mind* and loves talking to authors to find out what makes them tick. When she is not podcasting or delving into old newspaper files and archives, Emily enjoys reading crime fiction and horror, watching her children play sports and walking her two rescue greyhounds.

𝕏 @emilybwebb

◉ @emilywebbcrime

f @emily.webb.podcaster.author